ELEANOR OF AQUITAINE

Covering one of the most fascinating yet misunderstood periods in history, the MEDIEVAL LIVES series presents medieval people, concepts and events, drawing on political and social history, philosophy, material culture (art, architecture and archaeology) and the history of science. These books are global and wide-ranging in scope, encompassing both Western and non-Western subjects, and span the fifth to the fifteenth centuries, tracing significant developments from the collapse of the Roman Empire onwards.

SERIES EDITOR: Deirdre Jackson

ELEANOR OF AQUITAINE

Woman, Queen and Legend

LINDY GRANT

REAKTION BOOKS

For my brother, and in memory of his wife

Published by Reaktion Books Ltd
2–4 Sebastian Street
London EC1V OHE, UK
www.reaktionbooks.co.uk

First published 2025
Copyright © Lindy Grant 2025

EU GPSR Authorised Representative
Logos Europe, 9 rue Nicolas Poussin, 17000, La Rochelle, France
email: contact@logoseurope.eu

Printed and bound in India by Replika Press Pvt. Ltd

A catalogue record for this book is available from the British Library

ISBN 978 1 83639 086 2

CONTENTS

Detail of Eleanor from the tomb effigy at Fontevraud Abbey.

Prologue: Meeting Eleanor

The best place to meet Eleanor of Aquitaine face to face is the abbey of Fontevraud, near Saumur, in the Loire Valley, where she died and was buried in 1204. There she lies, in effigy, on her tomb in the middle of the nave of the great abbey church, with her husband and other members of her family. They are brilliantly, dramatically lit, as if players in some theatre in the round, while we, as tourists, peer at them from the surrounding gloom.

But when you look closely, when you do see Eleanor at close range, her tomb is a disappointment. She lies stretched out on a pleated sheet, as if she is on her deathbed. She holds an open book in her hands. Perhaps she is reading it, but her eyes are so roughly carved that one can't tell whether they are open or shut. She was famous for her beauty, but the sculptor couldn't rise to that. He gave her a long chin, a long sharp nose and a thin sulky mouth in a flat face. She was eighty or so when she died; perhaps the sculptor wanted to remind us that beauty fades. He was quite good at pleats. Her gown and mantle, made of finest wool or silk, flow softly over her body and ripple at her feet. But he was a second-rate artisan. Was he the best available to whoever commissioned her tomb? And was that Eleanor herself? Or the executors of her will, whoever they were? Or the nuns of Fontevraud? Or her last surviving son, John, king of England? He had other things on his mind in 1204, as he was driven out of Normandy and Anjou by the French king, Philip II Augustus.

Eleanor's tomb lies alongside those of her second husband, Henry II, king of England, and her favourite son, Richard the Lionheart. Both predeceased her: Henry died in 1189 and Richard ten years later. Shortly after Richard's death, someone, probably Eleanor, commissioned a matching pair of effigies for the two kings. This sculptor was not a provincial workman. His carvings of Eleanor's husband and son are sharply articulated and elegantly incised. If she commissioned them, Eleanor did both men proud.

Eleanor, like Henry II and Richard the Lionheart, was a legend in her own lifetime. Her beauty helped, but she had too, it seems, a charisma, a personal magnetism. She had a long career in the political theatre of the 'Angevin Empire' – the extensive dominions of Henry II and his sons, which stretched from northern England to the Pyrenees, and encompassed most of western France. She undertook diplomatic missions to Iberia, Rome and Germany. All contemporary commentators knew how far her sons, Richard and King John, owed their succession to the Angevin lands to her. But sexual scandal clung to her too. Henry II was her second husband. Her first was Louis VII, king of France. In 1152 he divorced her, after fifteen years of increasingly

Tomb effigy of Eleanor and Henry II, Fontevraud Abbey, France.

fractious marriage and, on her side, an indiscreet dalliance with an uncle on crusade. The marriage with Henry brought scandal too. This time the sexual dalliances were his – but that left her open to charges of jealousy – and in 1173 she joined, or it was rumoured incited, his sons in revolt against him. Within sixty years of her death, stories circulated that she was descended from a she-devil, and had had an affair with her son Richard's great Muslim adversary, Saladin, in a historically nonchalant elision of the Second Crusade, in which Eleanor took part, and the Third, in which she did not.

It is impossible to separate Eleanor the woman from Eleanor the legend. She fascinated contemporaries, and so those legends were building long before she died. Those who wielded power in the Middle Ages usually knew the importance of image, of the mystique of rulership. Henry, and above all Richard, were masters of the art of royal image. Louis vii lacked charisma and natural authority, but finally learnt to fashion the persona of a pious peacemaker. Eleanor too must have been complicit in the fashioning of her image. Perhaps she found an element of dangerous scandal amusing and sometimes politically useful.

Eleanor the woman is curiously elusive. What did she call herself? Her name varies even in her own charters – usually Alienor, but also Aleonore, Alinora, Alienordis, even Helienors. I have used the familiar modern English form Eleanor – as I have generally used modern English names throughout this book. She was heiress to the duchy of Aquitaine, but that was usually governed by her husbands or her sons. She was a queen consort, not a queen regnant or a king. Contemporary chroniclers told the story of their own times in terms of what rulers did. Their wives or mothers only feature if they did something extraordinary, like revolt against their husband, or rescue the kingdom when their son was imprisoned. The household accounts that often tell us so much about the everyday existence and the

ELEANOR OF AQUITAINE

material culture of elite women – and men – have not survived from the twelfth century in the way that they have from the later Middle Ages. There are long stretches of Eleanor's life when we don't know where she was, let alone what she was doing. And then suddenly she is there, as she is on her tomb, spotlit at the centre of the stage.

THE FIRST THREE CHAPTERS of this book tell Eleanor's story: the story of her unusually long and eventful life, as far as we know or can reconstruct it. The following six chapters search for her, exploring specific aspects of that life: her family; the tales of her sexual impropriety; the legend of her exotic Occitan otherness; her wealth, how she garnered it and spent it; her piety, her interactions with the Church and churchmen; and her power – how much she really had, and how and how well she used it. Her family – its pressures, networks and opportunities – is key to understanding her. The other aspects of her life are all problematic; they are clouded by legend, or by paucity of evidence, or by the expectations and assumptions of historians over the last 75 years or so. We want to think that she would have shared some of our assumptions about the place of women in society and politics, about the ways women should have agency and exercise power. But of course she did not, for she was born some nine hundred years ago.

ONE

Queen of France

We don't know when Eleanor was born. It was probably 1124 – a year of bad harvests and signs in the stars, according to a local chronicler.[1] Her father was Duke William x of Aquitaine, also count of Poitou.[2] He was tall and elegant. He had inherited the county and duchy in 1126 from his father, a famous troubadour and warrior, Duke William IX. Eleanor's mother, Aenor, was the daughter of a Poitevin aristocratic family, the viscounts of Châtellerault. They had three children, William, the heir, Eleanor and Aelith. Eleanor and her siblings probably lived mainly in the duke's ancestral territories in and around the city of Poitiers – in the comital castle at the centre of the city itself, or in the various residences in the fine hunting marshes and forests of Poitou and Saintonge. Aenor died around 1130 and was buried at the abbey of Nieul-sur-l'Autise; probably she died at one of the nearby ducal residences, Niort or Mervent. The heir, William, died soon after. Count/ Duke William was still young and was about to marry again, but his chosen bride, Emma of Limoges, was stolen from under his nose by the son of the count of Angoulême.[3] Eleanor was not groomed as his heir, in the way that King Henry I of England tried to establish his daughter, Empress Matilda, his sole legitimate child, as his heir.[4] Aquitanian inheritance customs probably dictated that William's lands should be divided between his two daughters in the event of his death without a male heir.

In spring 1137 Duke William went on pilgrimage to Santiago de Compostela. There, unexpectedly, at Easter, he fell ill and died. On his deathbed, with no male heir to succeed him, he named his oldest daughter, Eleanor, as his sole heir, giving her into the protection of his suzerain, the king of France, Louis VI, the Fat. When news reached the French court, Louis the Fat announced that his son and heir would marry the heiress to Aquitaine. He sent young Louis, with a substantial armed guard, and a group of trusted great barons and churchmen, to take possession of the heiress and her duchy. In July they found Eleanor at Bordeaux, where her father must have left her in the care of the archbishop. They were married in Bordeaux Cathedral on 25 July. Eleanor was probably thirteen, Louis a couple of years older. With their huge entourage, they processed to Poitiers, the true capital of the dukes of Aquitaine. There Eleanor was crowned queen of France. Louis had already been crowned and anointed in anticipatory kingship in 1131. Then came news that the old king had died. Between spring and summer, Eleanor was transformed from a child to a wife, from a carefree aristocratic girl to the heiress to a great principality and queen of France.[5]

Louis, now King Louis VII, raced back to Paris to secure his succession. Eleanor followed more slowly, probably with her sister, Aelith, and her own ladies, in the care of Geoffrey of Lèves, bishop of Chartres.[6] We do not know much about her life as the young queen of France. Chroniclers said little about her. At most they called her 'a very noble girl'. None commented on her beauty – perhaps she was just too young – though one chronicler praised her husband's 'elegance of body'.[7] Aelith, who was now often called Petronilla, accompanied her at the French court. Sometimes they stayed in Paris, in the ramshackle royal palace on the Île de la Cité. Sometimes they can be traced at the other royal residences around Paris, such as Moret-sur-Loing and Lorris, both in good hunting country to the southeast of the capital. Eleanor did not always travel with her husband: on one occasion he issued a charter in Paris, to which she and her sister assented soon afterwards at Lorris.[8]

Louis vii, like Eleanor, had had an elder brother, and had not expected to be his father's heir. He was educated at Notre-Dame in Paris, with the expectation that he would go into the Church, not as a monk, but as a secular churchman who would probably become a bishop. Louis would always be pious. Walter Map, a British churchman and chronicler, described him as simple but decent. He was never a natural warrior and leader in the way his father had been. He was bowled over by his bride. John of Salisbury, an English churchman and chronicler, who knew both Louis and Eleanor well, says that he loved her intensely, but 'in an almost childish way'.[9]

Eleanor was not the only queen at the French court. Louis' mother was Adela of Maurienne.[10] Adela had never been beautiful, but King Louis vi was devoted to her, and took her advice seriously. Unusually, royal acts were routinely dated by her regnal year, as well as his. She was an adept politician, able to precipitate the downfall of her husband's favourite minister, Stephen de Garlande. She soon remarried, to Matthew of Montmorency, the constable, an important member of the royal household. She retired from the court to her dower lands in Compiègne shortly after Eleanor's arrival, apparently unhappy that her son was wasting her wealth in kingly display.[11] Some have seen Eleanor's influence in Adela's retirement from court, but that is to expect a lot from a thirteen-year-old. Probably Adela's retirement was engineered by Abbot Suger of Saint-Denis. He had been a close advisor of Louis the Fat but had never liked Adela. Adela was soon back at court. When Louis vii went on two important ceremonial visits to Saint-Denis, for the consecration of the Abbey Church and to receive the banner of St Denis before leaving on crusade, Adela was there alongside Eleanor.[12] Perhaps Eleanor resented Adela's presence; perhaps Eleanor found the political queen dowager, who was a distant cousin, a tantalizing role model.

Young Louis' court, like most courts, was a place of poisonous intrigue. With the new king, there was a change of generation. Advisors who had been close to the old king, particularly Abbot Suger, struggled to retain their influence. Louis VII developed his own cadre of advisors, like the clerk Cadurc, his cousin Count Ralph of Vermandois, the seneschal, and lesser knightly courtiers such as Thierry Galeran. According to the well-informed gossip, John of Salisbury, Eleanor hated Thierry Galeran, whom she mocked as a eunuch. Thierry, though married, had no male off-spring, and finally became a Templar.[13] As a young queen, Eleanor would have found herself the object of courtiers' flattery, and their attempts to influence and control her. Before her marriage, Eleanor had probably been in the charge of Geoffrey of Loroux,

Tombstone from Poitou, c. 1140, with scenes on both sides, one showing a man hunting and this side showing an aristocratic woman, riding side-saddle and hunting with her falcon and dogs. Eleanor, like Henry II, was fond of blood sports.

archbishop of Bordeaux. On her journey to Paris, she was given into the charge of Geoffrey of Lèves, bishop of Chartres, a good friend of Geoffrey of Loroux. Suger was a close friend and colleague of both bishops. Perhaps he manoeuvred Adela into retiring from court to ensure that he, rather than the old queen, was the primary influence on Eleanor.

Louis VII took his new role as duke of Aquitaine in right of his wife seriously. In the mid-twelfth century, the king of France had little real power over much of his kingdom, for most of it was run, almost like separate polities, by great princes – the counts of Champagne, Flanders and Anjou, or the dukes of Normandy, Burgundy and Aquitaine. The counts of Champagne and Flanders and the dukes of Normandy were wealthier than the French king, running their realms more effectively politically, administratively and economically. The duke of Normandy was often also king of England. So the acquisition of Aquitaine was a real coup for Louis. The duchy had itself been a kingdom under the Carolingians, and some of that lustre still clung to it. It had impressive natural resources, especially wine, grain and above all salt, without which medieval meat and fish could be neither flavoured nor preserved. With income from those resources, and from lucrative rights of lordship, the duchy could make a substantial difference to the wealth of the French king.[14]

Louis made several visits to the duchy: in autumn 1138; December 1140; summer 1141; autumn/winter 1146; and December 1151 to February 1152. Usually he took Eleanor with him, though he left her behind in the Capetian lands in 1138. In 1140 Aelith accompanied her.[15] The daughter of the last duke was useful. She was related to many of the aristocratic families, and thus to many of the most important churchmen and women, in the duchy. Louis was careful to cultivate religious houses that had had close relationships with the dukes, such as Maillezais and Montierneuf in Poitiers, which had been founded by them and where some of them were buried; Notre-Dame at Saintes, where Eleanor's aunt Agnes was abbess, and Nieul-sur-l'Autise, where Eleanor's mother was buried; or Grace-Dieu, which had been founded by her father.[16] Usually, but not always, his gifts and confirmations were corroborated or assented to by Eleanor, for instance to the Templars of La Rochelle, to Fontevraud, Saint-Maixent and Saint-Eutrope at Saintes.[17] Occasionally, they were at Eleanor's request, for instance for her mother's burial house, and for her aunt Agnes.[18] But the wealth of Aquitaine came to Louis, not to Eleanor. Eleanor made few gifts on her own account since the wealth of Aquitaine was not hers to bestow – it was her husband's.[19]

Louis' visits to Aquitaine were usually to deal with problems there. In autumn 1138, for instance, he quashed a commune in Poitiers, with a violent enthusiasm that had to be moderated by Abbot Suger.[20] Louis left Duke William's officers – the seneschals of the counties, and provosts in towns – in place to run the duchy. He confirmed William of Mauzé as seneschal of Poitou until 1149, when he appointed Geoffrey of Rancon. When Louis thought there were problems, he would arrive in the duchy with a group of counsellors from the French court, and his entourage would be swollen by members of the retinue and household of Eleanor's father, including Hervey the Pantler, and other Aquitanian aristocrats and churchmen. In 1146/7 a small group of distinguished Poitevins, including William of Mauzé and Geoffrey of Rancon, met Louis and Eleanor at Étampes on behalf of the Poitevin abbey of Saint-Maixent.[21] Apart from this deputation, there is scant evidence for Aquitanians or Poitevins at Louis' court. Presumably Eleanor and Aelith had a small female entourage with some pages and chaplains from Aquitaine. Peter, described as Eleanor's chancellor and chaplain, witnessed an act that she issued in Paris in 1141 for Notre-Dame at Saintes.[22] He may be the Peter recorded as her chaplain between 1154 and around 1170, but there is no further trace of him at the Capetian court. Eleanor had limited opportunity to build a close relationship with the aristocracy or the major churchmen of her duchy.

Through her grandmother, Philippa of Toulouse, duchess of Aquitaine, Eleanor had a claim to the county of Toulouse, though the succession had gone to Duchess Philippa's younger brother. Eleanor's father and grandfather pursued the claim, in the end without success. In summer 1141 Louis led an army via Aquitaine to the walls of the city of Toulouse. It was well fortified, and Louis' army too small. He was forced into a humiliating retreat.[23] Perhaps Eleanor encouraged Louis into this unsuccessful escapade, but he needed little encouragement. As a young man Louis was restless, combative and rash, and Toulouse was a temptation to any ruler of Aquitaine.

The Capetian court was soon rocked by scandal. Louis' cousin, Ralph of Vermandois, married Eleanor's sister Aelith-Petronilla. From the Capetian point of view, it was a useful marriage, and Louis probably arranged it.[24] In customary law, Aelith had a valid claim to half of the Aquitanian inheritance. The marriage tied her closely to Louis and his immediate family. Louis must have given her a dowry, including lands or income from Aquitaine, for she made gifts to the abbey of Notre-Dame at Saintes.[25] Unfortunately, Ralph was already married to Eleanor, niece of Count Theobald of Champagne. Ralph tried to have his inconvenient first marriage annulled on the grounds of consanguinity – that by the dictates of canon law he and his first wife were too closely related. But most important churchmen, including the pope, and the formidable and influential Cistercian abbot Bernard of Clairvaux, condemned Ralph's marriage with Aelith as bigamous and Aelith herself as an adulteress. The union, fulminated Bernard, would be barren, and Ralph would have no posterity. Bernard's words proved horribly prophetic. Their only son was a leper, and their daughters died childless.[26]

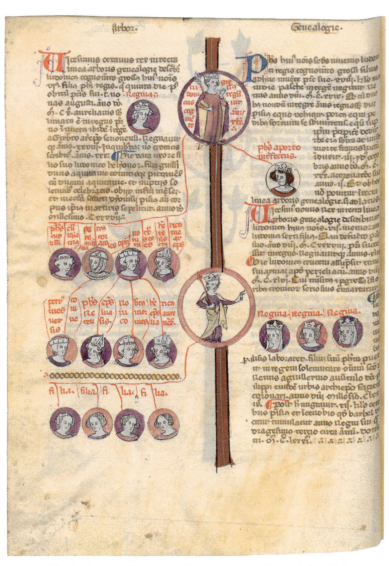

The family tree of Louis VI and Louis VII, from Bernard Gui, 'Arbor genealogiae regum francorum', early 14th century. The queens Adela of Maurienne, Eleanor, Constance of Castile and Adela of Champagne are all shown, labelled 'Regina', and Louis VII's four daughters, Mary of Champagne, Alixe of Blois, Margaret and Alice, are shown, simply labelled 'filia' (daughter). Louis VII's brother, Robert of Dreux, is named, as is Robert's son, Philip, the bellicose bishop of Beauvais.

Louis was already at odds with the French Church establishment, who objected to his attempt to appoint his favourite clerk, Cadurc, as archbishop of Bourges. His support of Ralph of Vermandois alienated Count Theobald of Champagne, who was incensed at the insult to his niece. Theobald was a great prince, nephew of King Henry I of England. He was highly regarded as a generous patron of the Church, especially of Cistercian monks, and was a close friend of St Bernard. By 1143 it had come to war, and Louis and Ralph invaded Champagne. A successful invasion became a propaganda disaster. At Vitry-en-Perthois, Louis' troops burnt down the church, which was full of women and children seeking refuge. Aelith-Petronilla's bigamous marriage had led to a terrible war crime.[27]

What was Eleanor's role in this disastrous scandal? Doubtless she supported her sister as far as she could. She named her second daughter, born in 1150, after Aelith. But there is no evidence that Eleanor pushed Louis to invade Champagne. The only evidence for Eleanor's active involvement in the affair is an account of a meeting between Eleanor and Bernard of Clairvaux at Saint-Denis in 1144, recorded by Bernard's secretary, Geoffrey of Auxerre. Bernard encouraged Eleanor to work and pray for peace between her husband and Count Theobald. Peacemaking was one of the roles expected of a queen. But Bernard suggested that prayers for peace would help Eleanor in the successful conception of a child. In a surprisingly intimate conversation between the queen and the abbot, Eleanor had lamented her inability to provide her husband with a son and heir. They had been married seven years. There had been an early miscarriage, then nothing.[28] A child did arrive in 1145, but it was a daughter.

In late 1144 came bad news from the crusader states: the city of Edessa had been captured by Muslim forces. The Church, urged on by St Bernard and Pope Eugenius III, called for a new crusade. Louis and Eleanor were quick to commit themselves to take part. Together they travelled to Vézelay to hear St Bernard preach at Easter 1146. There they took the cross, driven in part, probably, by a desire to atone for the horrors of Vitry-en-Perthois. A number of the French aristocracy joined them in taking the cross, but the only important Aquitanians to do so were, it seems, Hugh of Lusignan and Geoffrey of Rancon.[29] Much organization was required. In late 1146 and early 1147, Louis and Eleanor toured Aquitaine to raise troops and funds, and to ensure the duchy would be peaceful in their absence.[30] Louis arranged for the kingdom to be governed while he was away by the uneasy combination of Abbot Suger of Saint-Denis and the still excommunicate Ralph of Vermandois.[31]

In June 1147 Louis, accompanied by Eleanor and Adela of Maurienne, went to the abbey of Saint-Denis to receive the banner of St Denis and set off on crusade.[32] One of the abbey's senior monks, Odo of Deuil, went with them to act as Louis' chaplain, and provide a detailed account of the journey to the crusader states for Abbot Suger.

The crusade was a disaster. Eleanor was not the only aristocratic woman to take part, and there was a considerable non-military element. The crusaders seem to have assumed that they were going on a pilgrimage with some military action. But their provisions ran down as they were held up at Constantinople by the Byzantine emperor, who did not trust them any more than they trusted him. The empress wrote to Eleanor to try to break the deadlock. The emperor demanded one of Eleanor's attendants, a cousin of Louis, as a bride for his nephew, but the girl was spirited away from Eleanor's retinue, presumably with her connivance, by Louis' younger brother, Robert of Dreux. The crusaders lost more provisions and horses in the inhospitable mountains of Asia Minor, and then they were set on by the Seljuk Turks. Louis sent his cousin Amadeus of Savoy and Geoffrey of Rancon in the advance party. Rejecting the advice of the Templars, who knew how to combat the Turks, Geoffrey and Amadeus went too far ahead; their army was decimated, though Amadeus and Geoffrey escaped. Geoffrey was relieved of his command and sent back to France – surprisingly to run Aquitaine for Louis. Louis put the Templars in charge. We do not know how close Eleanor herself came to the fighting, but the final stretch of their journey through Asia Minor was gruelling. Battered, exhausted, deprived of their baggage, the French contingent, with Louis and Eleanor, finally made it to the coast, and thence to the safety of Antioch in March 1148.[33]

Antioch must have been paradise after the hellish journey. They were welcomed by Raymond, Prince of Antioch, who was Eleanor's uncle, the younger brother of Duke William x. Eleanor had not had many of her own relations around her, apart from her sister. She clearly delighted in her uncle's company; for Louis that delight was all too clear. We don't know whether Eleanor and Raymond's relationship was a mild familial flirtation or a full-blown affair. By the later twelfth century, most chroniclers assumed it was the latter. It precipitated a crisis in what was already a faltering marriage. Eleanor seized the initiative, claiming that the marriage was consanguineous and that she and Louis should divorce. Suger wrote to Louis advising him that, whatever the queen had done, he himself should not act rashly until they were home in France. Louis left Antioch for the Holy Land itself, forcing a protesting Eleanor to come with him. There followed an unsuccessful siege of Damascus, but they did get to Jerusalem.[34]

Having achieved nothing, Louis, Eleanor and the French crusaders sailed for home. Eleanor's ship was captured by pirates working for the emperor of Constantinople. She was rescued by a Sicilian fleet and reunited with Louis. She was ill and exhausted – and probably pregnant. King Roger of Sicily escorted them to Palermo, showering them with gifts. Then they proceeded north, staying with Pope Eugenius at Tusculum on the way. Like Suger, the pope hoped that their marriage could be saved; he more or less tucked them into bed together, according to John of Salisbury.[35] They arrived back in the Capetian heartlands in mid-November 1149. Shortly thereafter, Eleanor gave birth to her second daughter. Louis had enforced his marital rights. Eleanor named the daughter after her sister, Aelith, who died in early March 1150, probably around the time of the birth.[36]

The marriage was now irreparable. Eleanor had failed to produce an heir. Louis agreed that their marriage should be annulled. They made a tour of Aquitaine, spending Christmas 1151 at Limoges, returning to Capetian lands in February 1152. As during their other tours of Aquitaine, Aquitanian magnates and prelates attended them, alongside Louis' usual French entourage.[37] Presumably Louis hoped to impress upon the Aquitanians that he was their overlord and would remain duke of Aquitaine as ward of his daughters, the heirs to the duchy. Petulantly, he had city walls knocked down.[38] But it gave Eleanor the chance to reconnect with those who had supported her father. As they stopped close to her mother's burial house at Nieul-sur-l'Autise, Louis issued a charter in favour of the abbey of L'Absie with Eleanor's assent and at her request. It was witnessed by Poitevin aristocrats, including Brien Chabot and Saldebreuil, who would implement the donation made by Eleanor.[39]

On their return, Louis convened a court and a church council at Beaugency on the Loire between 18 and 21 March. It was Lent, time of fasting and abstinence. The council, presided over by the archbishops of Tours, Sens, Rouen and by Geoffrey of Loroux, archbishop of Bordeaux, declared the marriage void due to the fact that they were, as Eleanor had claimed, related within the degrees forbidden by the Church. Eleanor left immediately for Poitiers.[40]

TWO

Queen of England

Eleanor was a tempting marital prospect. Anyone who married her would claim the duchy of Aquitaine, despite Louis' pretensions. She evaded the clutches of two aristocratic younger sons, Geoffrey of Nantes and Theobald of Blois, and reached the safety of Poitiers.[1] She must have been well protected, presumably by a contingent of knights and nobles recruited on the recent tour of Aquitaine. She had, it seems, her own marital plans. On 18 May 1152 she married Henry, count of Anjou and duke of Normandy. They had met the previous year, when Henry accompanied his father, Count Geoffrey of Anjou, to the Capetian court. The speed of her marriage to Henry, having fought off his younger brother Geoffrey of Nantes, suggests that this was a carefully planned union.

Count-Duke Henry was around eleven years younger than Eleanor. Nevertheless, it was, at least for the first ten or fifteen years, a more successful marriage than that of Eleanor and Louis. Eleanor presented Henry with a son and heir in August 1153, and they had at least seven further children, including four sons, over the next thirteen years. Eleanor had emerged from her time as queen of France as a well-travelled woman of some diplomatic experience and proven courage, versed in the power-play of a court. Henry was energetic, determined, questioning and well educated. He was a match for her in way that the pious, indecisive Louis, who could appear weak-minded and simple, was not.

In the first two years of their marriage, they were based in Anjou and Normandy. Then, in late 1154, Henry inherited the English throne. The inheritance, like that of Normandy, came through his mother, Empress Matilda, the only surviving legitimate child of Henry I. On 15 December 1154 Henry and Eleanor were crowned king and queen of England in Westminster Abbey. Eleanor had once again the status of a crowned and anointed queen – and queen of a famously wealthy kingdom. Eleanor shared in that wealth. Henry gave her a generous dower settlement, with income from lands and rights in England, Normandy, Anjou and Aquitaine. Henry provided her with good administrators and clerks from his own household to form her household in England and Normandy, and to deal with her English and Norman revenues. The Norman John of Wauvray acted as her steward. Her chancellor until 1162, when he became dean of Angers cathedral, was the Angevin Master Matthew, who himself had tutored Henry and his aunts. Ralph of Hastings often dealt with funding and provisions for Eleanor and her children, as did Henry's own seneschal, Manasser Bisset, and chamberlain, Warin Fitzgerald. Eleanor never learnt to speak English. That did not matter, for the language of English courtly circles was Anglo-Norman, closely related to the French of Normandy, the Loire and northern Poitou. Henry himself usually spoke French or Latin, though he was said to understand all languages 'from the French sea [the Channel] to the river Jordan'.[2]

Henry, like Louis, saw himself as ruling Aquitaine in his wife's name. He had himself invested as duke of Aquitaine at Limoges in autumn 1152.[3] But his mother was Empress Matilda; he was used to politically active women. From the start he probably envisaged more political engagement from Eleanor than Louis had encouraged, and he made her an integral part of his government, in a way that Louis had not. She attested some of his acts, though fewer than might have been expected, and all at

the start of his reign.[4] Since 1066 the kings of England were
often also dukes of Normandy. They expected their queens to
act as regent, assuming the governance of England or Normandy
when they were absent. Now, ruler of a huge dominion, Henry
depended on his mother, Empress Matilda, to ensure the governance of Normandy, while Eleanor acted frequently as regent in
England, especially between 1155 and 1160. She worked closely
with Henry's impressive team of royal administrators, who issued
writs and mandates in her name, and she sat in judgement on
various cases.[5] Between spring 1165 and summer 1166, Eleanor
acted as regent for Henry in Anjou-Maine, while he dealt with
issues in England. But her authority in Anjou did not go uncon-
tested. The Bretons saw an opportunity to challenge Norman-
Angevin overlordship and refused to obey her orders. Henry put
down their revolt and brought Brittany under tight control.[6]

But Eleanor played a limited role in the governance of her
own inheritance of Aquitaine in her first fourteen years as queen
of England. Henry was, if anything, less scrupulous about obtaining her assent to acts issued for Aquitaine than Louis had been.[7]
Eleanor paid few visits there. She and Henry went via Fontevraud
to Saintes in spring 1154 and to Limoges and Bordeaux in late
1156, holding their Christmas court at Bordeaux. But she missed
his Christmas court at Poitiers in 1166: she was in England giving
birth to their youngest child, John.

In 1159 she accompanied Henry to Gascony as he, like Louis
before him, attempted to enforce Eleanor's claim to the county
of Toulouse. Henry's chancellor, Thomas Becket, organized the
expedition. It was no more successful than Louis' attempt eight-
een years earlier. Louis' sister was now countess of Toulouse; to
protect her and her city, Louis himself led troops to Toulouse.
Henry was overcome with feudal scruple, and retreated rather
than attack the king of France, accepting Louis as his suzerain for
Toulouse. Becket was, apparently, disappointed. So, presumably,

was Eleanor. Had she persuaded Henry to pursue her claim to Toulouse? He probably needed little persuasion. Possession of Toulouse was an obvious goal for a duke of Aquitaine who controlled Bordeaux and the lower Garonne. Henry and his sons kept up continual pressure on the counts of Toulouse through warfare and diplomacy until, in October 1196, Richard tied Count Raymond VI of Toulouse into the Angevin family by marriage with his sister Joanna.[8]

It was Henry who tried to impose himself on the more independent Aquitanian nobles, like the lords of Lusignan and viscounts of Thouars, the counts of La Marche and Angoulême and the viscounts of Limoges. He may have followed Eleanor's advice, at least in the early years. When he attacked the viscount of Thouars, Eleanor urged him to destroy the nobleman's town and castle, even though he was her cousin.[9] Like Louis, Henry appointed the local officials, the provosts, who dealt with local justice and brought in the revenues of the duchy, and the seneschals of Poitou, Saintonge and Bordeaux, who acted as the main representative of the ruler. Here too, he probably took her advice. After her return to Poitou in March 1152, Eleanor had formed her own household: a new chancellor, Bernard; as seneschal, Saldebreuil, who was also constable of Poitou; and Hervey as her 'pantler' (the officer in charge of the pantry and the provision of that vital staple, bread, to the medieval household). She had started to develop an entourage of Poitevin nobility, particularly her maternal uncles Hugh of Châtellerault and Ralph of Faye, and families including the Mauléon and Chabot, who had attended her father's court.[10] The seneschalcy of Poitou had been held by the Mauzé family under both Dukes William, and when Eleanor was queen of France. But Eble of Mauléon, who had been quick to join Eleanor's entourage on her return in 1152, was seneschal of Poitou in 1154. By 1163 Eleanor's uncle, Ralph of Faye, was seneschal of Poitou.[11] Nevertheless, Henry had no

Poitevins in his household or in his usual entourage, and Eleanor's household in England, Normandy and Anjou was stuffed with English, Norman and Angevin courtiers chosen for her by her husband. The only Poitevins in her household recorded with her outside Aquitaine were Bernard of Chauvigny, her chamberlain, who was a Châtellerault cousin, Philip her butler and Peter the chaplain.[12] Only two Poitevins were given estates in England – Ralph of Faye and her personal seneschal Saldebreuil. Saldebreuil lost his English lands when Henry established Eleanor in Poitou in 1168.[13]

Henry's court was full of strong personalities. These included John of Salisbury and, above all, Thomas Becket, the chancellor, until Henry arranged for him to become archbishop of Canterbury in 1162. Eleanor must have negotiated her way through courtly rivalry and intrigue more effortlessly, more confidently, than she did as queen of France: for, from the first, she was the mother of a future king. Their first child, William, was born in 1153. He died at Christmas 1156, and was buried at the feet of his great-grandfather, Henry I, in Reading Abbey. Henry was born in February 1155; Matilda in June 1156; Richard in September 1157; Geoffrey in September 1158; Eleanor in September 1161; Joanna in October 1165; and finally, John at Christmas 1166. Most were born in England, though Eleanor was born in Domfront and Joanna when Eleanor was acting as regent in Angers. The frequent pregnancies meant that she travelled less than her restless husband. By and large she kept to southern England, moving from one royal residence to another, particularly Westminster, Windsor, Old Sarum (the precursor of Salisbury), Oxford and Winchester. The exchequer rolls show her crossing the Channel from time to time, usually from Southampton, in the royal longship, the *Esnecca* (or 'Snake'), with her husband or going to join him. Usually she took part in the great plenary courts at Christmas and Easter, joining Henry for the Christmas courts at Bordeaux in 1156,

Cherbourg in 1158, Falaise in 1159, Le Mans in 1160 and Cherbourg in 1162. Whenever possible, her young children travelled with her, whether in England or on the always risky sea crossings.[14]

Whether she was travelling with her husband or holding court for him in England in his absence, she must have made a fine figure as his queen. The exchequer rolls record expenditure on her (and his) magnificent apparel: the samites and sables, the opulent gilded saddles and harnesses. Eleanor and Henry kept a fine table, with wines from Poitou, almonds and spices – cinnamon, pepper and cumin.[15] Chroniclers said little about her when she was queen of France, even during the crusade. But now, in her thirties, confident, experienced, spirited, powerful, fecund, beautiful and tainted by the rumours of her liaison with her uncle, she began to attract their attention. John of Salisbury worked with her occasionally when she acted as regent in England. His *Historia pontificalis*, written in the mid-1160s, provides the first detailed account of the incident at Antioch, and the return from crusade, together with an extended account of the scandal of Aelith-Petronilla and Ralph of Vermandois. Robert of Torigni, the abbot of Le Mont-Saint-Michel, who was gradually compiling a chronicle of Henry's reign, gives due acknowledgement to Eleanor's role as queen. He is not effusive, but he records her appearances at the great courts, and her role as matriarch of the family. Robert himself stood as godparent for Eleanor's daughter (also named Eleanor) at Domfront in 1162.[16]

The most idiosyncratic comment came from Stephen of Rouen, a monk of the Norman abbey of Le Bec. He was a great admirer of Henry and Empress Matilda and wrote a long chronicle-poem on the dynasty of the Anglo-Norman king/dukes, known as the 'Draco Normannicus', around 1170. Stephen was fascinated, as were so many at the Angevin court, by the tales of King Arthur, which had first been gathered together in literary form by Geoffrey of Monmouth at the court of Henry I. Geoffrey of Monmouth's *History of the Kings of Britain* purported to record a set of fantastic prophesies by Merlin. Ever since Geoffrey's book was written, commentators had read current events as fulfilments of Merlin's prophecies. Abbot Suger, for instance, had seen Henry I as 'The Lion of Justice'. Now Stephen of Rouen identified Eleanor as the fulfilment of the phrase: 'The Eagle of the Broken Covenant will paint a bridle with gold and will rejoice in her third nesting.' The broken covenant was her divorce from Louis, but Stephen of Rouen saw Eleanor and her marriage to Henry as 'painting a bridle with gold' – that is, bringing wealth and lustre to Henry's realm. Stephen made no attempt to explicate 'rejoicing in her third nesting'.[17]

Henry's court was more opulent, more cultured and more intellectual than the Capetian court.[18] His favourite pastime was hunting, which Eleanor also enjoyed, but he was well educated, as were many of his clerks. History writing, romances, political writing, even science, all flourished, often produced by those who hoped for, rather than actually obtained, patronage from the king. Some works were dedicated to Eleanor – Wace's *Roman de Brut*; Benoît of Sainte-Maure's *Roman de Troie*; a translation of the *Gynaecia Cleopatrae*, a gynaecological text thought to have been written for Cleopatra; and Philip of Thaon's *Bestiary*, originally dedicated to Henry I's second wife. Most were dedications by those in hope of support rather than the result of active patronage on Eleanor's part. Benoît of Sainte-Maure may have been introduced to the Angevin court through Hugh of Sainte-Maure, a connection of the Châtellerault family.

As queen of England, if not as queen of France, Eleanor had the resources to be a prominent patron of arts and culture. But her record as a cultural patron is unimpressive in comparison with that of other elite women, including her predecessors as queen of England, and with that of her daughters, her second

Wall painting from the Sainte-Radegonde Chapel, Chinon, which has often been taken to depict Eleanor and the Angevin family. It almost certainly shows scenes from the life of St Radegonde. It probably dates from the 1160s and reflects the rich visual culture of Henry and Eleanor's court circles at the height of their joint power.

husband and most of her sons. Nor was Eleanor a particularly generous patron of the Church. Empress Matilda, Henry and Richard were all thoughtful patrons of reformed monasticism, especially Cistercians, and regular canons. This manifestation of 'soft power' was exploited by most elite women. But Eleanor's recorded religious patronage was largely confined to Fontevraud, and mostly near the end of her life.

In 1167 and 1168 Henry was faced with a serious revolt in Aquitaine led by the count of Angoulême and the lord of La Marche, along with Poitevins led by the Lusignans. The revolt was encouraged by Louis VII.[19] Henry proposed that Eleanor

should be established in Poitiers, to govern Poitou and Aquitaine
as regent duchess alongside their second son, Richard, who would
inherit the dukedom of Aquitaine. The presence of the duchess
herself, and the future duke, might dampen disaffection.

The extent of the discontent in Poitou was demonstrated
immediately. In early spring 1168 the ever-troublesome lords of
Lusignan tried to capture Eleanor as she and her entourage rode
between Poitiers and the castle of Niort. Eleanor herself escaped.
The leader of her forces, Earl Patrick of Salisbury, was killed;
some of his knights, including the young William Marshall, were
captured. Earl Patrick was valued by both Henry and Eleanor.
Together they set up a commemoration of the anniversary of
his death at the church of Saint-Hilaire in Poitiers.[20] Eleanor
earnt the devotion of the young William Marshall by paying for

View of the castle of Niort. Eleanor often visited this important
stronghold of the dukes of Aquitaine. The impressive and unusual
double tower-keep was commissioned by either Henry II or Richard I
(before he became king) in the later 12th century.

his ransom and supporting him as one of the knights in her entourage.[21]

Eleanor's return to her home city of Poitiers, alongside her favourite son, who would inherit her father's lands, suited everyone. Eleanor was now well into her forties. Henry had less use for her, personally and politically, in England. He no longer needed Eleanor to act as regent in England. He himself spent more time there, and he had built a highly efficient administrative team. As she approached menopause, the age difference between them doubtless became more obvious. Henry had never been a faithful husband. He had perhaps already installed Rosamund Clifford as his mistress. He mourned Rosamund deeply when she died in 1176 and had her buried before the high altar at Godstow priory in Oxfordshire.[22]

For the next five years, Poitiers, and the surrounding comital residences, was Eleanor and young Richard's base. When he was fourteen, in June 1172 Richard was formally invested as duke of Aquitaine at the abbey church of Saint-Martial at Limoges with the ring of St Valery, and as count of Poitou at Saint-Hilaire at Poitiers with the comital lance and banner.[23] For the first time since her second marriage, Eleanor was in charge of the government of her own inheritance, though most documents were issued jointly with Richard. Her household and entourage was dominated by a small clique of Poitevin nobility, with whom she governed the duchy. These were the aristocratic families who had provided the entourage of her father, with whom she had made contact on her return to the duchy in 1152 and on her few subsequent visits. Relatives or associates of her mother's extended Châtellerault family were prominent in her household and in her wider entourage. Her household comprised Hervey, the old pantler of her father, Saldebreuil her seneschal and Philip her butler. Members of her retinue also included Porteclie of Mauzé, William Maingot, Theobald Chabot, Geoffrey of Taunay,

and her cousins Fulk of Matha (son of her aunt Amabilis of
Châtellerault, countess of Angoulême) and William and Hugh
of Châtellerault. To the latter, she gave valuable lands with a
hunting park. She relied above all, as Bishop John of Poitiers
observed to Thomas Becket in 1165, on her uncle Ralph of Faye,
the seneschal of Poitou.[24]

Reliance on Ralph of Faye was unwise: he upset everyone.
In 1163 he extorted coin and twelve marks' worth of silver chalices from the priory of Saint-Georges at Oléron. The prior sent
two monks to complain to Henry in England, who refunded the
priory from his own treasure at Chinon.[25] Eleanor herself had to
call Ralph out for his rapacious attitude to church property.[26]
John of Salisbury and his friend, the scholarly Englishman John
'Bellesmains', bishop of Poitiers, distrusted Ralph as the worst
kind of scheming courtier – a man of 'wiles and rash daring'.[27]
Bishop John had clashed with Ralph in 1164, in the fallout from
Henry's quarrel with Becket. In letters to Becket, Bishop John
denounces Ralph as 'our Luscus' – our one-eyed – 'whose men-
tal eye God has entirely blinded'.[28] This was not metaphorical.
Ralph was indeed one-eyed. When the court was at Woodstock,
Ralph had insisted on hunting on Good Friday, to the horror of
Henry ii, who knew how to observe religious proprieties. Divine
providence intervened: as Ralph rode through the woods, his
right eye was ripped from its socket by a thorn.[29]

There has been much speculation about Eleanor's court at
Poitiers. A vast new great hall was built at the comital palace
in the later twelfth century. It is tempting to see this as Eleanor's
initiative, but it was probably built after she left Poitiers in 1173.
Were troubadours, writing courtly poetry in the southern French
Occitan language, attracted to Poitiers from their more southern homelands in the Limousin, Auvergne, Toulouse and
Gascony, as they had been when Poitiers was the residence of
her father and her grandfather, the troubadour William? If they

Great Hall of the palace, Poitiers. This was probably commissioned by
Richard as duke of Aquitaine in the 1180s, but Eleanor would have
known it well in the last decade or so of her life, and likely attended
Richard's 1195 Christmas court here, resplendent in scarlet and green.

were, they left no traces. In the late 1180s Andrew, a chaplain
at the court of Eleanor's oldest French daughter, Countess Mary
of Champagne, wrote an entertainment called *De amore* (On
Love), the title referencing Ovid. Andrew the chaplain lists the
rules of love, dispenses advice like a good agony uncle (good legs
in men are not an indication of good character; love of nuns
has its dangers . . .) and purports to record the proceedings and
rulings of 'courts of love', presided over by Countess Mary, her
mother, Eleanor of Aquitaine, Queen Adela of France, Viscountess
Ermengarde of Narbonne and Eleanor's niece, Elizabeth of
Vermandois, countess of Flanders. But it was a satirical fantasy,
not a reflection of what actually happened at Eleanor and young
Richard's court at Poitiers.[30] Like all courts, there must have been
plenty of hunting, feasting, music-making and other entertainment. But nothing suggests that it was a centre of vibrant cultural
efflorescence.

Eleanor joined Henry from time to time, for instance at his Christmas court at Chinon in 1172. She was at his Christmas court at Bur in Normandy in 1170, along with their sons Richard, Geoffrey and John, when news arrived of the murder of Thomas Becket in Canterbury Cathedral.[31] She was much concerned in the future provision for their children. Their oldest daughter, Matilda, had been married to Duke Henry of Saxony in 1168. Eleanor probably helped to compile the magnificent dowry of riches that Matilda took with her to Germany, including splendid silks from Spain, sables, silver-gilt vessels for the table and seven gilded saddles and gilded harnesses. She accompanied her daughter at the start of her long journey, when they stayed together at the cathedral priory at Canterbury before crossing the Channel to Wissant, where Eleanor handed her daughter into the care of the duke's ambassadors.[32] Eleanor took the lead in negotiating the marriage of her second daughter, Eleanor, to King Alfonso VIII of Castile in 1170. She drew on the familial relationships with Iberian rulers developed by her father and grandfather, particularly with her cousin, King Alfonso II of Aragon. Young Eleanor's generous dower arrangements were finalized at Bordeaux, in Eleanor's presence, with the assistance of Alfonso II. Those witnessing for Eleanor included the archbishop of Bordeaux and his Aquitanian suffragens, and her Poitevin supporters, Ralph of Faye, William of Châtellerault, Theobald Chabot and William Maingot.[33]

Provision for Eleanor and Henry's sons was more problematic. Henry, doubtless with Eleanor's agreement, intended their oldest surviving son, Henry, to succeed to the patrimony: that is, the English throne, the dukedom of Normandy and the county of Anjou. Henry had him crowned as the Young King in 1170. The next eldest, Richard, would inherit his mother's lands: Poitou and Aquitaine. The next son, Geoffrey, was married to the heiress to Brittany, over which Henry, as duke of Normandy, claimed overlordship. This left little available for the youngest son, John. A solution presented itself. The count of Maurienne offered his daughter and heiress in marriage. Maurienne was a rich county, through which, as Robert of Torigni observed, everybody who went to Italy had to pass. Eleanor was undoubtedly involved in arranging the projected marriage. Adela of Maurienne had been her first mother-in-law: the present count's father had accompanied her on crusade. Indeed, there had been an earlier marriage between the counts of Maurienne and the counts of Poitou/dukes of Aquitaine. In February 1173 the families came together at Montferrand to finalize the marriage. Eleanor's involvement is underscored by the presence of Ralph of Faye, William Maingot and Theobald Chabot.[34]

But the complex diplomacy came to nothing. Henry the Young King refused to accept a treaty which saw three important fortresses which he had assumed would eventually be his – Loudun, Chinon and Mirebeau – assigned to John. From Montferrand, the Angevin family, including Eleanor, moved on to Limoges, partly to resolve the sibling rivalries, partly to insist that Count Raymond v of Toulouse do homage for some of his lands to Richard as duke of Aquitaine. Count Raymond got his revenge by telling Henry ii that Eleanor and his sons were conspiring against him.[35]

Young Henry stood to gain most when his father died, but in the meantime, despite his coronation, he resented the extent to which his own authority was constrained by his father's overall control.[36] Perhaps Eleanor too chafed under the constant presence of Henry's familiars in Poitou. Henry had ensured that one of his most experienced administrators, Richard of Ilchester, was a canon of the cathedral of Poitiers and treasurer of the abbey of Saint-Hilaire. Several Normans and Angevins who were close to Henry – notably Maurice of Craon, Joscelin of Bailleul, William of Lanvallay, Simon of Tournebu and Richard of Camville – witnessed charters issued by Eleanor in Poitou. Were they there to help Henry retain control? Or did they bring welcome administrative expertise to Eleanor's government?[37]

Her old husband, Louis VII, was perfectly placed, as notional overlord of the Angevin lands, to exploit the combustible relationship between Henry and his sons. Like herself, Louis was a more experienced politician than he had been in the early years of their marriage. He knew his limitations – he would never be a great warrior and leader in the way that Henry was, neither would he ever have Henry's energy, sharp intelligence and strategic grasp. But he had become a wily and patient politician, who learnt to build good relationships with the Church – which he exploited shamelessly during Henry's long standoff with Thomas Becket.

Louis focused his attention on Henry the Young King, all the easier since Henry was married to Margaret, Louis' daughter from his second marriage. The Young King and his wife spent much time in Paris at the Capetian court from 1169. Louis was fully aware of Young Henry's disaffection, of his desire for a larger share of Henry II's powers, lands and resources. In March 1173 the Young King fled to Paris. Richard and Geoffrey were with Eleanor in Poitou; she sent them to join him.[38] By April, a full-scale revolt against Henry II had broken out across his realms. Many contemporary commentators reported rumours that Eleanor had incited her sons against their father; two of the best informed reported that Eleanor herself had been persuaded to join the plotting against Henry by her uncle, Ralph of Faye, and his associate, Hugh of Saint-Maure.[39]

The forces ranged against Henry appeared formidable. Louis and the Young King had persuaded the king of Scotland, the count of Flanders and several prominent Anglo-Norman lords, especially those to whom marriage had brought French lands, to join the rebellion. The Bretons and several Angevin barons revolted, as ever. Some, but not all, of Eleanor's Poitevin relations joined the uprising. But many Normans remained loyal to the Old King, and the Aquitanians from south of Poitou stayed aloof. Henry fought back in Normandy, and the revolt crumbled in the Loire Valley. Eleanor tried to make her escape to Paris, but she was captured – dressed as a man, claimed the disapproving monk Gervase of Canterbury – in November 1173 on the road from Poitou to Chartres.[40] By summer 1174 Henry's opponents were defeated and in disarray. Henry forgave his sons. He reinstated Richard as count of Poitou and duke of Aquitaine. But he did not forgive Eleanor. He sent her to England and imprisoned her in Old Sarum castle.

Henry was not vengeful. He considered divorcing Eleanor and persuading her to retire as a nun at Fontevraud. Eleanor refused.[41] Instead, she remained under house arrest in the comfortable and elegant courtyard palace at Old Sarum. Henry took control of Eleanor's dower. Nevertheless, he funded Eleanor's living expenses with reasonable, and increasing, generosity, and ordered continual improvement works at Old Sarum. In 1178/9 Henry sent her a gilded saddle for hunting. She had a suite of ladies with her, including perhaps one called Bellebell, favoured, like Eleanor herself, with expensive clothing.[42]

In June 1183 Henry the Young King died of dysentery in the Limousin. He was fighting Richard over Aquitanian borderlands and had sacked nearby monasteries to pay his troops. On his deathbed, he wrote asking his father to forgive him, and to have mercy on Eleanor. Young Henry's chaplain, Thomas, canon of Wells, took the news of the death to Eleanor at Old Sarum. Perhaps with Eleanor's support, Thomas wrote a tract to promote Young Henry as a potential saint. He reported miracles generated by the Young King's dead body, and a dream in which Eleanor saw her son crowned not just with an earthly coronet, but with one that gleamed with heavenly light.[43]

Henry II himself was devastated at the sudden death of his wayward but charming oldest son.[44] He did, it seems, take seriously his son's request for mercy on his mother. From then on, Eleanor made more frequent appearances at court, though these were usually to Henry's advantage in the complex game of family politics. He insisted she progress through her dowerlands in 1183, to prevent the new French king, Philip, claiming any of them for his sister Margaret, the Young King's widow.[45] In December 1184 Eleanor attended a council at Westminster at which their younger sons, Richard, Geoffrey and John, still squabbling over territory and resources, were reconciled.[46] In April 1185 Henry demanded her presence at Alençon in Normandy, where he forced Richard to surrender the county of Poitou to his mother, and thus, effectively, back into Henry's own control. At Henry's request, Eleanor issued a charter assigning £100 worth of annual income from the county of Poitou to the abbey of Fontevraud, for her own soul, and the souls of her husband, Richard and all

Old Sarum, where Eleanor was imprisoned from 1174 until the early 1180s.

of her sons and daughters. Chroniclers felt these were momen-
tous times, confirmed by an earthquake that was felt throughout
England.[47]

Soon there were only two sons left. Geoffrey of Brittany went
to Paris, to enlist King Philip in his plot to acquire Anjou. Philip,
Louis VII's only son, succeeded his father in 1180 at the age of
fifteen. In spite of his youth, he quickly showed himself to be a
wily and ruthless politician. He shattered the dominance of the
two powerful factions at his father's court – the counts of
Champagne, including Philip's mother, Adela of Champagne,
and the count of Flanders, including Philip's wife, Isabelle of
Hainault. Then he turned his attention to the Angevins, exploit-
ing, as his father had done, the familial jealousies between Henry
and his sons. He developed a friendship with Geoffrey. At Paris,
in August 1186, Geoffrey was killed in a tournament, trampled
beneath the feet of his horse. Philip, deeply upset, had his body
buried in the choir of Notre-Dame in Paris.[48] But no contemporary suggests that either Henry or Eleanor suffered the intense
grief that the death of the Young King had brought them.

And in the meantime, their eldest daughter, Matilda, brought
them joy, which perhaps they sometimes shared. Matilda's husband, Henry the Lion, rebelled against Emperor Frederick
Barbarossa and had to flee with his family to seek refuge in
Angevin lands. Initially they were based in Normandy, but then,
from 1184, in Winchester. Eleanor spent much time with her
daughter and their children, Matilda-Richenza, Henry and Otto,
and a baby, William, born in Winchester. They all attended
Henry's Christmas court at Windsor in 1184.[49] By the mid-1180s,
Eleanor's life was one of familial and courtly pleasures. She had
no access to her own income and her political power was constrained, as was brutally apparent at Alençon, but she had resumed
her place as matriarch within the family.

THREE

Queen Dowager

In July 1189 Henry II died at Chinon. It was a miserable death, defeated by an alliance between Richard and King Philip of France. Richard immediately gave orders for the release of his mother. Her dower was returned to her, and she was given an augmented household to support her activities. Richard asked her to tour his English kingdom, doing justice, righting the wrongs of his father and preparing the way for Richard's coronation. She processed, wrote Roger of Howden, with a queenly court, freeing prisoners, because she herself understood so well the joys of freedom. When she heard Henry's horses stamping in the stable of an abbey, she ordered them to be distributed to those who needed them.[1]

At Richard's coronation in September 1189, Eleanor sported a mantle of the best green silk, lined with variegated furs and trimmed with sable.[2] She was accompanied by a well-dressed entourage of the important younger women of the court: Richard's fiancé, Alice of France; John's fiancé, Isabelle of Gloucester; and Denise, heiress to the lordship of Berry, who had just married Eleanor's cousin, Richard's close companion, Andrew of Chauvigny, in Eleanor's presence at Old Sarum.[3] Richard intended his mother to act as she had done in the earlier years of her marriage to Henry, as one of his most important counsellors, both in private and at plenary courts, and as a crowned and anointed queen who could assume the governance of any of his vast dominions in his absence – and Richard intended to be absent, for he had taken the Cross in 1187. A new interpretation of Eleanor as the 'eagle of the broken covenant' started to circulate. The broken covenant was no longer her divorce from Louis, but her betrayal of Henry. Now Eleanor fulfilled another of Geoffrey of Monmouth's ludicrous prophetic phrases, as the eagle who rejoiced in her third nesting – in her third son, Richard the Lionheart.[4]

In March 1190 Richard summoned Eleanor and his other advisors to a council at Nonancourt in Normandy to make final provisions for his realms before departing on crusade. The French king, Philip, was joining the crusade too: the lands of a crusader were under papal protection, so there should be nothing to fear from Capetian encroachments on Angevin lordship. Richard established his trusted and financially expert Norman administrator, William Longchamp, bishop of Ely, as justiciar of England. Richard clearly feared trouble from John and their illegitimate brother, Geoffrey Plantagenet, archbishop of York: both had to swear that they would not enter England during Richard's absence.[5] Eleanor was not given an official role as regent, but Richard doubtless trusted her to keep a watching brief and deal with trouble either familial or political during his absence.

He also depended on Eleanor to resolve his marital entanglements. Richard was betrothed to Alice of France, born of Louis VII's second marriage. She had been kept at the English court for many years. Since at least 1186/7 she had probably been in Eleanor's care, along with Matilda of Saxony's children, and Eleanor brought her to the council at Nonancourt. Alice brought the county of the Vexin as dowry, so she was an important political pawn. There were rumours she had been seduced, perhaps raped, by Henry II. Richard would use those rumours to extract himself from his obligation to marry her.[6] For he was now more concerned about problems in the far south of his

realms than French attacks on Normandy. He built an alliance
with Sancho VI of Navarre and proposed to marry his daughter
Berengaria. But these marital plans needed to remain secret, to
avoid alienating Alice's brother, King Philip. Richard entrusted
the finalization of the marriage negotiations with Navarre, and
the delicate commission to deliver Berengaria to him somewhere
on the journey to the Holy Land, to Eleanor.

Once again, Eleanor invoked her longstanding Iberian familial networks, for Berengaria's mother was Castilian. The project
needed to be planned meticulously and managed discreetly. It
was an epic journey. Leaving Richard at Chinon on 24 June 1190,
Eleanor travelled to Pamplona. Then, with Berengaria, Eleanor
crossed southern France, then the Alps in deep winter, arriving
in northern Italy in January 1191. There she undertook more
diplomacy for Richard, meeting Emperor Henry VI to assure him
that Richard would support his claims to the disputed throne of
Sicily. Eleanor and Berengaria met up with Richard in Sicily at
the end of March.[7] Eleanor was reunited with her youngest
daughter, Joanna, who had been married to William II of Sicily.
William died without a direct heir, and Joanna had been rescued
from the ensuing succession dispute by Richard. Richard was
determined to rescue Joanna's dowry too, which included a gold
throne, 'a gold table twelve-foot long' (3.5 metres) and a vast silk
tent. Now Joanna would accompany Berengaria on the rest of
her journey – initially to Cyprus, where Richard and Berengaria
were married. The monastic chronicler Richard of Devizes saw
the new queen as no rival to the old, dismissing Berengaria as a
girl more prudent than pretty.[8]

Eleanor remained in Sicily for four days.[9] Shortly before her
arrival, Richard had received news that William Longchamp was
struggling to impose his authority as justiciar and had fallen out
with John. Richard needed Eleanor's diplomatic expertise as he
tried to resolve the situation at a distance. She returned via Rome,

where she persuaded the new pope, Celestine III, to allow the consecration of her stepson, Geoffrey Plantagenet, as archbishop of York, and his appointment as papal legate to England, to keep an eye on Longchamp and John. She was accompanied by the archbishop of Rouen, Walter of Coutances, an experienced Angevin administrator, who travelled on to England. Eleanor herself remained, probably at Richard's behest, in Normandy, to ensure the stability of the duchy. She spent Christmas 1191 in her Norman castle at Bonneville-sur-Touques.[10]

The intervention of Walter of Coutances and Geoffrey Plantagenet only inflamed the situation in England.[11] Longchamp had been a loyal and effective administrator, and his understanding of royal finances was unrivalled. But he was clever, small, simian, of modest birth and Norman – and managed to alienate many of his fellow prelates and most of the magnates.[12] John put himself at the head of the disaffected magnates. Longchamp outmanoeuvred Walter of Coutances, dismissing as forgeries the letters from Richard giving Walter authority equal to Longchamp. When Geoffrey Plantagenet landed at Dover in September 1191, Longchamp had him arrested and flung into prison. John called a great council at Marlborough, at which Longchamp was deposed as justiciar and hounded out of the country. He fled to Normandy disguised as a woman, via Dover, where, it was rumoured, he was indecently assaulted by a fisherman.[13]

Walter of Coutances now headed the government of England as chief justiciar and set much value on Eleanor's advice.[14] Now there was a new threat to the Angevin realms. King Philip had not had a good crusade. He was continually outclassed, as king and as warrior, by the charismatic and decisive Richard. He left before Richard and was back in Paris by 27 December 1191. He was, more than ever, determined to impose royal overlordship over the French lands of the Angevin dynasty. There was no doubt about that overlordship in theory. Henry II had drawn back from attacking his king and overlord at Toulouse, and he had allowed his sons to do homage for his continental lands to the French king. Louis vii had never managed to make it more than theoretical. He lacked the wealth, and thus the military power, of Henry ii. But Philip was now much richer than his father had been. Through his marriage to Isabelle of Hainault, and through the failure of Aelith/Petronilla and Ralph of Vermandois' children to produce heirs, large, rich stretches of northeastern France – Artois, and parts of the Vermandois – fell to Philip. His clerical courtiers started to call him Philip 'Augustus' because he had increased (the Latin verb is *augere*, hence Augustus) the area of France under direct royal control – and, of course, it added Roman lustre to his name.[15]

Philip tried to seduce the ever-susceptible John by the offer of his sister Alice in marriage, and of Richard's French lands. As soon as she heard, in early February 1192 Eleanor sailed to England. She used all her maternal and reginal authority to insist that John did not leave England and talked him out of the alliance with Philip. Along with Walter of Coutances, she ensured that all magnates took an oath of fidelity to Richard. She persuaded Longchamp and Walter of Coutances to drop their mutual excommunications and interdicts against each other, their followers and diocesans. She was shocked by the misery inflicted on the people of the diocese of Ely by the interdict which forbad the sacraments, including the last rites and burial.[16] Longchamp tried to return to England, but Eleanor, judging this too contentious, ordered him back to Normandy.

In January 1193 news reached England that Richard had been captured on his way back from crusade. He was now a prisoner of Emperor Henry vi, who demanded a huge ransom for Richard's release. John seized the opportunity. He sped to France, did homage to Philip Augustus for Richard's French lands, promised to marry the unfortunate Alice and returned to England with a force of mercenaries. He declared Richard dead and demanded recognition of himself as king.[17]

Eleanor took control. Only she had the authority to do so: the authority of legitimacy as a crowned and anointed queen; the authority of long experience in politics and diplomacy; and the authority of a matriarch in dealing with her exasperatingly opportunist youngest son. She ordered the fortification of the Channel ports against a French invasion. She edged John into a truce: he surrendered most of the royal castles he had appropriated into Eleanor's custody.[18] When the archbishopric of Canterbury fell vacant in 1193, Richard charged Eleanor, in letters sent from captivity, with ensuring the successful election of his preferred candidate, Hubert Walter, bishop of Salisbury.[19]

Eleanor's principal objective was Richard's release. Three powerfully emotional letters to Pope Celestine III in Eleanor's name were drafted by the curial clerk and brilliant letter-writer, Peter of Blois. They have been much discussed.[20] Celestine was an old friend of Eleanor. She had met him at the papal court in 1149, when he was still Hyacinth, cardinal deacon of Santa Maria in Cosmedin, and had remained in contact.[21] Peter of Blois was one of the most renowned letter-writing specialists of the later twelfth century. He wrote on behalf of Henry II, King William of Sicily, and many of the busy bishops of the Angevin Church, including Archbishop Rotrou of Rouen and Walter of Coutances. Indeed, he penned a letter to Eleanor from Rotrou in 1173, reprimanding her for turning Henry's sons against him, and urging her to return to her husband before it was too late.[22] But in 1193 he was working alongside Eleanor, Walter of Coutances and the regency government.

The three letters demand action from Pope Celestine to ensure the release of Richard from imprisonment. They are very demanding. Why hasn't the pope sent a delegation of cardinal legates? Does he not remember how Richard's father supported

Pope Alexander III when the emperor's father supported the anti-pope? And Richard is a crusader, under the protection of the Church. He is the Lord's Anointed. The letters lay bare Eleanor's anger, her desperation and the profound, 'almost insane grief' of a mother whose son is in danger. She only has two sons left now, one in chains, the other ravaging his brother's lands. If there are sins to be expiated, they are her own and Henry's, not her son's. And she is ageing, her eyes dimming . . . No heartstring is left unplucked. Famously and irresistibly, Eleanor describes herself in one letter as 'Eleanor by the Wrath of God Queen of England'.

Some historians have taken these letters at face value and have heard the voice of Eleanor herself in them. Most have been more sceptical. The three letters are repetitive and overlap in content. They read like drafts for a single missive. There is heavy emphasis on Richard in chains – which he was not. Peter of Blois issued several collections of his letters. The Eleanor letters appear in the compilation issued around 1205, contained in an early thirteenth-century manuscript (BNF ms lat. 2605 and 2607). Peter intended his collected letters to show off his brilliant literary artifice. He edited his compilations heavily, improved genuine letters, crafted fantasy ones and never let inconvenient facts get in the way of a rhetorical flourish. Whether the three letters were commissioned by Eleanor, or were merely rhetorical inventions, Peter had to make them correspond to contemporary readers' and hearers' ideas of what Eleanor might say and how she might say it. They are strongly, desperately emotional. Is that because Eleanor was an emotional person; or because Peter thought that a queen of England whose son was imprisoned should be very emotional?

In fact, the powerfully emotive letter was Peter of Blois' speciality. His literary tone was always highly charged. He sometimes seemed drunk on words. Peter sent other letters demanding

Richard's release, one to the pope in the name of Walter of Coutances, and one in his own name to an old college friend who was now a key figure in the negotiations, the archbishop of Mainz.[23] They are shorter, but hardly more restrained than the Eleanor letters. 'What should you do for such a son, for such a prince? Whose utterly unjust imprisonment is lamented by provinces, grieves the people, is deplored by the Church, and is to be detested above all plots either ancient or modern?' thunders 'Walter of Coutances'. 'When, since the beginnings of the Church, has any other king – peaceful, innocent, a pilgrim – been so treacherously captured, so cruelly sold . . . where is the law of nature?', Peter asks the archbishop, concluding that this is the work of Antichrist.

Most medieval letters were not designed for private consumption, but to be read out in public before the intended recipient, and to circulate among the networks of senior churchmen who staffed the administrations of princes. They were propaganda tools. Eleanor's letters, as preserved in Peter's collection, are unlikely to be exactly as sent. But together with Peter's other missives, they suggest that Eleanor and Walter of Coutances orchestrated a sophisticated epistolary campaign to advocate and pressurize for Richard's release. To do so, they turned to one of the masters of the art, known to use a high emotional register.

Eleanor and Walter of Coutances had to raise the ransom demanded by the emperor – 150,000 marks. The Church contributed across the Angevin lands, giving gold where they had it (and most major ecclesiastical institutions did) or wool, if, like the Cistercians, they did not. One pound was levied on each knight's fee, and a tax of a quarter imposed on all moveable goods. In June 1193 Eleanor and Walter of Coutances called a council at St Albans, which determined that the ransom monies and treasure were to be stored in chests at St Paul's Cathedral in London, chests sealed with the seals of the queen and the archbishop. At Richard's request, a list of the hostages to be held against the payment were sent to him under his mother's seal.[24]

With the ransom raised, Eleanor set off for Germany to negotiate Richard's release. She was accompanied by Walter of Coutances and the new archbishop of Canterbury, Hubert Walter, by William Longchamp, by Savary, bishop of Bath (who was German and a relation of the emperor) and by the Aquitanian bishops Henry of Saintes and Sebrand Chabot, bishop of Limoges.[25] They arrived in Cologne on 6 January 1194 and went on to Speyer, where they met Richard. A great assembly was held on 2 February at Mainz to settle the terms of Richard's release, especially the handing over of prominent hostages on both sides. The imperial hostages, the archbishops of Cologne and Mainz, were to be given into Eleanor's custody. Two of her grandchildren, Henry of Saxony and Eleanor of Brittany, were to be married to, respectively, the emperor's daughter and the duke of Austria – who died in agony after the amputation of a gangrenous foot before young Eleanor arrived.[26] At the last minute, Henry vi demanded that Richard surrender England to him as an imperial fief. Eleanor persuaded Richard to agree: the important thing was the return of the king to his kingdom.[27] On 4 February 1194 Richard was released. One chronicler describes a rainbow around the sun welcoming the arrival of the king and his mother in England.[28]

Eleanor joined Richard's triumphal procession around his kingdom. She was prominent at his second coronation in Winchester Cathedral on 17 April, seated surrounded by her ladies in the north transept, opposite the king.[29] After that, Richard and Eleanor crossed over to Normandy. Richard had much to do to counter the incursions of Philip Augustus and the treachery of John during his absence. John threw himself on his brother's mercy at Lisieux in May. Eleanor persuaded Richard to forgive his brother.[30]

With John repentant and Richard back in control and dealing with Aquitaine, Eleanor, who was now around seventy, could retire. She chose the abbey of Fontevraud as her main residence. Henry was buried there, and it had been the recipient of patronage from her husband and, to a lesser extent, herself, and from both their ancestors. An ex-member of her household, Alice of Brittany, was prioress. Her granddaughter Alice of Blois, daughter of the baby Alixe that Eleanor left behind at the Capetian court in 1152, had recently entered as a nun.[31] Eleanor herself did not take the veil. Instead, she established her large household, with her many ladies, chaplains, clerks and knights, in what must have been a substantial residence close to, perhaps just within, the gates to the abbey. Her daughter Joanna, the ex-queen of Sicily, joined her.[32] Eleanor travelled to other residences from time to time: for instance, she issued acts at Chinon and Saumur in 1196.[33] She must have joined Richard at his Christmas court at Poitiers in 1195, since scarlet and green cloths and 39 furs for cloak linings were procured for her from London.[34] Perhaps she attended the marriage of Joanna to Raymond VI of Toulouse at Rouen in October 1196 – a marriage of even more naked political expediency than most, arranged by Richard.

Sometime in 1198 she visited Rouen. Philip of Dreux, bishop of Beauvais, one of the many sons of Louis VII's fertile and pushy brother, Robert of Dreux, had been captured in battle and was held prisoner in the ducal castle at Rouen. Eleanor asked for an interview with Philip of Dreux. His guards would not let him go to her lodging, so she came to speak to Philip in the castle. As his guards took him to see her, he escaped to a chapel and claimed sanctuary. He was soon recaptured. Richard had no sympathy for the bishop, who had advocated against his own release from imprisonment in the Empire. He despatched Philip to the castle of Chinon, where Philip languished until released in a prisoner exchange after Richard's death – despite a letter from Philip to

Celestine III making much of his fettered state, almost as emotive, if less finely turned, than those penned by Peter of Blois
for Richard's release.[35] The story is recounted laconically by two
well-informed chroniclers, Roger of Howden and William of
Newburgh.[36] Was Eleanor's intervention driven by misguided
sympathy with a prisoner? She must have been only too aware
of the bishop's attempts to counter her own negotiations for
Richard's release. Probably this was some kind of elaborate plot
to demonstrate Philip of Dreux's intentions to escape, to justify
moving him deeper into Angevin territory at Chinon. If so, it
demonstrates that Eleanor remained politically active despite
her semi-retirement.

In spring 1196 Richard conferred the duchy of Aquitaine and
the county of Poitou on his nephew, Otto, a younger son of
Matilda of Saxony.[37] It made no difference to Eleanor's income:
she continued to receive her dower revenues from the duchy,
while the rest, collected by the seneschals, went to Otto rather
than Richard. Richard's marriage to Berengaria showed no sign
of producing the desired male heir; Richard and Eleanor were
perhaps grooming Otto for this role. In 1189 Richard had tempted
the strategically important count of Perche into the Angevin
orbit, by giving Otto's sister, Matilda-Richenza, in marriage to
Geoffrey, the heir to the county. Otto would be well placed to succeed his uncle. But within a couple of years a more tempting
prospect opened before Otto – the kingdom of Germany and
the title of emperor. In late 1198 Otto resigned the duchy of
Aquitaine and went, with the blessing of his uncle, to Germany.

In March 1199 Richard was shot with an arrow as he besieged
the castle of Châlus while attempting to contain a rebellion by
the viscount of Limoges. It became clear the king was dying. He
summoned Eleanor to his deathbed. He died on 6 April. Eleanor
took his body back to Fontevraud, for burial, as Richard had
requested, at the feet of his father.[38] The family gathered for the

Detail of the imperial mantle of Otto IV, Eleanor's grandson, with the Angevin Lions.

funeral, including John, Berengaria and Matilda-Richenza of Perche.[39]

On his deathbed, Richard left the succession to the entire Angevin realm to his younger brother John.[40] But the succession was not indisputable. Customary law in Anjou and the Loire held that the rightful successor was Arthur, son of the brother senior to John, Geoffrey of Brittany, rather than Richard's youngest brother. Arthur, born just after the death of his father, had been brought up by his mother, Constance, countess of Brittany in her own right. In 1196 Richard demanded Constance hand Arthur over to him as a royal ward. Breton nobles, who had always chafed against Angevin dominion, smuggled Arthur to Paris and the protection of Philip Augustus.[41] Hence Richard's promotion of Matilda of Saxony's offspring. Eleanor was now determined that John should succeed to all the Angevin realms. If Arthur succeeded to Brittany and Anjou, it would have been very difficult for John to govern Aquitaine alongside Normandy

and England. But many Breton and Angevin lords declared for
Arthur. Eleanor and John acted quickly. They attacked Le Mans.
Then Eleanor, along with Richard's brilliant mercenary captain
Mercadier, captured Angers.[42] Like Richard, John depended on
his mother to secure his succession.

John concentrated on Normandy and England, where he was
crowned king on 25 May. Eleanor secured Aquitaine. She held
a great council of Gascon magnates and prelates at Bordeaux on
1 July, then went north to Tours, where she ensured that Arthur
would have no claim to the duchy by doing personal homage for
it to Philip August. John then agreed to give the entire duchy
over to her. She would have the governance of it; to her would
come its revenues. John's only proviso was that she should not
make major alienations of ducal property without his permission.
There was an element of co-rule. John had a tendency to micro-
manage from England and Normandy, sending several mandates
directly to Robert of Thurnham, the seneschal of Poitou, and
Martin Algais, the seneschal of Gascony, perhaps increasingly
as Eleanor aged. Nevertheless, in April 1203 John ordered Robert
of Thurnham that the moneys sent, presumably for the defence
of Aquitaine, were only to be distributed by the counsel, and in
the presence of Eleanor herself. Now, for the first time since
the brief interlude between her two marriages, Eleanor acted as
duchess of Aquitaine *suo jure*, in her own right.[43]

Eleanor's household scribes were busy as she issued a huge
number of charters. She made gifts to the great ecclesiastical institutions of the duchy, reminding them how much they owed to
her predecessors.[44] She issued generous charters to the urban and
merchant communities of Aquitaine – to Bordeaux, Poitiers,
Saintes, La Rochelle and the island of Oléron – to ensure their
support.[45] She appealed to the Poitevin nobility to support her
son, making enticing gifts of lands to Andrew of Chauvigny,
William Maingot and Ralph of Mauléon.[46]

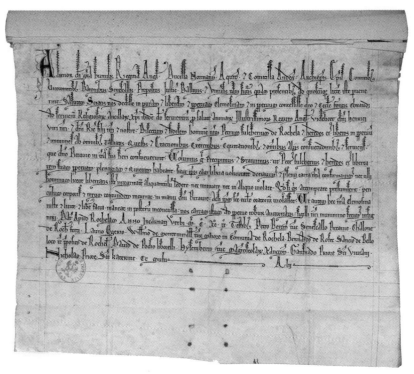

Act of Eleanor for Fontevraud, issued at La Rochelle in 1199, with unusually elaborate penwork. Witnessed by, among others, Master Isembert, master of the schools at Saintes, who built the bridges at Saintes, La Rochelle and London Bridge.

By May 1199 Eleanor had been joined again by her youngest daughter, Joanna. Joanna's second marriage had turned out little better than her first, and there was a rebellion in Toulouse. Joanna, heavily pregnant, sought refuge with her mother, accompanying her on her itineration around Aquitaine. In August, Eleanor and Joanna, with their entourage, went north to join John's court in Normandy. Here John and Eleanor issued their charters confirming the status of and succession to the duchy of Aquitaine: that she would rule Aquitaine during her lifetime and acknowledge John as her heir. But there was little time for celebration. Joanna became seriously ill. She made her will, witnessed by her mother.

She took the veil as a nun of Fontevraud and died giving birth
to a son who died shortly thereafter. She asked to be buried at
Fontevraud. Eleanor took her daughter's body to Fontevraud for
burial, as she had done so recently for Richard.[47]

Between them, Eleanor and John had stalled Arthur's claims.
A truce was declared between John and his nephew, and Philip
Augustus recognized John as the rightful heir to the Angevin
lands. It came at a high price. John paid a massive relief and recognized the French king as overlord for his French lands. Philip
insisted that the treaty be reinforced by a marriage between his
son and heir and a daughter of John's older sister, Eleanor, queen
of Castile. Philip had custody of Arthur and had married him to
his daughter Mary. Philip saw both the daughter of the queen of
Castile, and Arthur, as potential claimants to the Angevin lands,
or even the English crown, for John had no direct heir.

Once again, an Angevin king depended on Eleanor to finalize and finesse the negotiation of an important strategic marriage.
Now in her late seventies, Eleanor travelled to Castile in the early
winter months of 1200. The journey started badly. Hugh of
Lusignan detained Eleanor and her entourage just south of Poitiers
and forced her to hand the county of La Marche over to him.[48]
She saw her daughter Eleanor for the first time since Eleanor left
for Castile in 1170, though the Angevin family had remained
in touch with gifts and embassies. According to later Spanish
chroniclers, Eleanor of Aquitaine had to choose the most appropriate granddaughter to take back for the marriage. The oldest
and prettiest had a name – Urraca – which Eleanor deemed un-
pronounceable in Paris, so she chose the younger, less pretty
Blanca, which would transform into Blanche, instead. Whatever
the truth of that, the twelve-year-old granddaughter that Eleanor
took back with her was well chosen. Blanche of Castile, queen
of Louis VIII of France, mother of Louis IX, St Louis, queen regent
of France 1226–34 and 1248–52, would turn out to be an even

more formidable politician than her grandmother. Eleanor and young Blanche reached Bordeaux at Easter 1200. But there Richard's old soldier companion, Mercadier, was murdered. Eleanor was shocked and exhausted. At Fontevraud, Eleanor was too tired to go any further, and the archbishop of Bordeaux took her granddaughter on to Normandy and marriage.[49]

There was a short respite, but relations between John and Philip Augustus soon broke down. John had married Isabelle, heiress to the strategically important county of Angoulême. Unfortunately, she was already betrothed to Hugh of Lusignan. Hugh complained to Philip, as John's overlord. Philip called John before his court to answer. When John did not appear, Philip's court declared that all his French lands were forfeit to the king of France. Once more Eleanor tried to buy support for John among the towns, churches and barons of Poitou and Aquitaine. This time she had less success. She reminded Aimery of Thouars of their cousinship – but in October 1199 Aimery's brother Guy had married Constance of Brittany.[50] Perhaps they remembered that Eleanor herself had urged Henry II to destroy Thouars in 1158. Many Poitevins, even those who were closely related to her, or who had served the Angevins for many years, were tempted to support Arthur rather than tricky, treacherous John.

In summer 1202 Arthur, acknowledged by Philip as duke of Aquitaine, invaded Anjou and northern Poitou at the head of a French force. Eleanor, with a small group of her knights, fled Fontevraud for the safety of Poitiers, stopping at Mirebeau. There she was cornered and besieged by Arthur and his French forces. Eleanor sent word to John, who for once rose to the occasion. He sped across country with a small elite force of mercenaries and attacked the attackers. Arthur and his men were still eating breakfast. Arthur was taken prisoner, along with some of Eleanor's Châtellerault cousins, including Andrew of Chauvigny, who

ut sedeant mecum: ambulans in uia im
maculata hic michi ministrabat.
on habitabit in medio domus mee qui
facit superbiam: qui loquitur iniqua
non direxit in conspectu oculorum meorum.
In matutino interficiebam omnes peccato
res terre: ut disperderem de ciuitate domi
ni omnes opantes iniquitatem. Quintus

cognoscant misericordiam + dei peccata misericordiam.

NE EXAUDI
orationem meam:
et clamor meus ad
te ueniat.
Non auertas fa
ciem tuam à me in
quacūq; die tribu
lor: inclina ad me
aurem tuam.
Inquacunq; die inuocauero

Blanche of Castile, Eleanor's granddaughter, shown in her psalter,
produced for Blanche *c.* 1216, before she became queen of France.

had been so loyal to Richard, and her own previously devoted knight, Chalo of Rochefort.[51]

Eleanor was now nearly eighty. Once again, she returned to the peace of Fontevraud. She made occasional visits to Poitiers and strove to ensure the stability of her duchy. The news from further north was sobering. She must have known that more and more Angevin nobles were withdrawing their support from John, as rumours trickled through that John had murdered Arthur, who was, after all, her grandson. In 1203 Philip invaded Normandy, and by early 1204 much of it was in his hands. When Eleanor died at the turn of March and April 1204, Rouen, the capital of Normandy, had not yet fallen to Philip Augustus, but it was only a matter of time. As her life ended, so did the great *imperium*, the realm that she fought so hard to keep intact for her sons. The Capetian king of France won in the end.

FOUR

Family and Dynasty

leanor was heiress to a venerable dynasty. The dukes of Aquitaine were great princes of the French kingdom, equal in status to the dukes of Burgundy and Normandy. They were an old family, of Carolingian descent, counts of Poitou, who had taken the title of Duke of Aquitaine in the tenth century, and could call themselves Dukes of Gascony from 1063. Count/ Dukes William v, 'The Great' (r. 990–1029) and Guy-Geoffrey, who took the ducal name William (VIII, r. 1058–86), were particularly distinguished. They made their rule effective through a well-judged blend of alliance, warfare and the sort of demonstrative piety and generous religious patronage that induced admiration from monastic chroniclers.

Eleanor's grandfather, William IX of Aquitaine (r. 1086–1126), had a more colourful reputation – as a poet, warrior and adulterer.[1] His fame, or infamy, reached chroniclers in England and Normandy, like William of Malmesbury and Orderic Vitalis. His military activities attracted some approbation, for he fought in the Holy Land and in Spain, usually against the Muslims, but alongside Muslim kings if that offered better opportunities for wealth. His poetry was sung and written down in the Occitan language and the idiom of the southern lands of his duchy, of the Limousin, the Auvergne and Gascony, though his principal power base was in Poitou. His subject was war and illicit love. His personal life matched his poetry all too well.

He married Philippa, heiress to the county of Toulouse.[2] Through Philippa the dukes of Aquitaine traced their claims to Toulouse, claims pursued by William IX, by Eleanor's father and by both of her husbands – though after Philippa's death possession of the county fell to her uncle and cousins. Contemporary churchmen admired Philippa. She was an effective ruler when her husband was absent, and she was notably pious. An early patron of the charismatic if disorganized holy man, Robert of Arbrissel, the founder of Fontevraud, she eventually retired into a Fontevraudine house which she founded. She provided Duke William with children but no satisfaction. William left her and installed in her place at court in Poitiers the wife of the viscount of Châtellerault, a woman sometimes called Amalberge, but usually Dangereuse. Most churchmen regarded Duke William's relationship with Dangereuse as bigamous. The impression of a disorderly court was only reinforced when he married his son and heir, William, to Aenor, daughter of Dangereuse and her husband, Viscount Aimery of Châtellerault.

William the Young became count of Poitou and duke of Aquitaine at his father's death in 1126.[3] His father had had him well educated: his tutor was the sub-cantor of Poitiers cathedral. His marital history was unexceptional, but he found himself on the wrong side of a papal schism, and thus with a tarnished reputation among contemporary chroniclers. With Aenor, he had three children – William Aigret, the heir, Eleanor and Aelith. When Aenor and William Aigret died in the early 1130s, Duke William needed another wife to provide a male heir. The successor to the count of Angoulême ran off with his first choice, the heiress of Limoges.[4] He was probably seeking an Iberian bride when he set off on his fatal pilgrimage to Santiago de Compostela in early spring 1137.

Eleanor's father's marriage to a daughter of the regional Poitevin aristocracy was unique within the dynasty of the counts

Eleanor's grandfather Duke William IX, shown next to one of his poems:
'Since I feel like singing/ I'll write a verse I grieve over/ I shall never be a
vassal any more/ in Poitiers nor in Limoges.' This collection of troubadour
songs was written and illuminated in Italy in the later 13th century, and
was once owned by Petrarch.

of Poitou/dukes of Aquitaine. Their marriage alliances were usually more ambitious. William IX's wife was the heiress to Toulouse;
his mother, Audiarde of Burgundy, was the granddaughter of
King Robert II of France. Earlier duchesses came from the great
princely families of France – Provence, Blois, Gascony, Anjou,
Normandy, occasionally from the comital families of Aquitaine,
like the counts of La Marche or Perigord. The count/dukes usually obtained impressive marriages for their daughters and sisters
– to the kings of Aragon or Castile, the count of Maurienne, even
to the German emperor Henry III. Occasionally, younger sons or
daughters of the count/dukes were married to regional aristocratic
families, like Eleanor's aunt Agnes, who was married to Aimery,
viscount of Thouars. But after Aimery's death in 1127, she was
married to King Ramiro of Aragon.[5] On her father's side, Eleanor

was related, sometimes distantly, to most of the great princely families of France, to the ruling houses of Aragon, Castile and Navarre, to the German emperors, the kings of England and France, and even to her first mother-in-law, Adela of Maurienne.

But Aenor of Châtellerault's family were merely middle-ranking regional aristocracy. They came from the very north of Aquitaine.[6] Châtellerault protected Poitiers from Touraine, and the Châtellerault family were intermarried with other families from the northern marches of Poitou, the borderlands with Anjou and Touraine, like the viscounts of Thouars, and the lords of Blaison, L'Île-Bouchard, Faye-la-Vineuse and Chauvigny. The names Aenor and Alienor/Eleanor were frequent within this extended family.[7] The marriage was strategic. William IX was concerned to protect his northern border in the 1120s, hence the marriages of his son to Aenor of Châtellerault and his daughter to the viscount of Thouars. Presumably ducal marital strategy lay behind the marriage of Dangereuse's sister, Amabilis of Châtellerault, to Count Vulgrin of Angoulême.[8]

Aenor's family must have had a strong presence at the court of both Dukes William. Relatives of the family, especially from the Faye, Blaison and Chauvigny branches, and members of associated, if not traceably related, families, like the Surgères, the Maingots and the Chabots, formed the backbone of Eleanor's entourage and household whenever she was in Poitou – after her divorce, then again from 1168 to 1173, and then after Henry's death. Hugh of Saint-Maure, who, along with Ralph of Faye, encouraged her to revolt against Henry II, came from just across the border in Touraine, from a family with a long association with the neighbouring lords of Châtellerault, Faye and L'Île-Bouchard, visible through their support of the Benedictine abbey of Noyers, just north of Châtellerault on the river Vienne.[9]

The obscurity of her mother's family dogged Eleanor throughout her life. They were not powerful enough within Aquitaine to protect the dukes's two young unmarried daughters when William set off for Spain. So on his way to Spain, William left his two vulnerable young daughters in the care of Geoffrey of Loroux, archbishop of Bordeaux – which was where the Capetian contingent found them. On his deathbed, William had no choice but to give his territories and his daughters into the care of his overlord, the king of France.

The one member of the family who could have provided protection for William's daughters, his younger brother Raymond, had left for Antioch the year before. It was assumed that Raymond would inherit the county of Toulouse from his mother, Countess Philippa. He was given a name much used in the Toulousan dynasty in anticipation. When that proved illusory, Raymond was sent to the court of Henry I of England to be educated and knighted, for Countess Philippa's mother, Emma of Mortain, was Henry I's cousin. So Raymond was not at the Poitevin court in the 1130s as Eleanor grew up. She may not have met him until she arrived at Antioch in 1148. After Henry I's death, Fulk of Anjou, king of Jerusalem, arranged Raymond's marriage to the heiress to Antioch. This too depended on English court connections, for Fulk's son Geoffrey was married to Henry's heir, Empress Matilda, and his daughter Matilda was the widow of Henry's only legitimate son.[10]

With Raymond far away in Antioch, and her undistinguished maternal relatives, Eleanor had no strong familial support at the French court, apart from her younger sister, Aelith. It was an unusual position for a queen of France from one of the great French principalities. Louis VII's third wife was Adela of Champagne. Her position at court was buttressed by brothers. Count Henry 'the Liberal' of Champagne was married to Louis' eldest daughter – Eleanor's daughter, Mary; Count Theobald of Blois was married to Louis and Eleanor's younger daughter, Alixe; and William was archbishop of Reims, the archbishop who crowned and anointed the Capetian kings.[11] The first wives of both Philip I and Philip II were nieces of counts of Flanders. In both cases the counts of Flanders arranged the marriage when they had overwhelming influence over the young king. Both women began their role as queen with strong familial support – though both kings soon revolted against the Flemish stranglehold.[12] Constance of Arles, the third wife of King Robert II, arrived at the Capetian court with a large retinue of relatives and friends from the south, to the horror of northern commentators, who were outraged at southern mores and fashions, with men 'beardless like actors' wearing 'indecent stockings and shoes' – a phrase which tickles the imagination.[13] Adela of Maurienne's position as queen was reinforced by her august relations: her mother was daughter of the duke of Burgundy, her aunt was countess of Flanders and her uncle was Pope Calixtus II.[14] Eleanor had distinguished relatives too, on her father's side, but they were simply further away. No wonder she was overjoyed to see her uncle Raymond in Antioch. For the first time in her dealings with Louis, she had the support of a close relative with authority and prestige.

When Eleanor was based in Poitou in 1152, between 1168 and 1173, and after Henry II's death, her household was filled with her mother's relations and their associates. Outside Aquitaine, however, whether as queen of France or queen of England, her household and wider entourage included few Aquitanians. In England in 1164–5, Eleanor was attended by a 'cousin', Marchisia, probably a member of the family of the counts of La Marche.[15] Otherwise, as we have seen, her household was largely staffed with English, Normans and Angevins recommended by Henry II.

Arriving as a new queen with a heavy familial entourage was often resented. That was the case with Constance of Arles, and with some of Eleanor's successors as queens of England, notably Henry III's consort, Eleanor of Provence.[16] There could be clashes of culture. Constance of Castile, Louis VII's second wife, came

with a large Castilian entourage. When her seneschal struck and
killed a clerk at court, Louis insisted that the seneschal suffer
the designated punishment – the amputation of the offending
hand. Constance and her household begged in vain for mercy.[17]
Whether Eleanor was queen of France or queen of England, there
was no reported friction or cultural clashes between the king's
household and the queen's, because Eleanor's households were
dominated by her husbands' retainers, not members of her own
extended family.

The final visit to Aquitaine by Eleanor and Louis at the end
of 1151 and the beginning of 1152 gave her an opportunity to
reconnect with her Poitevin relations and the Poitevin Church
and aristocracy. They visited the abbey at Nieul-sur-l'Autise,
where her mother was buried. There, at Eleanor's request, Louis
made a gift from lands held in right of his wife to the abbey of
L'Absie.[18] Eleanor's uncle, Viscount Hugh of Châtellerault,
was in attendance when they visited the abbey of Saint-Jean
d'Angely.[19] One of Eleanor's first acts after her return to Poitiers,
and her marriage with Henry, was given in favour of the abbey of
Saint-Maixent, where her cousin Peter was abbot.[20] The act was
witnessed by her uncles Hugh, viscount of Châtellerault, and his
brother, Ralph of Faye.

Hugh of Châtellerault, who died in 1176, and his son William
appeared in her entourage from time to time. Hugh was the only
member of the Poitevin aristocracy to whom she gave lands,
before the hurried attempt to buy support for John in 1199 and
1200. It was a substantial gift – the strategically placed lord-
ships of Beaumont and Bonneuil on the rivers Clain and Vienne
respectively, and hunting rights in the hunting park in the forest
of Moulière in between.[21] The offspring of Hugh of Châtellerault's
sisters, one married to the lord of Chauvigny, the other to Count
Vulgrin of Angoulême – Bernard and Andrew of Chauvigny and
Fulk of Matha – were absorbed into Eleanor's entourage. She

promoted the careers of members of the extended Châtellerault family who had gone into the Church. Her nephew, Hugh of Châtellerault, was made dean of Saint-Hilaire at Poitiers; Maurice of Blaison (Dangereuse of Châtellerault's mother was a Blaison) became bishop of Poitiers in 1198, and thenceforth a close supporter of Eleanor.[22]

Eleanor grew particularly close to her disreputable one-eyed uncle, Ralph of Faye, who died around 1186. It was on his unwise advice that she rebelled against Henry in 1173. Ralph acquired the lordship of Faye-la-Vineuse through marriage to its heiress, Elizabeth – whose mother enjoyed the evocative nickname of 'Rumpsteak'.[23] Faye-la-Vineuse is close to Châtellerault, and this was probably not the first marriage between the families. Ralph was given lands in England; his second wife, Philippa, still held them in the mid-1190s.[24] By 1163 Ralph was seneschal of Poitou and a dominant presence at Eleanor's court in Poitou between 1168 and 1173. His sons Ralph and William, and to a lesser extent Peter and Philip, attended Eleanor assiduously between 1199 and her death.[25]

In Poitou, Eleanor's family provided her with essential political support. Some, particularly members of the Chauvigny family, found favour with Richard.[26] But none of them were significant enough to find a place in Henry's entourage and the English court, apart from Ralph of Faye, and that only occasionally. Even as queen of England, Eleanor had to operate without powerful and distinguished relatives of her own.

The presence of Eleanor's maternal relations in her entourage may have alienated other Poitevin aristocratic families who had supported the dukes in the past. Members of the Lusignan, Parthenay, Mauléon and Thouars families rarely appear in Eleanor's charters, even though the latter were cousins.[27] Cousinship did not guarantee loyalty and friendship. It was apparently at Eleanor's behest that Henry brought the Thouars to heel in 1158. Eleanor

invoked their cousinship in an effort to persuade Aimery of
Thouars to support John rather than Arthur – unsurprisingly in
vain. Richard alienated Eleanor's cousin, the younger Hugh of
Châtellerault, high-handedly seizing from him a strategically
placed castle in 1196.²⁸ Both Hugh of Châtellerault and Andrew
of Chauvigny supported Arthur in 1202 and were captured at
Mirebeau.

ELEANOR WAS RELATED TO BOTH of the families into which
she married – the Capetians and the Anglo-Norman Angevins.
Indeed, the annulment of Eleanor and Louis VII's marriage was
predicated on the fact that both were descended from King
Robert II. Henry II was an oldest son, brought up from the start
to rule his inheritance. From his father, that was the county of
Anjou; from his mother, the duchy of Normandy, with the prospect of inheriting the kingdom of England. From a young age,
he was involved by his mother, Empress Matilda, in her campaigns to conquer England from her cousin, King Stephen. It
was a tough upbringing. When he married Eleanor, Henry was
already inured to battle and experienced in diplomacy. Louis VII
was brought up in the shadow of his older brother, Philip, who in
1130 was crowned as associate king. The next year, Philip died,
to great mourning at the French court, crushed when his horse
tripped over a 'diabolical pig' – Suger's description – in the streets
of Paris.²⁹ Young Louis was crowned as associate king in his
place. Whereas Henry of Anjou was brought up to knighthood
and to rule, Louis was educated at Notre-Dame in Paris for a
career in the Church.³⁰ However, it was Henry of Anjou who
had received the better education. Both his parents came from
families which valued education: an Angevin predecessor had
once dismissed an undereducated Capetian king as 'an unlettered
king and a crowned ass' – *rex illiteratus, asinus coronatus.*³¹

Henry and Louis had younger siblings. Two of Louis' younger brothers went into the Church. Robert, count of Dreux, proved rebellious when Louis was in the Holy Land, but settled down thereafter.[32] Henry's youngest brother, William, was a loyal supporter, who died in 1164 apparently of a broken heart when forbidden to marry the countess of Warenne on grounds of consanguinity.[33] The second brother, Geoffrey, was troublesome. He tried to capture and marry Eleanor, as she travelled back to Poitou in 1152, and he rebelled in both 1152 and 1156. Fortunately for Henry II, in 1158 he died.

Both of Eleanor's mothers-in-law were formidable personalities and active politicians. With neither did she have obvious clashes. Adela retired from court as Eleanor arrived, but soon returned. Later, both women attended important courtly occasions together, like the reception of the crusade banner at Saint-Denis. Suger thought that Adela urged her younger sons, especially Robert of Dreux, to chafe against Louis' authority. Her relations with Louis were cooler than with her other sons.[34] Henry, on the other hand, was devoted to his mother. Neither Matilda nor Henry forgot that she was an empress. Walter Map thought she had taught him how to rule.[35] It was probably fortunate that Matilda spent most of her time in Normandy. Matilda and Eleanor cooperated, at least initially, to reconcile Henry and Thomas Becket.[36]

The primary duty of the aristocratic wife, even more of the wife of a ruler, was the provision of children to inherit and ensure the continuation of the dynasty. For a queen like Eleanor, the coronation orders made this explicit: 'that she, like Sarah, Rebecca, Lia and Rachel, should be worthy to be fecund and rejoice in the fruits of her womb for the glory of the kingdom'.[37] The failure to provide posterity, even if the failure came in the next generation, was seen as punishment for sin, as for Aelith and Ralph of Vermandois. The churchman Gerald of Wales became a bitter critic of the Angevins, largely because they did not support his ambitions for ecclesiastical preferment. In his last work, *Instruction for a Ruler*, Gerald gleefully notes the lack of male grandchildren of Eleanor and Henry II as God's punishment for their sinful lives.[38]

Eleanor's difficulties in producing children at all, never mind male children, with Louis would have been deeply distressing, not just because it undermined her position as queen. According to Geoffrey of Auxerre, Eleanor was brutally frank in discussing her problems of conception with Bernard of Clairvaux. She asked him why the Lord had closed up her womb – her 'vulva'. She had lived with the king for nearly nine years, she said: in the first year, she conceived, but miscarried; since then, she had remained sterile and now she despaired of her fecundity.[39] The failure to conceive would have been blamed at the French court on Eleanor, at least at first.

William of Newburgh, writing in the late 1190s, claims Eleanor said that marriage to Louis was like being married to a monk.[40] By then, Eleanor's fertility was not in doubt, neither were Louis' difficulties in fathering a male child. William of Newburgh's comment points up the virility of Henry II, while suggesting on Eleanor's part an improper insouciance towards a pious husband. By the late 1140s there were probably rumours in Capetian circles that Louis, with his 'childish' love, was not up to producing an heir. Doubtless they informed Robert of Dreux's apparent bid for the throne while Louis was still away on crusade. Male infertility was clearly discussed at the Capetian court, for Eleanor despised Thierry Galeran as a eunuch.[41] Sexual insecurity explains Louis' over-reaction to flirtation with an uncle. And it is hard to imagine the ambitious Duke Henry of Normandy marrying Eleanor if she was widely regarded as infertile.

Her fertility with Henry must have seemed like God's blessing on their marriage. But the stress of infertility was replaced by

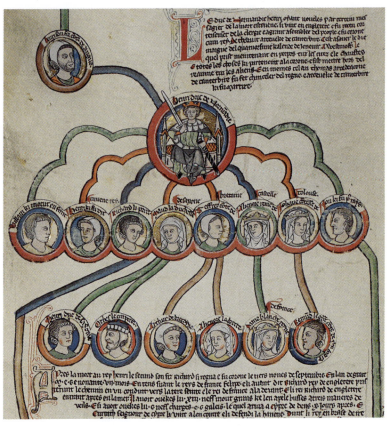

A genealogical roll of the kings of England, *c.* 1300, shows Henry II and his children, all of whom, including the daughters, are named, but Eleanor is not shown.

the exhaustion of almost continual pregnancy and the horrors of childbirth. A translation into Latin of a Greek gynaecological tract, usually known as the *Gynaecia Cleopatrae*, was dedicated to Eleanor by a scholar called Henry. He describes himself as a courtier of Emperor Manuel of Constantinople, but was probably the Sicilian translator Henry Aristippus, who was attached to the court of William I of Sicily. The text has much advice on conception – ironically no longer an issue – and successful pregnancy. A book written for one of the most famous queens of the

classical past made a handsome gift for the new queen of England
– and incidentally suggests that Eleanor, like many elite women
of her day, had been educated to read Latin.[42]

The naming of children was governed by a sort of established
dynastic etiquette, which the names of most of Eleanor's children
with Henry follow. Robert of Torigni observed that the name of
their first son, William, was 'virtually the property of the counts
of Poitou and the dukes of Aquitaine'.[43] It reflects the importance
that the duchy of Aquitaine assumed in Henry's plans, at a stage
when succession to the English throne was still uncertain. Henry,
after King Henry I, was the obvious name for the son born after
the accession to England. Richard commemorated some of the
earliest Norman dukes. Geoffrey honoured Henry's father, and
Matilda honoured his mother, the empress. Eleanor was named
after her mother. Joanna and John were not dynastic names on
either side. John was born near the feast of St John the Evangelist
and was named accordingly. John and its feminine version celebrated saints' names; both, along with other saints' names like
Margaret and Catherine, suddenly became popular from the
mid-twelfth century.[44]

The names of Eleanor's children with Louis do not follow
expected naming patterns. Their first daughter was named after
the Virgin Mary. Mary was born in 1145, after Eleanor had con-
fided her distress at her childlessness to Bernard of Clairvaux,
who was particularly devoted to the Virgin.[45] The name was
unknown in either dynasty and was surprisingly rare before the
twelfth century. Normally, the first daughter would have been
named after the husband's mother: she should have been Adela.
The second daughter would be named after her maternal grandmother: she should have been Aenor. Instead, she was named
after Eleanor's sister, Aelith, introducing a version of that name,
Alixe/Alice, to the Capetian line. It is surprising that Eleanor's
choice prevailed. Perhaps Louis too mourned Eleanor's tragic

sister, for he used it again for the daughter whose birth caused the death of his second wife, Constance of Castile.[46]

Eleanor has sometimes been regarded as a distant, almost neglectful, mother to her own children.[47] She had no choice but to leave her two small daughters behind at the French court after the divorce. As overlord, Louis insisted on keeping the heirs to the duchy of Aquitaine under his protection: as their protector he could call himself Duke of Aquitaine until Eleanor produced a son – as she did in 1153.

English pipe-roll evidence tells us quite a lot about the childhood and upbringing of Eleanor's children with Henry, and of the children of Matilda of Saxony, who spent so much time at the English court.[48] For Capetian France, there is no such evidence. The pipe rolls reveal how much Eleanor kept her Angevin children with her when they were young, though like all elite women in the Middle Ages Eleanor had her infant children fed by wet-nurses. All the children would have been well educated, for that was the tradition within the Angevin family.[49] As an Angevin chronicler gloomily observed, Eleanor's daughters had to be prepared to put up with living in dreadful lands – Saxony, Spain and Sicily – where food, dress, customs and houses were quite different from those in England. In a heavy-handed play on Eleanor's name, 'Alienor', the author says they rose to the challenge, inspired by the nobility of their formidable grandmother, the empress, and, as 'Alienor's' daughters, imbibing alien air from childhood so that they were more easily taught the diversity of alien languages.[50]

Matilda and Eleanor stayed in their mother's household until they were despatched to their future husbands, Matilda at the age of eleven, and Eleanor at the age of nine. Young Henry was sent at the age of seven to the household of the chancellor, Thomas Becket, for his education – until 1163, when Henry II and Becket fell out. As chancellor, Becket spared no expense on a lavish and luxurious household. Young Henry, under Becket's influence, grew into a notorious spendthrift.[51] John's earliest education was at Fontevraud, where he was within easy reach of his mother at Poitiers; after the 1173–4 revolt, Henry sent John to be educated by Ranulf Glanville, the justiciar.[52] Geoffrey accompanied his father to Brittany for betrothal to the heiress, Constance, in 1166; by 1169 he was established in Brittany under Henry's tutelage. Richard's education as future duke of Aquitaine occurred within Eleanor's own household after they were established in Poitiers in 1168, when Richard was eleven. Young Eleanor probably resided at Poitiers too, since her mother negotiated her marriage arrangements, and it was from Aquitaine that the princess set off for Castile. Joanna, like John, was educated at the not-too-distant Fontevraud; both were taken back to England with their captive mother in 1173. So all of the children saw much of their mother in their early childhood, but only for Richard was she a permanent presence after the age of eleven.

The personalities of Eleanor and Henry's sons were caught in acute if spite-tinged character sketches by Gerald of Wales in his *Topography of Ireland*, when Gerald hoped for preferment at the Angevin court, and in his *Instruction for a Ruler*, when disappointed hopes had turned to hatred. Henry the Young King was handsome, chivalric, easily loved and followed, overgenerous with funds that he did not have. Richard was a focused warrior, with a seriousness of purpose that his elder brother lacked. Geoffrey was intelligent, eloquent, hypocritical, untrustworthy. John combined the negative qualities of all three.[53]

Richard, the longest under Eleanor's guidance, was most likely to reflect her influence. Both could be tenacious for power and possession. Under Eleanor's tutelage, Richard got to know and rule Aquitaine. He was undoubtedly her favourite son, and he depended on her counsel and support in the way that his father had depended on the empress. Eleanor probably saw a good deal of John in his early years at Fontevraud, until the disaster of 1173. His treachery to Richard exasperated her, but she always sought forgiveness for John from, and reconciliation with, Richard. She was determined that John rather than her grandson Arthur should succeed Richard. Young Henry had the fecklessness of the spoilt older child. Relations between the Young King and Richard deteriorated into open conflict from the later 1170s.[54] But Eleanor, like Henry II, mourned their charming but worthless oldest surviving son, and was perhaps behind attempts to have the young man made a saint. There is little direct evidence for her relationship with Geoffrey. Contemporaries certainly saw her as a strong influence on her sons, able to entice Henry, Richard and Geoffrey into rebellion against their father in 1173.

One cannot overstate the position of Eleanor as a matriarch for the Angevin family, both immediate and extended, even during her imprisonment. Young female royal relatives and prospective daughters-in-law were placed in her household. The prioress at Fontevraud in the 1190s, Alice of Brittany, had been a loved protégée in her household.[55] In the late 1180s Alice of France, betrothed to Richard, Isabelle of Gloucester, betrothed to John, and the heiress Denise of Châteauroux, betrothed to Eleanor's Poitevin kinsman Andrew of Chauvigny, seem to have been under Eleanor's tutelage, for sumptuous clothes were purchased for all of them together.[56] Margaret of France, at her betrothal to Young Henry, was initially placed in the care of a member of the Perche family, rather than in the household of her future mother-in-law – whose own marriage to Margaret's father had been annulled less than ten years previously. But Margaret was increasingly in Eleanor's company when not with her husband. The two queens waited together in Normandy while the Young King was crowned in 1170 and were brought back to England together in 1174 after the failure of the rebellion.[57]

Eleanor was involved in all the family marriage arrangements, except that of Joanna to William of Sicily in 1177. The two-year negotiation of Matilda's marriage to Henry the Lion was largely Henry's preserve, but Eleanor accompanied her daughter across the Channel at the start of the long journey to northern Germany and probably chose Matilda's luxurious dowry. Eleanor's role in the projected marriage of John to Alice of Maurienne was considerable, and in the marriage of young Eleanor to Alfonso of Castile essential. Richard probably consulted his mother when he arranged Joanna's second marriage in 1196, with Raymond of Toulouse. He depended on Eleanor to fetch his own bride from Navarre, just as John depended on her to bring a Castilian niece to marry the heir to the French throne in fulfilment of John's treaty with Philip Augustus in 1200. In both cases, Eleanor was much more than a companion to the young bride. Berengaria's marital arrangements, including dowry and dower, required delicate diplomacy. Eleanor was involved in the Castile marriage from the start. Richard began the negotiations before his death. In May 1199 Guy de Paré, abbot of Cîteaux, a churchman closely associated with Richard, came to visit Eleanor at Niort; six months later, Guy went on to the court of Alfonso and Eleanor of Castile in Burgos, doubtless preparing the ground for Eleanor's arrival.[58]

No letters survive to prove that Eleanor or Henry kept in touch with their daughters in their distant marriages. But the building of diplomatic networks was the point of marriage, and connections were doubtless maintained. Both Henry and Eleanor were overjoyed to welcome Matilda back, though Matilda and her husband came as exiles seeking refuge at her father's court. No expense was spared for them and their children, Matilda-Richenza, Henry, Lothar and Otto, and William, who was born at Winchester in 1184. They were provided with rich clothes and horses. Henry funded their households, and the nurses and masters for young William. Eleanor, although not at full liberty, spent much time with Matilda and her children at Winchester, London, Windsor and Berkhamsted. Duke Henry, and perhaps Matilda, accompanied Eleanor to the family summit at Alençon in 1185. Matilda-Richenza and William were left behind with their grandmother when their parents returned to Saxony in 1185.[59] Doubtless both parents regretted Matilda's return to Saxony. Her death, shortly after her father's in summer 1189, must have hit Eleanor hard.

Eleanor of Aquitaine and Eleanor of Castile did not meet until the former went to collect the Castilian granddaughter who would marry the heir to the French throne in 1200. But Henry and Eleanor kept in contact with their distant daughter, who named two of her children after them. In 1187, probably with Eleanor's support and intervention, Matilda-Richenza was despatched to the Castilian court with a baggage train almost as magnificent as that sent with her mother to Germany. Presumably marriage to an Iberian king was under discussion, for Castilian ambassadors had been staying at the English court. But Matilda-Richenza returned and in 1189 was married by Richard to the heir to the count of Perche.[60] Eleanor did not see Joanna between 1174 and 1190, when they met briefly in Sicily. Eleanor welcomed Joanna warmly when she joined her in Poitou in 1194, and again in 1199. Eleanor was with Joanna when she died in childbirth at Rouen in August 1199. Joanna made Eleanor the executor of her will.[61]

What of Eleanor's relations with her Capetian daughters, Mary and Alixe, left behind at the French court? Alixe married Count Theobald v of Blois. A year or so after Alixe's death in 1197/8, Eleanor established a commemoration for 'her very dear daughter' at Fontevraud. Was 'very dear daughter' merely a pious formula – it was the phrase she used for Joanna – or had Eleanor and Alixe been in contact? Eleanor also provided funds to support Alixe's daughter, Alice, who had recently entered Fontevraud as a nun.[62] In 1197/8 Richard enticed Alixe of Blois' son, Count Louis of Blois, into alliance with the Angevins against Philip Augustus.[63] It looks as though Eleanor played her part in the diplomatic realignment. But there is no evidence that Eleanor had contact with her older Capetian daughter, Mary, countess of Champagne, after 1152. Mary became close to her half-brothers, Henry the Young King and Count Geoffrey, when they frequented the Capetian court, but by then Eleanor was imprisoned in England.[64]

Eleanor and Henry were indulgent grandparents to the offspring of Matilda of Saxony. William, born in Winchester, was called English William on the pipe rolls; probably his grandparents assumed that he would have a future at the English court. Eleanor refused to send William to Germany as a hostage for his uncle.[65] Matilda-Richenza, now countess of Perche, joined Eleanor and Joanna at Fontevraud in 1194 or 1195, and mourned Richard alongside Eleanor in April 1199.[66]

Geoffrey of Brittany was the only son to produce children during Eleanor's lifetime. After Geoffrey's unexpected death, Henry took his daughter, Eleanor of Brittany, into wardship. She probably joined the family group around Eleanor. Various marriages were proposed for her during Richard's reign, including Saladin's brother, provided he were prepared to convert to Christianity – but he was not. After Richard's death, Eleanor of Brittany, like her brother, was a potential threat to John's rule, and was kept in close if comfortable confinement in England for the rest of a long, empty life.

Geoffrey's second surviving child – a son – was born shortly after his death. Constance of Brittany, Geoffrey's widow, called this child, the heir to the county of Brittany, Arthur. The name had never been used in the Anglo-Norman/Angevin dynasty or the dynasty of the Breton counts. It made bold and blatant reference to Arthur, the legendary king of Britain. During the crusade,

Richard named Arthur as heir to the Angevin realm, and betrothed Arthur to the heiress to Sicily. But Richard was about to get married and assumed that he would have sons to succeed him. When no son materialized, Richard promoted his other nephew, Otto of Saxony, as his heir – until Otto became emperor. When Richard died, Eleanor was determined that Arthur should not succeed to any of the Angevin inheritance.

Historians have speculated that Eleanor did so because she and Constance hated each other. But Geoffrey and Constance's first child, born around 1184, was named to honour her grand-mother; there was no hatred then. The crisis came in 1196. Richard demanded that Constance hand Arthur over as his ward. Constance refused, and was then imprisoned by her own husband, the Earl of Chester. Breton nobles managed to smuggle Arthur to Paris, to the court of Philip Augustus, who betrothed the young Breton heir to his own daughter, Mary. From that point, Arthur was a pawn of Philip Augustus. Eleanor's attitude to Arthur was driven by fear of Philip Augustus rather than hatred of Countess Constance.[67]

The Angevin family became famous for their quarrels. Richard of Devizes compared them to the 'confused house of Oedipus'.[68] The Capetian family had tensions too, but Angevin chroniclers knew or cared less about them. Adela of Maurienne supported her younger sons as they challenged the authority of Louis VII; Philip Augustus violently rejected his first wife's Flemish rela-tions, and his mother's Champenois relations. Louis VII's low fertility meant that Philip had no younger brothers to deal with. Philip's own marital failings – he spent many years trying to divorce his second wife and was accused of bigamy with his third – meant that he only had one legitimate son to provide for. Empress Matilda and Eleanor had better and more politically fruitful relationships with their royal sons than did either Adela of Maurienne or Adela of Champagne.

Whatever the tensions, family produced a spider's web of connection. Those connections might be dormant for some time, to be revived when useful and/or feasible, like Eleanor's connections with her daughters, Eleanor, Joanna and Alixe. Marriages of younger sons and daughters are often untraceable, at the level of the princely families, let alone the regional aristocracy of northern Poitou. Distant and untraceable relationships were sometimes invoked – like that of the mysterious Marchisia. Family might mean tension and rivalry, even hatred, but it could also mean affection, forgiveness and love, and it mattered.

Detail of illumination from the Gospel Book of Henry the Lion and Matilda of Saxony, probably late 1170s. Behind Matilda of Saxony, as she is crowned by the Hand of God, stand her father, Henry II, and the grandmother after whom she was named, the Empress Matilda, as well as a mysterious uncrowned and unnamed woman. Is this Eleanor?

Poitiers Cathedral, east window: Eleanor and Henry II as donors of the window, with four of their sons. The window can probably be dated to the late 1160s.

Two famous images encapsulate the importance and the challenges of family ties. In the late 1170s Henry and Matilda of Saxony commissioned a great gospel book for their new cathedral church of St Blaise at Brunswick. One page shows them receiving their ducal crowns from God. Duke Henry is flanked by his parents and his imperial grandparents. Duchess Matilda is described as the daughter of King Henry of England, who stands behind her. Next to him is Empress Matilda, here described as 'Queen Matilda' – as she was often known in Germany. Behind her stands another female figure. This woman is uncrowned and unnamed. Is this Eleanor? Is this mysterious ghost the woman who had so recently torn the family apart?[69] More happily, in the late 1160s Henry and Eleanor donated a great east window to Poitiers Cathedral. At the base of the window, they had themselves portrayed as donors. Behind them stand their four living

sons – Henry, Richard, Geoffrey and John. There was no room
for the daughters. But it was an image of the king and queen,
with those who would succeed to their complex realm, together
in brief familial and dynastic unity before the ruptures of the
1170s.

uif que ma dame
de champaigne.
vialt q romant
afeire anpraigne.
Je lanprendrai
mlt uolentiers.
come cil qui
est siens antiers.
o e quan cil puet el monde ferre

Eleanor's oldest daughter, Mary of France, countess of Champagne, shown as a patron of Chrétien de Troyes in a collection of romances, produced c. 1230, probably for the family of the counts of Champagne.

FIVE

Marriage, Sex and Scandal

ichard of Devizes was a monk of Winchester, and knew Eleanor, who often resided in the city. He admired her, calling her 'an incomparable woman, beautiful yet virtuous, powerful yet gentle, humble yet keen-witted'. But even Richard could not resist a satirical aside in the margin of the page: 'Many know what I would that none of us knew. This same queen, during the time of her first husband, was at Jerusalem. Let no one say any more about it. I too know it well. Keep silent.'[1] Richard confused Jerusalem with Antioch, but no one would miss the snide reference to Eleanor's dalliance with Raymond of Antioch.

Marriage, love and sex were for Eleanor wreathed in scandal – and not just her own. Her grandfather, William IX, was notorious for his sexual improprieties. A northern French chronicler, Guibert of Nogent, claimed that he went on crusade with 'crowds of girls'; Geoffrey of Vigeois called him 'a passionate lover of women'; William of Malmesbury said he took nothing seriously, making his audience roar with laughter, and built a 'convent of prostitutes' beside his castle at Niort.[2] That he had deserted Philippa of Toulouse for the wife of the viscount of Châtellerault was well known. According to Orderic Vitalis, Philippa (Orderic calls her Hildegarde) denounced her husband's adultery at a church council held in Reims by Pope Calixtus II in 1119.[3] William of Malmesbury claimed that William had an image of his mistress painted on his shield, saying 'that he wanted to be beneath her in battle just as she lay beneath him in bed'.[4] Nevertheless, the sins of her grandfather were invoked by chroniclers in relations to Eleanor only after her death. Gerald of Wales made the connection, of course, claiming that the viscountess of Châtellerault had been abducted by force, and confusing Eleanor's grandfather with her father.[5]

Nobody mentioned her grandfather's amorous reputation when she married Louis in 1137. But she was soon touched by the scandalous marriage of her sister Aelith/Petronilla to Louis' cousin, ally and seneschal, Ralph of Vermandois. The fullest account of the scandal is given by John of Salisbury in his *Historia pontificalis*. John wrote this wry memoir of the papal court in the mid-1160s to amuse fellow churchmen. John launches his book with an account of the Council of Reims in 1148, at which Ralph finally obtained a divorce from Eleanor of Champagne, together with absolution from the pope for his sins of, as John puts it, 'adultery . . . with the queen's sister . . . a concubinage condemned by three popes'. John thought the absolution and divorce were obtained by bribery, and he condemns the greed and moral vacuity of Pope Eugenius and the Capetian bishops as well as the adulterous couple.[6]

It is John who records St Bernard's prophesy that 'no worthy fruit' would result from Ralph and Aelith's marriage, and that they would not enjoy each other for long. Bernard was vindicated: Aelith died in early 1150, their only son died of leprosy and neither of their two daughters had children. The younger daughter, named Eleanor after her aunt, was married at least four times. When she died in 1213, the Vermandois inheritance fell to the king of France. The older daughter, Elizabeth, became the object of scandal herself. Her marriage to Count Philip of Flanders was unhappy and infertile. In 1175 Count Philip accused her of adultery with a knight, Walter of Fontaines. The knight was hung upside down to drown in a cesspit.[7] Elizabeth brought too valuable an inheritance to divorce. She died in 1183. As for Ralph of Vermandois, he married again, to Laura of Flanders, but died because he could not refrain from sex with his young bride despite his doctor's orders – or so John of Salisbury could not resist telling us.

John of Salisbury does not implicate Eleanor in her sister's affair at all. In his letters, St Bernard blames Louis' youth and lack of wisdom and the 'diabolical advice' given to him. Bernard thought the king's brother, Robert of Dreux, a malign influence, and even accused Suger of giving bad advice, but he never suggests Eleanor was among the diabolical advisors.[8] Geoffrey of Auxerre, in his account of the conversation between Eleanor and Bernard at Saint-Denis, suggests she has some responsibility for her sister's scandal. Bernard promises Eleanor that she will have the longed-for child if she works for peace, 'the king himself recognizing, through the words of the queen, when the reconciliation is complete'. But Geoffrey is explicit that the lack of peace is due to the wickedness of Ralph of Vermandois, who 'holds the queen's sister'.[9] Here Aelith is an unwilling victim; however, she was denounced as an adulteress, and she lived under the cloud of excommunication and infidelity for six difficult years. It must have added to a perception that, for Eleanor and her family, sexual gratification mattered more than marital propriety, and made Capetian courtiers all the more likely to believe the worst of her relationship with Raymond in Antioch.

It is impossible to know what really happened between Eleanor and Raymond in Antioch. That it posed an existential threat to Eleanor's marriage is clear from Suger's letter to Louis, written before Easter 1149, to persuade the king to return to France. Almost as a postscript, Suger wrote:

With regard to your queen, we venture to praise [her] to you . . . whatever the rancour in your soul, you should try

to hide it . . . then when you have returned to your
kingdom, you can, God willing, deal with this and
with everything else.[10]

Suger must have heard of the marital tensions in letters from
Louis and Odo of Deuil, and from returning crusaders like Robert
of Dreux. Tellingly, Odo ends his account of the crusade with
the safe arrival at Antioch, though he remained with the king
until they returned home.

The first chronicler to mention the episode was a German
Augustinian abbot, Gerhoh of Reichersberg, in a disquisition on
the calamities of the Second Crusade, written around 1160. He
paints Raymond as a wicked seducer who abducts Eleanor and
wants to deprive her husband of her companionship by treachery, fraud and force. She escapes and returns to her husband.
Although she has kept to her marriage vows, Louis refuses to
take her back as his wife.[11]

John of Salisbury provides, once again in the *Historia
pontificalis*, the fullest near-contemporary account of the scandal.[12] John reports that 'the intimacy [*familiaritas*] of Prince
Raymond with the queen, and his constant and almost unin-
terrupted conversation with her, made the king suspicious.'
Louis wanted to leave, Eleanor wanted to stay and Raymond
'made every effort to keep her, if the king would accept it'. When
Louis tried to drag her away, Eleanor countered by declaring
their marriage invalid because they were too closely related
according to canon law – they were both descended from King
Robert II. John observed that rumours to that effect were already
circulating in France – indeed, Bernard had referred to it during
the scandal of Aelith's marriage.[13] But Louis' trusted courtier
Thierry Galeran, whom Eleanor 'had always hated and mocked'
as a eunuch, persuaded Louis to take Eleanor to Jerusalem with
him by force. A few pages later, John takes up the story of their

return to France, via Sicily. At Tusculum, Pope Eugenius III, 'having heard the accounts of their quarrels from each of them separately', tried to reconcile them. He 'made them sleep in the same bed, which he had had decorated with his own most precious fabrics' and forbad any future discussion of their consanguinity. John insists throughout on Louis' love for Eleanor: his love was 'almost excessive'; he loved her 'violently, in an almost childish way'.[14] Louis comes out rather worse than Eleanor in John's account of the affair. He is either indecisive or overreactive. His childish love turns violent when thwarted. John does not applaud the violence with which Louis drags her away from Antioch.

For John of Salisbury, Eleanor was a queen with a mind of her own, an over-attentive uncle and an inadequate husband. But the next detailed surviving account of the incident, William of Tyre's *History of Jerusalem*, depicts a more sinister Raymond and a more complicit Eleanor. William, the archbishop of Tyre, wrote most of this book between 1179 and 1184. By then, Eleanor had left her pious first husband for a king who had murdered his own archbishop and led a revolt against her second husband. William claims that Raymond planned to take her 'by force or by secretive plotting from her husband'; too much avuncular attention has now become intended rape. Eleanor, claims William, was prepared to comply 'for she was . . . just as she showed both then and later, an unwise woman, who, against royal dignity, ignored the laws of marriage, forgetful of the faith of the marriage bed.' William makes it clear that Raymond and Louis had argued over the direction of the campaign. Raymond wanted Louis to stay and defend Antioch, while Louis was determined to press on to Jerusalem. For William, the 'foolish' and flighty Eleanor is her uncle's pawn in the game, while Louis, advised by his magnates, has no choice but to leave Antioch as fast as he can, dragging his wife with him.[15]

Which of these accounts gets closest to what really happened? Gerhoh of Reichersberg implies that he has heard an account of the disasters of the crusade from Emperor Conrad III himself, but the German contingent were not at Antioch with Louis and Eleanor. William was writing almost forty years after the incident. His account reflects gossip in the court circles of the Kingdom of Jerusalem. John of Salisbury was given to gossip too, but he was the best informed of the three. He was at the papal court when Eleanor and Louis arrived. He knew Louis and Eugenius well, and by the time he wrote the *Historia pontificalis* he had worked with Eleanor when she acted as regent of England.

William's Eleanor is a feckless pawn; Gerhoh's Eleanor an innocent victim of abduction and suspicion. John's Eleanor has more agency. It is Eleanor who takes the initiative to end the marriage. What did she hope for? She can hardly have contemplated marriage with Raymond, since he was married already, and far more closely related to her than Louis. But had Raymond, acting as the close family advisor and protector that she lacked in France, offered to arrange an advantageous marriage for her? It was a risky strategy, but she was not in a position to negotiate herself out of her marriage in France. Both Eleanor and Raymond must have hoped that she would have a son to inherit Aquitaine and knew that to do so she would need a different husband. Raymond had himself been extracted from a difficult position at the English court after Henry I's death, when Fulk of Anjou, king of Jerusalem, arranged Raymond's marriage to the heiress to Antioch. Did Raymond have in mind a husband for Eleanor in the crusader states? Or did he suggest that young Henry Plantagenet, grandson of both Fulk and Henry I, might make a suitable match?

But the damage to Eleanor's reputation was done. Poems by the troubadours Marcabru and Cercamon, both of whom had been supported by Eleanor's father, appear to show the Antioch gossip circulating almost immediately. In a poem addressed to his fellow troubadour and crusader, Jaufré Rudel, an Aquitanian aristocrat from the Bordelais, Marcabru observes: 'She who takes two or three lovers and does not pledge herself to one alone . . . her reputation and worth decrease with each month.' Cercamon's 'Ab lo pascor' is more sharply pointed, defaming, as it does, a lady 'worthless from now on' whose sin is 'gossiped of as far as Poitou'.[16]

When Bishop John of Poitiers warned Thomas Becket about Eleanor's reliance on Ralph of Faye, he continued: 'Every day many tendencies come to light which make it possible to believe that there is truth in that dishonourable tale that we remember mentioning somewhere else.'[17] Did Bishop John mean Eleanor's tendencies, or Ralph of Faye's? Is he invoking Antioch, or dishonourable antics by the disreputable Ralph? Is he implying that Eleanor is once again altogether too entwined with another uncle? Nevertheless, apart from innuendo from Richard of Devizes, Gervase of Canterbury and, of course, Gerald of Wales, the Angevin chroniclers are remarkably circumspect about the Antioch scandal.[18] With good reason – after Henry's death, Eleanor was more powerful than ever, and gratuitous attacks on her would alienate Richard and John.

William of Tyre's *History*, and a French translation of it, circulated widely in the early thirteenth century. His version of the Antioch incident, and his dismissive judgement of Eleanor, had become influential by the time Gerald of Wales revised his malicious *Instruction for a Ruler*, though that had limited circulation. Chroniclers writing after Eleanor's death had no reason to hold back. In the 1240s the English monk Matthew Paris introduced two new elements to the charge sheet, claiming Eleanor was 'defamed for adultery, including with infidels, and she was of devilish stock'.[19] A contemporary Flemish writer, Philip Mousques, tells the legend of Eleanor's 'devilish stock'.

Once upon a time, a count of Aquitaine married a beautiful but mysterious woman he found in a wood. She would never stay for the mass in church. One day, the count locked the doors of the church, so that she would be forced to attend mass. With a fearsome scream, the woman flew off through the windows, taking two of her children with her – for she was a devil. So, after her divorce, claimed Mousques, Eleanor called her barons of Aquitaine together to repudiate Louis' claim that she was 'not good enough for his bed' because she was a devil. Eleanor stripped naked to show them she was not. Mousques was the first to attach this colourful legend to the Aquitanian dynasty. In earlier versions of the story, as recounted by Gerald of Wales for instance, the mysterious beauty brought her 'devilish stock' to the Angevin family into which Eleanor married, rather than to her natal Aquitanian dynasty.[20]

The most entertaining version of the incident at Antioch was confected by an author known as the Minstrel of Reims around 1262. The Minstrel confuses the Second Crusade with the Third, and has Eleanor tempted into an affair with Richard the Lionheart's great foe, Saladin. Eleanor is 'a wicked woman', married to 'spineless' Louis. Impressed by Saladin's chivalric reputation, Eleanor falls in love with him and tells him that, if he can find a way to capture her, she will renounce her Christian faith and acknowledge him as her lord. Louis is alerted to Eleanor's elopement and manages to prevent it. Eleanor tells him why she wanted to leave: 'In God's name, you are worthless, even worse than a rotten apple . . . you will never again hold me in your arms.' Back in France, Louis asks the advice of his barons: 'Let her go, she is the very devil, and if you keep her any longer we fear she may have you murdered. But above all you have never had a child of her.' Eleanor returns to her lands and sends for Henry. The Minstrel of Reims wrote to amuse a courtly audience. He had no pretensions to serious history, but like Philip Mousques and Matthew Paris, he shows us how quickly salacious legends clouded Eleanor's reputation.[21]

The divorce from Louis and subsequent marriage with Henry damaged Eleanor's reputation more than it did Louis' or Henry's. Clerical chroniclers were always predisposed to blame the woman rather the man, Eve rather than Adam. One wrote that after Eleanor's remarriage 'the thorn of slander could not be removed from the heart of the French king.'[22] Her divorce made her 'the eagle of the broken covenant'. Although the *Draco Normannicus* claims that the eagle will bring wealth to England, the breaking of covenants was not to be encouraged. Two Angevin chroniclers, Walter Map and, of course, Gerald of Wales, cast the divorce and remarriage in the worst light. Map implies that they were plotted by Eleanor, who 'managed to secure a divorce' after 'she cast glances of unholy love on Henry.' 'King Henry', wrote Gerald, 'dared to pollute the queen of France . . . with an adulterous liaison . . . he took her away from her lord and joined with her in a de facto marriage' – though even he notes this was 'according to rumour'. Both writers claim that the failure of their sons to have sons is divine judgement on an immoral divorce and marriage. Neither can resist the additional rumour that Eleanor had sex with Henry's father, Geoffrey of Anjou. Map observes that this charge was 'made secretly against her' as she tried to obtain her divorce from Louis.[23] Both Map and Gerald had close connections at the Capetian court, where such accusations would undermine the legitimacy of Eleanor's second marriage and buttress Louis' claim to the duchy of Aquitaine.

Eleanor's final sin against the institution of marriage was her rebellion against her second husband, made more heinous still by the fact that she persuaded her sons to join her betrayal of him. Most of the Angevin chroniclers handled her revolt with discretion during her lifetime, adding 'as was rumoured' to the assertion that she induced her sons to revolt. Robert of Torigni, personally close to both Henry and Eleanor, and godfather of their daughter Eleanor, observed with studied restraint that Eleanor and her sons were 'alienated from' Henry.[24] Roger of Howden was less generous: this was 'nefarious treachery' by 'as was said by some, Queen Eleanor herself'.[25] Ralph of Diceto followed his account of Eleanor's role in the rebellion – he put in the usual 'as is said' disclaimer – with a litany of classical and biblical examples of sons who revolted against their fathers, especially when women fomented insurgence within the family. Ralph included Semiramis, who retained power by marrying her son; Jeptha, son of a prostitute, whose sons threw him out saying 'You cannot inherit, for you were born of an adulterous mother'; and Eurydice of Macedon, grandmother of Alexander the Great, who tried to kill her husband to marry one of her sons. Ralph finished his excursus on destructive wives with more recent examples, including Constance of Arles, the colourful third wife of Robert II of France, who plotted with her sons against their father. He brought things close to home by claiming that Eleanor's father rebelled against his own father in disgust at William IX's liaison with Dangereuse of Châtellerault; there is no other evidence for this.[26] Ralph appreciated Eleanor's role in stabilizing the realm during Richard's imprisonment and negotiating Richard's release. His long disquisition on families destabilized by dangerous women reflects the miasma of scandal, scandal with hints of glamour, through which even well-disposed churchmen saw her by the time Henry died.

Andrew the Chaplain's book *De amore* capitalizes on the scandal-wreathed yet glamorous reputation that Eleanor had accumulated by the later 1180s. Its presentation of Eleanor judging romantic and sexual dilemmas would raise knowing smirks in its readers. To show her unfortunate granddaughter Elizabeth of Vermandois doing so, perhaps felt too close for comfort for many. Eleanor's judgements are rather sensible: women should stick with an older man of good character rather than chasing a worthless youth and should not try to preserve an incestuous love which had begun as an honest mistake. But Andrew did not restrict himself to women whose reputation was sullied, for he included Adela of Champagne, Louis VII's third wife, and his impeccable patroness, Mary of Champagne, Eleanor's daughter, who makes some of the saucier pronouncements.[27]

The revolt encouraged new interpretations of Eleanor as the eagle of the broken covenant – which was now her marriage with Henry rather than with Louis. One of the first to do so was a Cluniac monk, Richard the Poitevin – though Richard thought Henry had it coming to him.[28] A French poet, Guernes of Pont-Saint-Maxence, was the first to link Eleanor with the entire eagle prophecy: 'The Eagle of the Broken Covenant shall paint the bridle with gold and will rejoice in her third nesting.' For Guernes, the eagle gilded (funded?) the plot against Henry, and particularly rejoiced in her third nest, England – the other two being Aquitaine and France. The king, continued Guernes, has ceased to fear the eagle, and she will never nest in another place, because she has lost her plumes.[29] Ralph of Diceto wrote late enough to bring a positive twist to the eagle prophesy: the 'third nesting' in which the eagle rejoiced was now revealed as her third son, King Richard.[30]

Louis, with his passionate but childish love for Eleanor, did not take mistresses. He was a 'chaste' husband in both of his other marriages, presumably due to low libido and his religious upbringing. By the thirteenth century, pious laymen had internalized the idea of the 'chaste marriage', for marriage was defined as a sacrament of the Church at the Third Lateran Council in 1179. But in the earlier twelfth century most elite laymen saw no reason why they should not take lovers. Henry II, while not as productive a sexual athlete as Henry I, had several mistresses. The most famous was Rosamund Clifford, whom he loved deeply. When she died, he had her buried beneath a beautiful tomb before the high altar at the abbey of Godstow. Bishop Hugh of Lincoln had the tomb dismantled and her body removed to the graveyard.[31] By the fourteenth century, legend had it that Eleanor had poisoned the 'Fair Rosamond'.[32] In fact, Eleanor appears to have regarded Henry's sexual relationships with indifference; they were hardly exceptional among his contemporaries. In general, Henry looked after his mistresses and their offspring well. His illegitimate children were usually brought up at court, and the girls given in strategic marriages. His son Geoffrey was placed in the Church, eventually becoming the archbishop of York. Roger of Howden claims that Eleanor persecuted Geoffrey Plantagenet 'with the hatred of a stepmother', but she worked with him during the crisis of Richard's imprisonment.[33]

Henry was accused of inappropriate sexual relations with two young princesses in his care. In 1166 a Breton noble, Eudes of Porhoët, accused Henry of violating his daughter while she was at Henry's court. The girl, Alice, was a hostage for negotiations between Henry and her parents, Eudes and Bertha, countess of Brittany. Eudes quickly came to terms with Henry and dropped the claims of sexual abuse. There may have been no substance to them. Alice was placed in Eleanor's household, and thence, perhaps after Eleanor's disgrace, as a nun at Fontevraud. By the late 1190s she was prioress and received gifts from Eleanor, who called her 'her dearest protégée'.[34]

The more problematic case was Alice of France, daughter of Louis VII and Constance of Castile and sister of Philip Augustus. In 1169 she was betrothed to Richard and handed, as was normal, into the care of the family into which she would marry. She brought with her a valuable dowry, the strategic county of the Vexin. She was kept at Henry's court, which meant he could keep the Vexin, but the marriage was postponed indefinitely. In 1191 Richard refused to marry her, saying that she had been his father's mistress. The accusation stuck; it was widely reported and grist to Gerald of Wales's mill.[35] Whether it was true is another matter. In the later 1180s Alice, along with John's fiancé, Isabelle of Gloucester, were generously provided for; both were probably under Eleanor's care. Alice was splendidly dressed for Richard's coronation.[36] But he had already decided to make a strategic marriage alliance with Navarre, and he needed an excuse for his sudden rejection of Alice. So both accusations of predatory sexual behaviour against Henry were politically driven and remain unproven.

The French call the legends that accumulated around Eleanor her 'black legend'. A 'black legend' also accumulated around her granddaughter, Blanche of Castile.[37] In both cases, the legends concern sex and a powerful woman. In both cases they emerge from the anxieties, sometimes the fantasies, of men, usually churchmen, faced with a woman with power. Both queens feature in a legend of disrobing. Philip Mousques has Eleanor strip to prove to the court that she is not a she-devil. The Minstrel of Reims has Blanche throw off her clothes and twirl on the table in council to prove that she is not pregnant by the papal legate, as the bishop of Beauvais has insinuated.[38] But the differences are revealing. Eleanor is accused of adultery, with Raymond of Antioch, with Henry of Anjou and/or his father, Count Geoffrey, or, at its most sensational, with Saladin. The accusations were not conjured out of thin air: something happened at Antioch, and the marriage with Henry followed very fast on the divorce and must have been carefully planned. Blanche's married life was above reproach. She was not accused of adultery, but of sexual relations that were inappropriate for the queen-regent and mother of the future king of France – with the papal legate, Romanus, and with her cousin Count Theobald of Champagne. Blanche is unlikely to have had affairs with either man; it would have been too risky. But she was certainly close to both and enjoyed their company. By the later thirteenth century, it was widely believed that Count Theobald, one of the finest French poets of his time, addressed love poems to her. Both Philip Mousques and the Minstrel of Reims claim that her second son, Robert of Artois, resented Count Theobald's flirtation with his mother, and punished the count with a runny cheese in the face in the manner of a custard pie (Minstrel), or a bucketful of ox innards and faeces (Mousques).[39]

The accusations against Blanche circulated in political songs. They were essentially political mud-slinging by a baronial faction hoping to overthrow her as regent. There was a political element to the accusations against Eleanor. Louis and his advisors probably developed the rumours of adultery with Henry and Geoffrey of Anjou to undermine the legality of her marriage with Henry, and thus their hold on Aquitaine. But Eleanor's 'black legend' was burnished among Angevin courtiers and commentators who – apart from Gerald of Wales – had no interest in her political destruction, and indeed who admired her interventions in Richard's reign.

A black legend was not inevitable for a woman of power. Tales of sexual misconduct did not cling to Empress Matilda, nor to her mother, Queen Matilda II, nor to Eleanor's daughter Mary, who ruled as regent countess of Champagne from 1181 to 1187, and from 1190 to 1198. All of these women were politically prominent. Why were Eleanor and Blanche different? Probably because there is no smoke without a few sparks at least. Both seem to have had considerable personal charm, and deployed it politically, in a way that the empress did not. Blanche was very close to both Romanus and Count Theobald. There was an incident at Antioch: Eleanor did remarry suspiciously fast, and she did revolt against her second husband.

And Eleanor's legend was all the more potent because it was not just about her, but about the whole Oedipal Angevin family.

Henry and all their sons except Geoffrey captured the imagination of contemporaries, though their reputations were blackened
more by tales of violence and treachery than of sex. In his book
of *Instruction for a Ruler*, Gerald of Wales argues that the fall
of the house of Anjou was the result of a decadent and immoral
family heritage. He pulls his 'evidence' together in a chapter
headed: 'The origins of both King Henry and Queen Eleanor,
and the totally corrupt root of their offspring'. It is here that Gerald
relates the story of Henry's ancestress, the beautiful countess of
Anjou 'of unknown descent', who flew out of the church window
when forced to stay for mass. Richard, said Gerald, particularly
relished this legend of his family's origin, and joked that 'from
the devil they had all come, and to the devil they were all going.'[40]
Perhaps we should not see Eleanor as the victim of rumour: perhaps, like Richard, she relished and connived in her own legend.

Remains of the Cluniac priory on the Île d'Aix, where the chronicler Richard the Poitevin lived and wrote of Eleanor as *Aquila bispertita* – the eagle with the spread wings – captured by the 'king of the north', Henry II.

SIX

The Eagle with the Spread Wings

Richard the Poitevin was one of many writers who identified Eleanor as the 'eagle of the broken covenant' from the prophesies of Merlin after her revolt against Henry. He also described her as the *Aquila bispertita* – the bipartite eagle – the eagle who spread her wings over two realms, France and England, and over her own land of Aquitaine and the lands of her husband, Henry II. Richard the Poitevin called Henry the *Rex aquilonis* – the king of the north. The king of the north had captured the eagle, after she and her sons revolted against him, and now he held her prisoner in his northern lands, where the people were uncultivated and unknown to her, where she, who had been surrounded by maidens singing sweet music in her own warm lands, was now silenced.[1]

Richard the Poitevin was a well-travelled and well-connected member of the Cluniac order, but he retired to and wrote from a small priory on the tiny windswept island of Aix just off the coast south of La Rochelle. Perhaps he felt Eleanor's isolation only too keenly; his writings suggest he had lost touch with reality. None of his contemporaries wrote about Eleanor as a creature of the south imprisoned by the king of the chill north. But Richard's hallucinatory vision has influenced many historians. Eleanor is often seen as a daughter of the south, faced, both as queen of France and as queen of England, with cultures, indeed with versions of the French language, which were alien to the granddaughter of the troubadour Duke William IX of Aquitaine. In fact, she was largely brought up in the north of Aquitaine, in Poitou, surrounded by her mother's family, who came from the northern borders of Poitou. She must have spoken the sort of French current in the western Loire area. There would have been no great culture shock when she married the count of adjacent Anjou, or when she married the king of France. But Eleanor was *bispertita*: she was countess of Poitou and duchess of Aquitaine. She and her family did look, politically and culturally, both north and south. And many cultural historians have speculated on the role that Eleanor might have played in transmitting southern culture to northern courts, for princesses often did act as agents of cultural transmission, as they married from one culture to another.

Once the counts of Poitou became dukes of Aquitaine in the late tenth century, they were bound to concern themselves with southern regions of the kingdom of France. Aquitaine retained the prestige of having been a separate kingdom under the Merovingians and Carolingians, stretching far to the east to include the Auvergne. But it was an elastic spatial concept. The power base of the dukes of Aquitaine was their original county of Poitou, including the Saintonge. They were overlords of the Limousin, Angoulême and parts of Berry, though they had trouble imposing anything resembling political control there. In 1063 they obtained Gascony, with its cathedral city of Bordeaux. William IX was married to Philippa, the heiress to the county of Toulouse. Countess Philippa's uncle and then cousins took and held the county, disinheriting her. But the Aquitanian claim to Toulouse through her was never forgotten. William IX and Philippa named their second son Raymond, a name frequently used by the counts of Toulouse and not at all by the dukes of Aquitaine, because they intended him to succeed to his mother's inheritance. Both Louis VII and Henry II tried – in vain – to take Toulouse as Eleanor's rightful inheritance.

Possession of Gascony and claims to Toulouse meant that the dukes of Aquitaine became involved in Iberia. Eleanor's great grandfather Guy-Geoffrey, and grandfather William IX, campaigned against the Muslims in Spain. Duke William was an opportunist warrior rather than a crusader. Like many of the Spanish lords, he was happy to ally with Muslim princes in search of reward. In 1120 he fought alongside the Muslim king of Saragossa, Imad al-dawla abd al-Malik ibn-Hud, who gave him a precious rock crystal vase in thanks.[2] William IX's sisters were married to the kings of Castile and Aragon. His daughter Agnes was married to a later king of Aragon. William X died on a pilgrimage to Santiago de Compostela, probably prospecting for an Iberian bride as well as salving his soul.

Eleanor's Iberian family connections had real political import, especially after her marriage to Henry. Her strongest family relationships were with the rulers of Aragon. Eleanor's cousin, Petronilla, was queen of Aragon, ruling with her husband, Raymond-Berengar, count of Barcelona. Henry developed an alliance with Aragon, doubtless with Eleanor's help, in the late 1150s, not least to enable his attack on Toulouse in 1159. The counts of Barcelona had claims on Provence, and the county of Toulouse was squeezed by Aquitaine to the north and Provence to the south. When Raymond-Berengar died in 1162, he named Henry II as guardian of his young son, Alfonso II of Aragon. Alfonso II attended the great court at Montferrand in February 1173 to finalize the marriage between Prince John and the heiress to Maurienne. In 1170 young Eleanor of England was married to Alfonso VIII of Castile, developing ties with Castile as well as Aragon. The terms of young Eleanor's generous dower, with the stipulation that she would be crowned as queen or empress whenever her husband was crowned, were negotiated at Bordeaux under her mother's aegis. The witnesses for Eleanor included the Aquitanian bishops and a clutch of Aquitanian aristocracy, prominent among them Ralph of Faye and William of Châtellerault. The resulting Castilian charter was issued at Tarazona, in Aragon, in the presence of Alfonso II of Aragon, who, as a close relative of both parties, in effect stood surety for the marriage. Richard continued the close relationship with Alfonso II.[3]

Eleanor's revolt and imprisonment did not impede Henry's relationships with her Iberian cousins. In 1177 Henry was invited to arbitrate between the kings of Castile and Navarre. The 1187/8 pipe roll shows Castilian ambassadors supported for some time at the English court. Henry sent ships to the king of Castile, and prepared to send his granddaughter, Matilda-Richenza of Saxony, to Castile with a substantial suite of men and women and magnificent garments and accoutrements.[4] This must have been arranged with Eleanor's connivance. By this time, Eleanor was acting as materfamilias for Henry, especially with regard to the Saxony family. Both Richard and John depended on their mother's Iberian connections to bring important diplomatic marriages to fruition. This was straightforward enough where collecting the young Blanche of Castile was concerned. But the marriage of Richard to Berengaria of Navarre required serious diplomatic realignment. Aragon and Castile tended towards enmity with Navarre; Richard needed to avoid incurring their enmity too, as he allied with their old enemy. We might surmise that Eleanor's connections and experience were deployed in avoiding a breakdown of relations with the long-standing Aquitanian allies.

But the count/dukes of Poitou/Aquitaine did not neglect their northern neighbours. They saw themselves as princes of the kingdom of France and they recognized the importance of the economic nexus created by Atlantic coastal trade. William IX brought his troops to help Louis the Fat repel an invasion of the kingdom of France by the emperor in 1124, and in a poem

written around 1111 he hoped that the king of France and Count
Fulk of Anjou would protect his young son in the event of his
own death.[5] William IX's mother was Audiarde of Burgundy,
granddaughter of King Robert II; his mother-in-law, Emma of
Mortain, was a niece of William the Conqueror. Emma's sister,
Sibyl, became abbess of the wealthy ducal abbey of Notre-Dame
at Saintes.[6] The Anglo-Norman connection allowed William IX
to despatch his younger son, Raymond, to England to be brought
up at the court of Henry I. Between 1033 and circa 1050, Poitou
was ruled by the countess, Agnes of Burgundy, and her second
husband, Geoffrey Martel, count of Anjou. As a result, Angevin
religious houses, especially La Trinité at Vendôme, had substantial properties in Poitou. Nevertheless, relations with the counts
of Anjou and Blois were often confrontational, hence the importance of the Châtellerault and associated families, all of whom
defended the northern border of Poitou.

Just as the political outlook of the Poitevin court was both
northern and southern, so was its culture. Religious and intellectual culture was tied into that of the Loire. Robert of Arbrissel,
the founder of Fontevraud, visited Countess Philippa in Toulouse
and persuaded her to found the Fontevraudine house of L'Espinasse
close by. Gerard of Salles, from the Limousin, was a close associate
of Robert of Arbrissel, and the houses founded by him in Poitou/
Aquitaine, often with ducal support, shared a similar approach to
eremitic and reformed monasticism. Poitiers, like Angers and
Chartres, was an important intellectual centre, and was in the late
eleventh and early twelfth century the site of a series of major
Church councils. Many of its bishops, notably Gilbert de la Porrée,
were distinguished scholars. The Angevin scholar Geoffrey of
Loroux moved south to live first as a hermit, then as a ducal advisor and finally as archbishop of Bordeaux, while maintaining his
connections with the churchmen of northern France, St Bernard,
Bishop Geoffrey of Chartres and Abbot Suger.[7]

On the other hand, an important aspect of the literary culture and literary networks of the Poitevin court was meridional. Eleanor's grandfather, William ix, was known as one of the first troubadours. Some have seen the influence of Spanish Islamic love poetry on troubadour poetry, particularly the obsession with the distant, unobtainable lover. William doubtless had opportunities to hear such poetry in the company of the prince of Saragossa. Cercamon and Marcabru, from the next generation of troubadours, attended William x's court at Poitiers.[8]

Cercamon and Marcabru, both in need of patronage, went south after William x's death: Marcabru to Spain, probably to Castile. Both bemoaned Louis vii's acquisition of Poitou and his lack of interest in crusading in Spain. Cercamon wrote a lament on Duke William's unexpected death in Santiago, which deprived Cercamon of a patron, Spain of a crusader and Poitou of a generous soldiering lord. It also deprived Eleanor and Aelith of a protective father, though Cercamon saw Eleanor merely as the means by which Aquitaine and Poitou were transferred to the rule of the king of France. Far from following Eleanor and seeking her patronage, both wrote poems which seem to condemn her behaviour in Antioch. Jaufré Rudel, the aristocratic younger son of the lord of Blaye, was the other prominent poet of this second generation. There is no evidence that he followed William x's daughters to the Capetian court. He did join the Second Crusade, but probably sailed with his immediate lord, William Taillefer, count of Angoulême, rather than joining Louis and Eleanor's French overland contingent.

William ix had a rival in the first generation of troubadours, Ebles of Ventadorn, all of whose poems and songs have disappeared. Ebles of Ventadorn apparently encouraged a courtly poetry, celebrating love for the unobtainable woman in a way that paralleled Islamic courtly verse. What survives of Duke William ix's poetry tends rather to celebrate conquest in war and

in love. Duke William could be crude, lascivious and scatological. One famous poem involves sadomasochistic foreplay
between our hero, two women he deceives and their big red cat.
Duke William's verse is technically brilliant, structurally subtle
and inventively playful with words, but on the whole, courtly
love it is not.

Had Eleanor and Aelith heard their grandfather's unsuitable
songs, or the more courtly Jaufré Rudel, Cercamon and Marcabru
at their father's court? Perhaps. All of them, including Duke
William, produced their songs in Occitan, the language of the
south. Rudel was the son of the lord of Blaye, just across the
Gironde from Bordeaux. Cercamon and Marcabru were from
Gascony; Ebles of Ventadorn from the Limousin. In all these
areas, Occitan was probably the principal vernacular language.
But the vernacular language in Poitiers and Poitou was northern
French, akin to the French spoken in the Loire. At the Poitevin
court, Occitan must have been seen as a – or *the* – language of
song. William IX's wife, Philippa of Toulouse, probably spoke
Occitan, but her mother was Norman, and the other important
women at the Poitevin court were northerners. William IX's
mother was a niece of the Capetian king Henry; his mistress,
Dangereuse, and William X's wife, Eleanor's mother, were from
the northern marches of Poitou. Eleanor and Aelith may well
have heard, and perhaps enjoyed, Occitan songs at the Poitevin
court, but the prevailing court culture was Ligerian rather than
Occitan.

None of the troubadours followed Eleanor to the Capetian
heartlands. They sniped at Louis, and perhaps Eleanor herself,
from Iberia or Gascony. There is no evidence that they joined
Louis and Eleanor's entourage when the two of them toured
Aquitaine. Troubadours did appear at the Angevin court. Henry
the Young King, Richard the Lionheart and Geoffrey of Brittany
attracted into their entourages troubadours singing in Occitan.

The Limousin troubadour Bertran of Born praised their sister, Matilda of Saxony, as the only thing that relieved the tedium of the court at Argentan in 1182. Bertran was in contact with all three princes, especially when they came to the Limousin. Sometimes he praised them; sometimes he criticized them. He wrote laments on the deaths of both Young Henry and Geoffrey.

But there is no direct evidence that Eleanor, as the queen of England, attracted troubadours to her entourage. Bertran of Ventadorn addressed one of his poems to her as the Queen of Normandy, and seems to have visited England. His poems can be read – 'can' is the operative word – to imply that Eleanor is the distant and unobtainable lady he loves from afar. Bertran was either a younger member or a retainer of the Ventadorn family, into which Ralph of Faye's daughter Sybil had married.[9] No other troubadour saw Eleanor as a subject for their fantasies of courtly love as Bertran of Born vaunted her daughter Matilda. But Eleanor spent many of her early years as queen in England and frequently pregnant. By the time she was established back in Poitou as regent duchess for Richard in 1168, she was in her forties, too old to be an obvious subject for an intrinsically misogynistic art form which played on the untouchable but sexually attractive – that is young – woman. Indeed, Bertran of Born lumped the old queen in with the old king – Henry, who should be replaced by the younger generation.[10]

Nevertheless, her position as queen ought to have facilitated their appearance at the Angevin courts, and the court she and Richard ran at Poitiers, even if she was too old to be the object of their desires. A court must be entertained. Days could be occupied by hunting, but guests expected music, song and storytelling while they feasted. Long dark nights in winter must be whiled away, as the closest entourage huddled round the fire in the queen's chamber. Many lay elites were well educated and might be able to read. Some, like Eleanor's daughter Mary and her

husband, Count Henry of Champagne, commissioned impressive libraries. But reading was best done by daylight, not guttering
candlelight. Entertainers were an integral part of the courtly life.
Like present-day social media or television, they ranged from
the sublime to the scatological, from the religious to the ridicu-
lous, from the obsequious to the subversive. Some managed to
be all of those at once.

Troubadours performing their songs in Occitan were not
the only entertainers at court. By the later twelfth century, the
northern Francophone world had its own purveyors of courtly
love songs, the trouvères. The subject-matter was similar, but the
language was Old French, not Occitan. The earliest trouvères,
Chrétien de Troyes, Gace Brulé, Conon of Béthune, Le Châtelain
de Coucy and Blondel de Nesle, were attached to or frequented
the courts of Count Henry and Countess Mary of Champagne,
of Count Philip of Flanders and of Henry II's sons, especially
Richard and Geoffrey. Richard and Geoffrey were trouvères
themselves. Even more than the troubadours, many northern
trouvères were associated with Eleanor's children and grandchildren. As with the troubadours, there is no evidence that
Eleanor herself patronized them, or inspired their poetry.[11]

That has not stopped speculation that it was Eleanor who
brought the troubadours north, and that it was in Eleanor's entourage that northern trouvères discovered the joys and woes of
courtly love from their Occitan colleagues. Andrew the
Chaplain's *De amore* was often held to be proof that Eleanor
hosted her daughter Countess Mary of Champagne, her niece
Elizabeth of Vermandois, countess of Flanders, and Viscountess
Ermengarde of Narbonne, who was indeed a patron of troubadours, at her court at Poitiers: that there the women had sat in
judgement on issues of love, and that there northern poets in the
entourage of the countesses of Champagne and Flanders found
inspiration in the love poetry of the troubadours in the trains

of Eleanor and Ermengarde. But it is highly unlikely that these women and their poets ever gathered together at Eleanor's court at Poitiers. Eleanor was neither an active patron of poets, either northern or southern, nor does she seem to have fired their imagination. Her role in the transmission of the poetic and amatory culture of the south to the northern courts rests at best on optimistic speculation. The real agents of cultural transmission were her sons, Henry the Young King, Richard and Geoffrey.

And whatever Richard the Poitevin had to say from his island fastness, Eleanor found a rich courtly culture in the lands of the king of the north. The Capetian court probably did seem dull and the entertainment there tame in comparison to Cercamon, Marcabru and Jaufré Rudel. But the Angevin court had plenty of sophisticated entertainment, as well as its share of buffoons, purveyors of bawdy songs and female dancers known as *saltatrixes* for their somersaulting.

Although none of the troubadours bothered to attract Eleanor's cultural attention, writers from the Anglo-Norman and Angevin realm did. A strong tradition of dedicating literary works, especially in the vernacular, to the Anglo-Norman queens, and of Anglo-Norman queens commissioning literary works, was well established. As Henry's queen, Eleanor partook of this tradition. The Norman cleric, Philip of Thaon, wrote a new dedication to his *Bestiary* in honour of Eleanor; it had originally been dedicated to Henry I's second wife, Adela of Louvain. Henry II commissioned the *Roman de Rou*, an Anglo-Norman history of the Norman dukes, and the *Roman de Brut*, an Anglo-Norman version of Geoffrey of Monmouth's *History of Britain*, from the Norman poet, Wace. The *Roman de Brut* was dedicated to the 'noble Eleanor, queen of the great king Henry'. The *Roman de Rou* was begun around 1160, and still in progress in the late 1170s, when Wace was replaced by a writer called Benoît – probably Benoît of Sainte-Maure. Between 1160 and 1170, Benoît

of Sainte-Maure wrote the *Roman de Troie*. This was dedicated
to 'the noble wife of a noble king', who 'has high birth, worth
and valour, integrity, intelligence and honour, goodness, moderation and virtue, noble largesse and beauty', in whom 'the
misdeeds common in other women are effaced by her inherent
goodness, in her all knowledge abounds . . . she is second to none
on this earth.' Eleanor is the only possible candidate for this
florid encomium with its delicate sting – her misdeeds effaced by
her inherent goodness. Benoît of Sainte-Maure came from the
Touraine-Poitou marches, possibly from the household of Hugh
of Sainte-Maure. If so, it seems likely that Eleanor introduced
him to the Angevin court.[12] The early troubadours who had
sung at her father's court produced works that seem appropriate
for a masculine audience, an audience who fought and fantasized
about sex with unobtainable women. Perhaps Eleanor found the
elegant vernacular romances of the Angevin court, with their
powerful stories and their nuanced approach to sexual desire,
more beguiling.

Like Henry II, Eleanor was seen by contemporaries as a fulfilment of the prophesies of Merlin. The Angevin court was, like
most of the northern French courts in the second half of the
twelfth century, entranced by 'the matter of Britain', the Arthurian
legends, including Merlin's prophesies, first gathered into literary
form by Geoffrey of Monmouth at the court of Henry I. Indeed,
Wace's *Roman de Brut*, dedicated to Eleanor, was a translation into
Anglo-Norman of Geoffrey's *History of Britain*. The Arthurian
canon was most fully developed in the 1170s and '80s in the
works of Chrétien de Troyes, a clerk first attached to the court of
Count Henry and Countess Mary of Champagne, and then associated with Count Philip of Flanders. For Count Philip, Chrétien
wrote his last work, *Perceval*; for Countess Mary, Eleanor's oldest
daughter, he wrote the *Knight of the Cart* or *Lancelot*, probably
around 1180. As with Andrew the Chaplain's *De amore*, historians

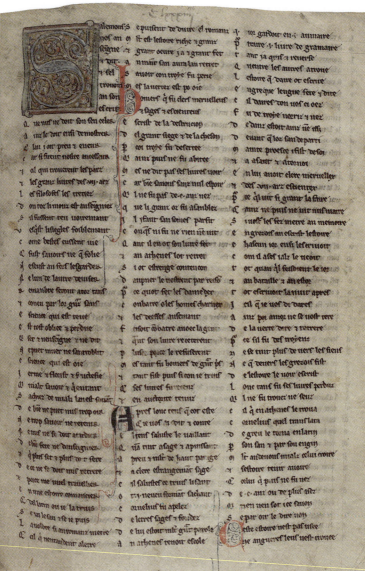

Opening page of Benoît of Sainte-Maure's *Roman de Troie*, addressed to Eleanor of Aquitaine as 'the noble wife of a noble king' ('riche dame de riche rei'), in the same collection of romances, produced *c.* 1230 at the court of the count of Champagne, in which Mary of Champagne is portrayed.

have often assumed that a relationship between a mother and her long-deserted daughter lies behind the transfer of Arthurian legend from the Angevin court to the court of Champagne, but of that relationship there is no evidence. If Eleanor herself was not implicated, her children perhaps were. Countess Mary got to know Henry the Young King, Richard and Geoffrey when they visited the French court to plot against their father. Indeed, the grand finale of Chrétien's first poem, *Erec and Enide*, written around 1170, takes place at Nantes, and seems designed to remind its hearers of one of Henry II's great Christmas courts. There were many ways in which Arthurian culture might spread to the court of Champagne.

Much of the 'matter of Britain' concerned forbidden love, often adulterous, and, on the woman's side, the sexual betrayal

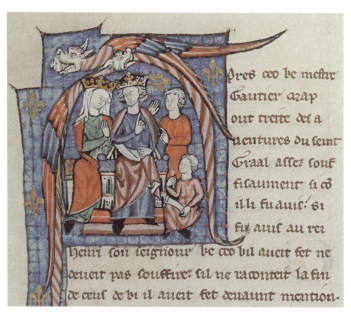

Walter Map presents a book to Henry II and Eleanor of Aquitaine, miniature from a compilation of Arthurian legends produced *c.* 1275 for the marriage of their descendants Blanche of Artois, a granddaughter of Blanche of Castile, and Edmund of Lancaster, son of Henry III.

of her husband. Did courtiers, family, political enemies and political allies hear the tales of Queens Iseult and Guinevere and think of Eleanor's chequered marital history? Did writers intend a frisson of recognition as their romances were performed at court? Perhaps – but we can't go further than that.[13]

What about the material culture – the things – that surrounded Eleanor? The rock crystal vase given to her grandfather was unlikely to have been the only Islamic luxury item from Spain to reach the Aquitanian court. There would have been rich patterned silks for clothes and hangings, and fine ivory caskets. There must have been gold in the form of tribute money – which was one of the main attractions of joining the Iberian crusading wars. Many historians have assumed that young Eleanor and her sister were removed from a court of exotic Islamic cushioned comfort and riches to the chill, threadbare, uncouth interiors of Capetian castles. Doubtless Capetian castles and residences were draughty and damp in winter. No Capetian charter records that it was issued in the shade of an umbrella in a castle courtyard, as does one issued by Eleanor's father – in which, in exchange for substantial properties, the abbot of Saint-Jean d'Angely gave the duke a gold chalice weighing 100 ounces.[14] But the Capetian lands offered fine hunting and game, and the Capetians had luxury objects of their own. They had inherited impressive treasuries from their Carolingian predecessors and from their own early links with Lotharingia and the Empire. Their treasures were imperial rather than Islamic, but not unimpressive, as an account of the travelling chapel of King Robert II shows.[15] They too could source silks, but through the Empire, rather than Spain. And when Eleanor became the 'noble wife of a noble king' Henry, she lacked for nothing.

Did Eleanor bring the material culture of the south to the north? Almonds, cumin, cinnamon and chestnuts were procured for Eleanor in England in the 1150s. Was this a novel demand, or

The Eleanor Vase, now in the Louvre, Paris, with Abbot Suger's inscription on the base: 'Hoc vasa sponsa dedit Aanor regi Ludovico, Mitadolus avo, mihi rex, Sanctisque Sugerus' ('As a bride, Eleanor proffered this vase to King Louis, Mitadolus to her grandfather, the King to me and Suger to the Saints') – 'Mitadolus' standing for Imad al-dawla abd al-Malik ibn-Hud.

just what any self-respecting northern court would have acquired from the thriving spice trade? She had her own *cordubanarius* – a worker with the finest leather from Cordoba – perhaps providing her with beautiful shoes in 1155/6. Is that evidence of exotic Iberian taste? Perhaps.[16]

The rock crystal vase given to her grandfather, known as the 'Eleanor Vase', now in the Louvre, is an indisputable case of cultural transmission, in which Eleanor acts as a prime agent. The vase is crafted from a transparent rock crystal, cut to look almost like a pine-cone. It was designed to hold perfume, was perhaps Persian and probably part of the collection of the Caliphate in Fatimid Cairo. So it was precious, profane and Islamic. It was given to Eleanor's disreputable grandfather by his ally, Imad al-dawla abd al-Malik ibn-Hud, the Muslim king of Saragossa. Eleanor and Louis gave the vase to Abbot Suger for the abbey of Saint-Denis. Suger commissioned a bejewelled gold base, neck and lid for the crystal vase, and transformed the perfume jar into an object for the altar, to hold holy water in its clear crystal body. He made the profane sacred. A verse on the base tells us how the vase arrived at Saint-Denis: 'As a bride, Eleanor gave this vase to King Louis, Mitadolus to her grandfather, the King to me, and Suger to the Saints.' Mitadolus was a scrambled attempt at Imad al-dawla abd al-Malik ibn-Hud. Suger stressed its exotic provenance, both in the verse which revealed it, and in the unusual and distinctly Islamic arabesques of his goldsmith's work. Was this done after discussion with Eleanor? Did he think it might please or flatter her? Did she insist on this remembrance of her grandfather and his exotic connections? We can never know. But the object seems inconceivable without conversation, reminiscence and understanding between the abbot and the queen.[17]

SEVEN

Riches

The Welsh courtier, chronicler and gossip Walter Map recounts a conversation with Eleanor's first husband, Louis VII of France, on the riches of kings. Louis felt himself very much the poor relation. The king of India, said Louis, was rich in precious stones, the emperor of Byzantium and the king of Sicily in gold and silks, the German emperor in soldiers and war horses. The king of England had everything – men, horses, gold, silks, gems, even a menagerie of exotic beasts. 'We in France', ended Louis complacently, 'have nothing except bread, wine and joy.'[1]

There was no room for complacency. Wealth mattered. The French kings were painfully aware of their disadvantage against the superior wealth of the Anglo-Norman kings. Louis the Fat, Philip Augustus and Louis VII himself battled to develop and accrue the wealth of their own lands. Eleanor found herself married first to a king who saw himself as poor, then to one who was widely seen as conspicuously rich.

A queen, just as much as a king, needed wealth. She needed resources to attract courtiers into her entourage, and to reward members of her household. She needed wealth to advertise her piety, her care for her people and to ensure the power of prayer for her soul after death by founding or patronizing churches, monasteries or hospitals. She needed wealth to commission cultural artefacts – buildings, liturgical objects, precious books,

music, poetry or histories. A queen's wealth, like that of other
elite women, derived from two sources: her dowry, provided by
her family as they gave her in marriage, and her dower, provided
by her husband, to support her if she survived him. But for enjoy-
ment of her properties and income, a queen was dependent on
the king. In Eleanor's case, her 'dowry' was her inheritance, the
county of Poitou and the duchy of Aquitaine. The dowry was
often absorbed by the husband, so that the woman had no direct
access to it. Sometimes women had no access to their dower until
after their husband's death – and then had to fight or negotiate
for it with their sons.

It is difficult to know precisely how royal income and expenditure worked during Eleanor's lifetime. The kings of England ran
a sophisticated administration and system for recording royal
income and expenditure from the early twelfth century, partly
because they inherited an Anglo-Saxon system geared to raise
taxes, and partly because they often ruled multiple realms. The
pipe or exchequer rolls from England, together with a few surviving rolls of the Norman exchequer from 1180 onwards, record
the income and expenditure of royal officials, the sheriffs in
England and the bailiffs in Normandy. But they don't give a full
picture of royal finances. Many payments and gifts – even substantial ones for building projects, alms and expenses, for food,
horses or clothes – were paid out by members of the royal household in money from coffers in the royal chamber and go effectively
unrecorded. French royal administration and record-keeping
lagged far behind, hence the relative poverty of the French kings.
The system was overhauled by Philip Augustus in the 1190s,
when important documents were entered into new Registers.[2]
But surviving French royal income and expenditure accounts
are few and far between until the late thirteenth century. As for
Aquitaine, there is only fragmentary evidence for the income
and expenditure of the duchy, even once it was in the hands of

the Angevins. Permanent gifts of properties or revenues were usually recorded in formal documents – charters – not least because the recipient wanted a charter to prove their ownership. But the survival of these documents is haphazard, and generally better for England and Normandy than for Capetian France or Aquitaine. In short, we have much more information for Eleanor's finances as queen of England than as queen of France or duchess of Aquitaine.[3]

Eleanor brought the duchy of Aquitaine and the county of Poitou as, in effect, her 'dowry' to both marriages. Aquitaine was a richly productive land, with seaports and rivers for fishing, abundant game in marsh and woods, good soils for wine and grains, valuable metals, especially silver mines at Melle, and most valuable of all, great salt pans – for salt was essential for flavouring and preservation. Ralph of Diceto, the dean of St Paul's in London, lauded the wealth of the duchy. He was well informed, for he was a friend of John Bellesmains, bishop of Poitiers from 1162 to 1181. Ralph thought the people of Aquitaine were rather

Abbey of Notre-Dame, often called the Abbaye aux Dames, at Saintes, where Eleanor's aunt was abbess, and to which both Eleanor and her sister made gifts; detail of early 12th-century portal.

too fond of the pleasures of the table, cooking beef with pepper, wild apples and green grape juice, roasting duck on wood fires and feasting frequently on the royal fish (sturgeon) – all of which were readily available.[4]

Both of Eleanor's husbands treated Poitou and Aquitaine as theirs to administer as they wished, as count/duke in right of their wife. Both assumed that the wealth of Aquitaine and Poitou was theirs to control, to receive and to give. Eleanor had some control over the resources of the duchy when she ruled it as regent and then in co-rule with young Richard, but required Henry and Richard's assent to major disposals. After Henry's death, Richard, and then Otto of Brunswick, drew the revenues for themselves, as count/dukes. Only after John gave Poitou and Aquitaine to Eleanor for her lifetime in 1199, provided she did not make major alienations of land without his permission, did Eleanor enjoy the full resources of her inheritance. Both of Eleanor's husbands must have assigned some properties and revenues within Aquitaine to her, possibly regarding it as dower. In 1139/40 she gave revenues from 'our lands' to the Templars at La Rochelle.[5] A papal privilege for the abbey of Notre-Dame at Saintes, where Eleanor's aunt was abbess, confirms whatever Eleanor and her sister Aelith have given or will give to the abbey.[6] Presumably Louis had provided some dower from Aquitaine for Aelith, as well as for Eleanor. From 1189, Eleanor held Jaunay, the island of Oléron and the castle of Mervent as dower; probably, she held them as dower during Henry's reign, at least until her revolt.

Louis VII must have set up dower from his own lands for Eleanor, but we do not know what it was or whether she enjoyed the income from any of it while she was queen of France. She assented to or approved three of Louis' acts concerning properties in Capetian territory, possibly because they involved her dower interests. Two were confirmations of gifts to Cistercian abbeys, Chaâlis and Echarlis, and one involved urban houses

belonging to the bishop of Paris.[7] Louis had the problem that his
mother was still alive and unprepared to give up any of her dower,
which included the prosperous town of Compiègne with its
Carolingian palace. It led to the financial squabble at the beginning of Louis' reign recorded by Suger. Suger says that Louis
generously suggested that Adela could stay in the royal palace,
with her son and his new wife. Adela, thinking that this was a
trick to deprive her of her revenues, retreated to Compiègne,
perhaps to ensure it could not be taken off her. The king, his wife
and his mother must have come to a mutually acceptable arrangement, since Adela soon returned to court – but she kept
Compiègne.[8]

Henry demonstrated his wealth by providing Eleanor with
a generous dower, which Eleanor enjoyed until her imprisonment, when Henry took some or most of it back into his own
hands. He used some for his religious foundations at Waltham
and Amesbury in contrition for the murder of Thomas Becket.[9]
Richard restored Eleanor's dower after Henry's death and substan-
tially increased it, adding the dower of the queens of Henry I and
Stephen, according to Roger of Howden. 'Now,' said Richard of
Devizes, 'where formerly she had lived from the government
income [*de fisco*], she would live off her own [*de proprio*]' – a sim-
plification, since Eleanor had had plenty of her own income to
live on before the fateful revolt.[10]

We are much better informed on her dower, especially the
continental dower, under Richard and John than under Henry.
Both had to carve out dower arrangements for their own queens,
Berengaria in 1191, then Isabelle of Angoulême in 1200, by
which time three living queens required support. The dower
arrangements for Berengaria and Isabelle provide us with evidence
for Eleanor's dower. Moreover, Philip Augustus needed to know
what was or had been due to all three queens, as he conquered
Normandy and Anjou in 1204.[11]

Eleanor's continental dower under Richard, and probably Henry, included Jaunay, the castle of Mervent and the island of Oléron from her own inheritance, and the castles and towns of Bonneville-sur-Touques, Domfront and Falaise in Normandy, of Château-du-Loir in Maine, and of Loches and Montbazon in Touraine. Eleanor's income from Bonneville-sur-Touques was £160, from Falaise £540 and from Domfront £180. Richard was careful to leave his mother's dower intact as he organized Berengaria's dower in 1191. Berengaria would inherit Eleanor's dower after her death; in the meantime, her income came from Gascony beyond the Garonne. John was less careful: Château-du-Loir was transferred to Isabelle, as were the wealthy towns of Saintes and Niort from Aquitaine. Eleanor's English income included the port of Queenhithe in London and Queen's Gold, both, as their names imply, traditional dower of the queen of England; the barony of Berkhamsted; the cities of Exeter and Chichester; and lands in and income from several, mainly southern, counties. In addition to her own revenues, Eleanor often received expensive gifts like a gilded saddle, or luxurious clothes, and her living expenses at court from Henry's income. She always lived *de fisco* as well as *de proprio*.[12]

As queen of England, Eleanor, with her generous dower, even before Richard's augmentations, and periodic access to her Aquitanian inheritance, was extremely rich – apart from the lost years under house arrest. She was as wealthy as the greatest of Henry's barons.[13] It was very different as queen of France. Then, she was probably dependent on Louis' generosity for her household expenses, and Louis had less room for generosity. She made no major donations to religious houses or gifts of

Folio from Matthew Paris, *Liber additamentorum* (Book of Additions), c. 1250, with the list of jewels from the treasury of St Albans, showing the ring, with its 'oriental sapphire of intense colour', which once belonged to Eleanor.

prior de Walingefford deo 7 eccle sci Albani
Casto aut contulens eandem gemam unonu 7
ipe lapis ad maiorem cancellam 7 sedita-
tem eiusdem aureo ectulo cum anigitur
prout in capite huius capituli figurat.

Ponderat autem Ser denar. De Saphiro

Hunc lapidem precosum dui Nich.
videlicet saphirum fere rotundu
et coloris remissi dedit domin
Nicholaus aurisab de sco Alba
no oriundus deo 7 eccle s. albi. H gema
esteq; fuit be Admundi cam archiepi
Postea uero Sci Robti frs ei. Postea in
memorati dni Nicholai. In libo eiusd
castonis sbtilissime lite isculpuntur
nigellate. et erur cui euerso figurat.
Ponderat autem Ser den. De Anulo Archid.

Hunc anulu cotinere acont Johis.
num Saphirum orientale intensi
coloris dedit huic eccle dus Johis
de Wmudha huius eccle Archidiac
Que de dono dui Rogi eccle hi prior
optinuerat. In una q parte anuli ad
memoria hi nois Johis perpetuandam
isculpit 7 nigellat hi lira J. ex alia uero
O. **Ponderat autem noue den.** 7 ob. De anulo Ric.

Hunc anulu cotinentem Animal.
Saphirum orientale coloris intensi
dedit dus Ric cognometo Animal
deo 7 huic eccle. Que de dono cuis
dam regine alienore optinuerat
eiusa oscolares 7 sua inuentire ertirio
et sodales. fuerat aut gema antea ipsi
regine A. In una q pte anuli isculpi
tur R. In alia A. R. po Ric. A. parial.
Ponderat autem dece den. de Anulo epi Johis

Hunc anulu dedit deo cum magno
et huic eccle dus Johis Saphir.
epe quida Ardsertensis. In cui
castone otinet saphir eiusd orien
tal pulcherrimi muuere magnitudis
quatuor tenaculi que uulgarit petonu
dicunt cousseptus. Qui dies Saphir per
cquatuor Anguloz 7 surgit i medio
sumitate. Deputatur principuis festiuis
tatibz. Inscribiturq; hoc nome Johis.
Ponderat autem xviii den.

Hunc lapide in precosu de peridoro
qui uulgarit dr peridos. Qui et
subuiridis coloris est. et in cui me
dio saphir mure pulcherudis collo
catur. cum nomine Johis incial sculp
tur: dedit dus Johis epe quida Ardsensi
deo 7 huic eccle. Pronatur aut. Et iuxta
hr spasmu potir resreuandi. Et utiq;
forma fere elipeale. Et ponderat xvi den.

Hunc lapide precosu De Saphiro et
videl. saphirum orientale dom epi
dedit deo 7 huic eccle pie recoda
tuis memorie dus Johis epe quida
Ardsensis. In cui castone oblongo
et fere tangulari dst saphir cotinetur
In longu re ui eius sumitate pronatur.
Casto aut hac notula signatur.
Ponderat autem Ser den. Hec 7 alia multa
bona cotulit dus epe huic eccle. q alibi
diligens perscatorr inuenire potir anno.

Hunc anulu De magno anulo
nobilissimu rotundo 7 gema
maria 7 ope precosu. In cui
medio saphir remissi colo
ris ine nu. aureos floseulos
collocat. 7 i circuitu ei octo gem
ge. cquatuor. s. perle. 7 cquatuor gnate: dedit
dus Henr epe Wintonn frs dni Angl regi
deo 7 huic eccle ad memoria sui tea d
pretianda. Ipsius 7 nome ebut ceu
lo anuli. Assignat aut ornatui abbis
principuis festiuitatibz. Pondar xxviii d.

Hunc lapide pre
ciosum qvidel.
costar. et sar
donice cal
cedonio et
onic pt
hoc qd in
tinsecu la
tee veru
ipse toti
vulgarit
kaadimau
appellat. de
dit deo 7 eccle

properties that might attract courtiers to her entourage – probably because she was in no position to do so. Her one major recorded gift as queen of France was the precious Islamic rock crystal vase which she and her husband gave to the abbey of Saint-Denis. Doubtless Louis ensured that his wife dressed, dined and lived in queenly comfort, and was provided with an adequate household. He must have provided money for her coffers, which she could hand out as alms to the Church, or directly to the poor and sick who converged on the court, or with which she could reward poets or minstrels who entertained her. But this was small change for an heiress who had brought her husband so much.

But even as queen of England, Eleanor was careful, almost stingy, with her wealth – at least as far as we can tell from charters recording her gifts. She gave property to support members of her household, usually from her English dower. Her handmaid and foster child, Amiria Pantolf, received lands in Devon and woods in Hemel Hempstead; her nurse Agatha, lands in Hemel Hempstead and Devon; the chief administrator of her English lands, Henry of Berneval, lands in Wiltshire; and her cooks, Roger and Adam, property at Berkhamsted and Cumberland respectively.[14] Normans in her service, such as Andrew of Domfront, who was sent to serve her daughter Eleanor, queen of Castile, or William her almoner, were supported by property from her Norman dower lands.[15] Once she had received Poitou from John, she could provide support from Poitiers itself for her chaplain and notary, Roger.[16] Occasionally, she made grants to nobles, but most of those were after 1199, when she was not restricted to her dower and was trying to build support for John.[17] She did, however, presumably with Henry's agreement, give the fief of Beaumont and the lordship of Bonneuil, with its game park, to her uncle Hugh of Châtellerault, perhaps in the late 1160s.[18] Her gifts to ecclesiastical institutions follow a similar pattern: until 1199, she was, relative to her resources, distinctly tight-fisted.[19]

Probably her prodigious income was spent on ephemeral things, paid for from her coffers, and not recorded in charters – gifts of jewels, silks, horses, hunting dogs, lapdogs and falcons, and on the maintenance of a court appropriate to the 'noble wife of a noble king'. There must have been many small but precious gifts to valued servants like Amiria Pantolf. Also to the women of the extended royal family – Alice of Brittany, her 'protégée'; her daughters and granddaughters, like Matilda-Richenza; her daughters-in-law, Margaret and Alice of France, Isabelle of Gloucester; or Denise of Châteauroux. Men appreciated gifts of jewels too. The treasury of the abbey of St Albans contained a gold ring with 'an oriental sapphire of intense colour'. It had been given by a churchman with the curious name of Richard Animal. He obtained it from an old college mate from Eleanor's household. The ring originally belonged to Eleanor.[20]

Eleanor had a great deal of her own wine, which was often moved at Henry's expense. Doubtless her table was always laden, the food enhanced with luxuries like almonds, cumin, chestnuts and pepper – the latter a key ingredient of Aquitanian cuisine according to Ralph of Diceto. She had many cooks in her house-hold.[21] Her entourage and guests had to be entertained by musi-cians and storytellers, even if she was not herself a discerning patron of troubadours or trouvères. She probably enjoyed hunting as much as Henry: a gift to the abbey of Luçon in 1156/7 pro-tected her hunting rights, and her gift of lands to her uncle Hugh of Châtellerault specified rights in a hunting park.[22] Hunting was an expensive pastime. It required well-trained dogs, horses, fal-cons and sparrowhawks, and well-maintained and stocked hunt-ing parks. The *History of William Marshal* claimed that Eleanor's name was an amalgam of the word gold – *or* – and *ali* (meaning pure): she had a lot of gold, pure or otherwise.[23]

Indeed, William Marshal thought Eleanor 'very worth and courtly' when she paid his ransom and provided him with the accoutrements of knighthood after he was captured by the Lusignans.[24] Eleanor had a large contingent of household knights, including younger members of the Faye and Chauvigny families, and sergeants whenever she operated or resided in Aquitaine, and could not depend on knights of the royal household. The necessity for them was all too clear: in 1168 and 1200 she was ambushed by the Lusignans; in 1202 she was besieged by her grandson at Mirebeau. The maintenance of a substantial contingent of household knights, with their horses, tack and arms, must have been a heavy drain on Eleanor's income.[25]

Whether one was a queen, a king, a duchess or a duke, it was all very well to own properties and revenues. One could only enjoy the fruits of these resources if one had good administrators and an effective infrastructure; that was why Henry II was known as the king who had everything, while Louis VII had so little. Accounts must have been produced for Eleanor by her clerks, though none have survived. Did she insist on checking through them with her clerks herself? We know her granddaughter, Blanche of Castile, did – though we only know that from a throwaway comment on a single surviving building account for an abbey Blanche founded.[26] Or did Eleanor leave that to her household staff?

Eleanor's revenues mainly came in coin, but there were still some in kind. In 1156/7 she surrendered to the Hospital at Surgères, perhaps with some relief, an annual income comprising generous measures of wine, a small measure of oats and one chicken.[27] For revenue in kind, good barns and cellars for storage and well-run local markets – which would generate more income for the astute lord or lady – were essential. Local officials collected her revenues and organized their safekeeping (if chickens or grain), or their transport to her (if coin), or their payment to someone else if she ordered it. They are occasionally mentioned in texts. Robert the Saucier rendered the account for her dower castellany of Domfront to the Norman exchequer and ensured that the revenues due to Eleanor were sent to her in Poitou.[28] When she herself governed Poitou, briefly in 1152 and after Richard's death, and presumably during her co-rule with Richard from 1168 to 1173, ducal officials, particularly the provosts, ensured that the resources of the duchy came to her coffers. A system of ducal provosts had been in place since the late eleventh century, including in Poitiers, Chizé, Benon, Saintes, Surgères, Oléron, Saint-Jean d'Angely, La Rochelle, Talmont, Montreuil-Bonnin, Bordeaux and possibly Mervent. Hervey the Pantler was provost of Poitiers between 1157 and 1175, in addition to his duties within Eleanor's household. The vital role of the provosts in managing the ducal revenues – and the problems when a provostship is vacant – emerges powerfully from a series of letters sent to Abbot Suger, when he acted as regent when Louis VII was on crusade.[29]

Like all medieval elites, Eleanor moved from residence to residence, feeding her entourage and guests on the provisions in her stores, and filling her coffers from moneys raised in the locality. But she had too much property, too widely scattered, for itinerating to absorb all her revenue, whether it came in kind or, as most of it did, in coin. Cartloads of silver pennies or ingots of silver must have been shipped across the Channel to her, and then driven along the roads, from Oléron to Berkhamsted, from Devon to Fontevraud, from Domfront to Poitiers. Presumably her household knights helped to protect her riches as they trundled across England and France to her coffers. Did she have her own treasuries in the places she most frequented? Or did she use the king's treasuries at Winchester, Caen and Chinon? Either way, managing Eleanor's wealth was a complex logistical challenge. Her staff had to ensure she got her monies and income in kind, that they were stored safely, accounted for and distributed as the queen ordered. Her gifts of properties, relatively few though they were, had to be recorded in charters by her household staff.

A queen's household staff managed not just her wealth, but her life and lifestyle. When the queen was with the king, some of this logistical challenge was handled by his household, and at his expense. When Eleanor crossed the Channel with Henry or at his command, her expenses, including the special royal ships, the *esneccas*, are recorded on the pipe-roll accounts. The costs were carried by the king's revenues (*de fisco*), and the arrangements made by members of his household. When Eleanor was actively governing, for instance as regent in England or Anjou for Henry, or as effective regent in England during Richard's imprisonment, her household was subsumed, or even completely displaced, by royal administrators. This was probably just as well, for the political acumen of her own Poitevin household and entourage was not impressive.

The daily running of an aristocratic or royal household, like Eleanor's, was controlled by the seneschal or dapifer, supported by the butler or pincerna, the pantler and the chamberlain. Between them, they ensured that she and her household dined in the appropriate manner, whether entertaining guests or observing one of the many fast days that littered the calendar; that she dressed regally, and that her ladies and household were robed; that she had cushions, draught-excluding curtains and comfortable bedding; that she had warm fires, and candles or oil lamps for light. Curiously, oil for her lamps in England was always bought out of the king's London income.[30] Her seneschal and chamberlain oversaw the arrangements to move from one residence to the next, ensuring her goods were loaded on to sumpter carts, and the next residence was prepared for her arrival. The constable managed her stables and the military rather than domestic aspects of the household – the household knights and sergeants. A chancellor and a set of clerks, some of whom might be identified as notaries, or scribes, would deal with the writing and issuing of charters, with correspondence, and with accounts.

Almost nothing is known about the personnel of Eleanor's household when she was queen of France. Most of her few charters were issued by the king's chancellery, but in one charter, her chaplain, Peter, is designated as her chancellor.[31] In the two months when she was countess of Poitou and duchess of Aquitaine in her own right in-between marriages, she must have appointed her own Poitevin household. It included Hervey the Pantler, who had served her father. He was an adept old survivor. He avoided implication in the 1173 revolt and transferred his loyalty to Henry II.[32] An early act shows Saldebreuil in the role of her seneschal, but he was soon, perhaps under Henry's influence, demoted to her constable. He continued as constable until 1173 and was one of the few members of her Poitevin household to attend her in England and was given property there.[33] In 1156 Porteclie of Mauzé was her seneschal in Poitou, his name – 'the carrier of the keys' – invoking the importance of the role, but at the same time Ralph of Hastings was seneschal for her English household. In 1163 John of Wauvray was listed as her seneschal on an act issued in Normandy and on the English exchequer rolls. By 1163 her butler Philip, perhaps a Poitevin, had been replaced by Luke, at least in Normandy. Her first chamberlain, a cousin, Bernard of Chauvigny, was soon replaced by Warin FitzGerald. In the early 1170s her chamberlain was Adam FitzJordan. Her first chancellor, Bernard, probably a Poitevin, was soon replaced by Master Matthew of Angers. Matthew travelled with her to England and Normandy. Matthew retired from her household to become dean of the cathedral of Angers around 1162. After that, she never appointed another chancellor to her household, even when she ruled Aquitaine with young Richard. In fact, her acts issued in Poitou between 1168 and 1173 do not

specify any other household officers. Almost certainly, Henry
ensured that her household was filled with his own administrators and clerks, but she undoubtedly had different entourages,
and perhaps different household officers, in England, Normandy,
Anjou and Poitou.[34]

Her post-1189 household had few named officers. Henry of
Berneval oversaw the administration of her English properties,
but he had no official title. In England, Ingelran was her butler
and Geoffrey of Wancy her constable, and she employed multiple
cooks. At the end of her life, her household seneschal was Geoffrey
Galion or Julian. The clerk Geoffrey, probably from Chinon, was
the clerk of her chamber. Her household knights were prominent,
witnessing her acts and aiding her in judgements. Laonno Ogero
and Chalo de Rochefort seem to have been particularly active.
Some of the churchmen in her household, such as Roger, her
chaplain, or the clerks Master Richard and William of Saint-
Maixent, issued her acts as a chancellor might, but did not hold
the office. William of Saint-Maixent, the clerk Jordan and Roger
the chaplain were sometimes called 'notaries' when they produced or wrote charters for Eleanor. No almoner is recorded in
her household before 1189. But throughout the 1190s, Master
William 'our almoner' was often with the queen, and there is
brief mention of Richard the almoner.

The clerks were clergy, often in lower orders well below
priesthood, who had trained in the schools, often at Paris, in
Latin and the mathematical arts, and who pursued careers as
administrators. Jordan, described as 'her clerk', worked for her in
Poitou between 1168 and 1173, and then joined her again in 1189.
Their numbers expanded exponentially in the 1190s, when at
least nine named 'clerks' can be identified. Several clerks had
attained the level of 'Master' in the schools, including the English
clerks Master Thomas of Chichester and Master Richard of
Knowsale.

We have to trace Eleanor's household through the acts and letters that she issued, and through odd references in the English and Norman exchequer rolls. The evidence is fragmentary, and conclusions drawn from it are at best provisional. But it looks as though there was always more structure – more specified offices – to her household in England, and perhaps Normandy. In Poitou, that 'office' structure was lost by 1168. Does that reflect a lack of organization in Poitou? Or a more fluid approach to the running of the household – an acknowledgement that the work of the seneschal, the chamberlain and the butler often overlapped? By her last years, her household had a strong military tone, dominated by her knights and sergeants, though this was offset by at least six identifiable chaplains and nine identifiable clerks.

The Angevin kings attracted gifted administrators to their households and government. Eleanor worked closely with them – people like Thomas Becket, John of Salisbury, Richard of Ilchester, William Longchamp or Walter of Coutances – when she acted as regent for Henry and Richard. She must have known how indispensable such gifted administrative clerks were, for the running of one's household, for generating income from and the ruling of one's territories. Surprisingly, her own administrative staff were undistinguished. The most effective were those imposed on her by Henry II, or dealing with her English or Norman lands and working within an Anglo-Norman administrative framework. Few of her own clerks went on to distinguished careers in the royal administration or the Church, apart from her chancellor Matthew, who was imposed by Henry II, or William of Saint-Maixent, who entered John's administrative cadre. None of her own clerks, as opposed to those appointed for her by Henry, obtained the bishopric with which so many effective royal clerks were rewarded. Some of the lay members of her household, like Bernard of Chauvigny, the chamberlain, were absorbed into

Richard's household. Perhaps she made little effort to attract the best administrators. Perhaps her stinginess with gifts put them off.

It put her at a disadvantage. It left her open to too great a dependence on ill-chosen advisors, like Ralph of Faye and later the brutal mercenary Mercadier. Although she chose to reside largely in Poitou in her later years, she needed her well-administered and dependable income from England and Normandy. And it was counter to the trending growth of administrative rulership in the later twelfth century. The Anglo-Norman realm under Henry I had led the way here, but all late twelfth-century rulers appreciated organization, administration and careful recording, and valued and rewarded those who could produce it. This was true of Henry II, of Richard and John, of Philip Augustus and even of Louis VII in his later years. It was true of the counts of Toulouse and Flanders and of the counts of Champagne, including Countess Mary, Eleanor's daughter, who ruled Champagne as regent. It is not difficult to see why. Administration produced the goods – literally. It meant that a ruler could realize the potential wealth of their realm, the wealth that allowed them to live like a king or a queen. For all her delight in the things and activities of the regal life, Eleanor showed little interest in the administrative structure that provided them.

EIGHT

Prayer

Eleanor's father and grandfather both had eventful relationships with the Church. William ix was careless with his women, and his and their marital status – for which he was excommunicated – and infamous for his sexually explicit songs. His expedition to the Holy Land in 1101 was unsuccessful. In Spain he fought alongside the Muslim prince of Saragossa, who rewarded him with the famous rock crystal vase.[1] William x supported Anacletus ii, the pope who eventually lost out in the disputed papal election of 1130. By early 1131 Bernard of Clairvaux, helped by Suger among others, had persuaded Louis the Fat and Henry i to support Innocent ii.

William x did not change sides as nimbly as Louis, Henry i and the other French princes.[2] Bishop Gerard of Angoulême, papal legate to Aquitaine since 1107, and once regarded as a distinguished scholar, supported Anacletus. Despite a visit by St Bernard, Gerard persuaded William to do so too. In a display of blatant lay pressure on the Church, William engineered the election of Anacletus-supporting bishops at Limoges and Poitiers, imposing Dangereuse's uncle, Peter of Châtellerault, at the latter. William, and the Aquitanian prelates and magnates who supported Anacletus, were excommunicated. Innocent ii appointed Geoffrey of Lèves, bishop of Chartres, as legate to Aquitaine. His duties included smashing all altars consecrated by the discredited Gerard of Angoulême.[3] Rescuing Duke William from Anacletian inclinations became a project of the reformists of the northern French Church, led by Geoffrey of Lèves and Bernard.

They were aided in Aquitaine by Geoffrey of Loroux. He had been a distinguished scholar and theologian at Angers Cathedral, despite a bad stammer. By the 1120s he was living a religious life of eremitical hardship as an Augustinian canon in Aquitaine. Surprisingly, he was close to Duke William x. Together they established the Augustinian houses of Sablonceaux and Fontaine-le Comte.[4] The burial of Eleanor's mother, Aenor, at Augustinian Nieul-sur-l'Autise may reflect Geoffrey of Loroux's influence at the ducal court. Geoffrey organized another attempt by St Bernard and Geoffrey of Lèves to persuade William to support Innocent, at a meeting at Parthenay. Faced with Bernard's harangues, William had some kind of physical, perhaps epileptic, collapse and capitulated.

When Gerard of Angoulême died in early 1136, support for Anacletus in Aquitaine withered. William now adopted a belated but enthusiastic pro-Innocent stance. He supported the election of Geoffrey of Loroux as archbishop of Bordeaux. Archbishop Geoffrey and Geoffrey of Lèves acted as witnesses when William founded the Cistercian abbey of La Grace-Dieu in the presence of St Bernard.[5] But the Church disapproved when William joined Geoffrey of Anjou in a violent attack on Normandy in 1136–7, and William's final fatal pilgrimage to Santiago de Compostela was made in penance for it.

William left his daughter and heiress in the care of Archbishop Geoffrey at Bordeaux. When Louis rushed back to Paris on the news of his father's death, Eleanor travelled more slowly in the care of Bishop Geoffrey of Chartres. Both must have seen it as their duty to keep Duke William's daughter and heiress on the right religious path. At the French court, their friend and colleague, Abbot Suger of Saint-Denis, saw himself as an advisor to, and perhaps a protector of, William's daughter. Eleanor took part in all the ceremonial royal visits to Saint-Denis – the consecration of the choir, at which Archbishop Geoffrey of Bordeaux consecrated the principal altar in the crypt, and the ceremonies of departure for the crusade. Saint-Denis gave Eleanor the space to discuss sex with Bernard of Clairvaux. When Louis complained about Eleanor's behaviour in Antioch, Suger 'dared to praise the queen'. Suger stressed Eleanor's ownership of her grandfather's precious rock crystal vase; he could just have mentioned Louis. Suger took an informed interest in Poitou. He had studied in the Loire and knew Fontevraud well. Saint-Denis had a priory close to Châtellerault, and stored a charter by which Eleanor's Châtellerault grandparents, Aimery and Dangereuse, abnegated customs they had imposed on the priory. The young Suger and his abbot attended a great church council at Poitiers

The church of St Pierre at Parthenay-le-Vieux, outside which Eleanor's father, Duke William x, collapsed when St Bernard of Clairvaux harangued him for his support of the anti-pope Anacletus ii.

in 1106, and the charter may be linked to their visit. If so, Suger had met Eleanor's notorious grandmother.[6]

Louis VII became famous for his piety, and for his offer of refuge to exiled churchmen, including Pope Alexander III and Thomas Becket. But in the first fifteen years of his reign, Louis' relationship with the Church was fractious, culminating in Ralph of Vermandois' marital scandal and the disastrous war against Champagne.[7] The Church was not disposed to take Louis' side rather than Eleanor's as their marriage fell apart. Pope Eugenius III took his line from Suger. He was protective of Eleanor when she finally arrived at the papal court, exhausted, ill and probably pregnant, along with her irate husband, and tried to patch up their marriage.

At the papal court in 1149, Eleanor met Hyacinth Boboni, then the dynamic young cardinal deacon of Santa Maria in Cosmedin, who had studied in Paris with Abelard.[8] When Hyacinth came to France with Pope Alexander III in 1162, she wrote to him as if to a personal friend, seeking his help for her relative, the embattled Abbot Peter of Saint-Maixent. In old age, Hyacinth was elected pope, as Celestine III. Eleanor met him in Rome on her way back from Sicily in 1191 to negotiate confirmation of Longchamp as papal legate, and permission to consecrate Geoffrey Plantagenet as archbishop of York. She arrived at Easter, just in time for Celestine's inauguration as pope. It was to Celestine that Peter of Blois' emotive letters in Eleanor's name were addressed. Whether they were sent or not, Celestine did what he could to secure Richard's release, despite opposition from his cardinals.[9]

As queen of France, Eleanor consorted with the pope, with cardinals and with great churchmen who were widely admired as the ecclesiastical leaders of France, and in the case of St Bernard, western Christendom. It stood her in good stead. In later life, whatever her reputation among dyspeptic clerical writers, she dealt easily, directly and personally with the uppermost Church hierarchy, whether ensuring the election of Hubert Walter as archbishop of Canterbury or negotiating with the archbishops of Mainz and Cologne.

Henry II's reputation has never recovered from Becket's murder. But Eleanor's second husband was, in his own way, as pious as her first. Henry was always susceptible to holy men, like the Carthusian bishop Hugh of Lincoln. Henry had been schooled by his mother, the empress. Like his mother, he was a generous patron of monastics and regular canons, above all of those orders emerging from the monastic reforms of circa 1100 – Carthusians, Grandmontines, Fontevraud, Cistercians, Augustinian canons, including Premonstratensians – and the poor, sick and lepers. Richard shared many of his father's religious enthusiasms: for Fontevraud, Grandmont and in particular the Cistercian order. Despite his support for the wrong pope, Eleanor's father was also a generous religious patron, conscious, as indeed was Henry, of maintaining the patronal reputation and the commemoration of the dynasty. Under the influence of Geoffrey of Loroux, William X favoured reformed orders: his foundations were Augustinian and Cistercian. In 1134, in the depths of the papal schism, in the hall of his castle at Niort, he made substantial gifts to the Fontevraudine priory of St Bibien, in the presence of his Châtellerault brothers-in-law.[10]

Eleanor's maternal relations could not pretend to this level of princely patronage, but they were consistent supporters of institutions in their vicinity. The Châtellerault, Faye, Blaison and L'Île-Bouchard families all supported Fontevraud from the start. Two Blaison, one L'Île-Bouchard and one Châtellerault daughter entered Fontevraud as nuns. Ralph of Faye was recorded in the Fontevraud necrology.[11] The Châtellerault, Faye, L'Île-Bouchard and Sainte-Maure families supported the Benedictine abbey of Noyers. Eleanor's grandfather, Viscount Aimery, was buried there. Realizing he was close to death, the viscount asked to be taken by boat from his castle to the abbey, where his sister, Girberga, the nun of Fontevraud, cared for him in his last hours. He was buried in the chapter house. His son Hugh, Eleanor's uncle, established anniversaries for his father and became, in his place, advocate for the abbey. The patronage of Fontevraud and Noyers by these families developed a community, a social solidarity between them, as they witnessed each other's donations, and attended each other's burials. Hugh of Sainte-Maure, who joined Ralph of Faye in persuading Eleanor to revolt in 1173, was also buried at Noyers when he died in 1180.[12]

The demonstration of piety was an important weapon in the armoury of most powerful medieval women. Several duchesses of Aquitaine, most famously Agnes of Burgundy, were renowned patrons of monasticism. Eleanor's grandmother Philippa of Toulouse supported the reformist monastic movements of Gerard de Salles and Robert of Arbrissel, the founder of Fontevraud. She retired to, and was buried at, either Fontevraud itself or the Fontevraudine priory of L'Espinasse that she had founded. Geoffrey, abbot of Vendôme, wrote to her about the state of her soul – as indeed he wrote to her raffish husband.[13] Eleanor's mother persuaded her husband to make important donations, though she probably lacked the resources to make them herself.[14] The women of the Anglo-Norman dynasty – the queens of England, Matilda I, Matilda II, Adela of Louvain, Matilda of Boulogne, Empress Matilda and Henry I's sister Adela of Blois – were all prominent patrons of religious institutions. All founded religious institutions, often using income from their dower to purchase lands, so that the dower itself was not depleted. Some of the institutions were relatively modest, but Matilda I's Holy Trinity Caen and Matilda II's Holy Trinity Aldgate, not to mention Empress Matilda's foundations, were substantial. Eleanor's first mother-in-law, Adela of Maurienne, may have clashed with

Abbot Suger, but she supported reformist churchmen, as befitted the niece of Pope Calixtus II, and founded, with the generous support of her husband and some income from her dower, her own burial house of Benedictine nuns at Montmartre.[15]

Many of these women commissioned pious literature. Distinguished churchmen wrote to them, sometimes asking for their intervention, but always assuming their engagement with matters spiritual. The admiration of churchmen lent an indefinable lustre to their position, and they often deployed this clerical capital to political advantage. The siting of their monastic foundations was often highly political, in border zones or disputed territory. These women could obtain places at court for sympathetic churchmen and promote clerics from their entourages to important positions within the Church hierarchy. Eleanor's mothers-in-law, her daughters and her granddaughters, notably Mary of Champagne, Matilda of Saxony, Eleanor of Castile, Matilda-Richenza of Perche and Blanche of Castile, made personal piety and judicious ecclesiastical patronage a hallmark of their political persona and activity. Everything suggests that all these women took religious matters seriously; that was why this worked.

Eleanor does not fit this pattern. The Church had been protective of her as queen of France. But when she was queen of England, distinguished churchmen did not write to give her religious advice, in the way that Anselm wrote to Matilda II of England and Adela of Blois, Geoffrey of Vendôme to Duchess Philippa, or Adam of Perseigne to Alixe of Blois and Matilda-Richenza. When they did write to her, like the monks of Canterbury, they wanted her protection or her intervention on their behalf.

As queen of France, her resources were limited, but as queen of England, apart from the years of imprisonment, her resources were substantial. Nevertheless, her patronage of religious institutions is underwhelming. She did not found her own abbey or

priory, apart from, possibly, the Fontevraudine priory of Ste-
Catherine at La Rochelle. She did not fund building campaigns,
apart from Fontevraud, where she built a precinct wall and a
small chapel for her private devotion.[16] She showed no interest
in Noyers, where many of her mother's extended family were
buried. Most of her acts for religious houses confirm existing
rights and properties granted by her predecessors as dukes of
Aquitaine, her husbands, sons and her nephew, Otto.[17] She made
restitution for wrongs committed by Richard at Ste-Croix and
Ste-Radegonde at Poitiers and Maillezais.[18] There were a handful
of new donations, but outright gifts were few and far between,
except when Eleanor was trying to drum up support for John.
As queen of France (and again in 1199), she assented to gifts
to the Templars of La Rochelle and the Cistercian abbey of
La Grace-Dieu, founded by her father to mark his acceptance
of Innocent II, and to the abolition of bad customs for Vendôme.
As queen of England, she made new donations to Luçon, La
Sauve-Majeure, the hospital at Surgères and Turpenay.[19]

   Eleanor's religious patronage was focused on Fontevraud.[20]
The major gifts of revenues from lands came at the very end of
her life, mostly after Richard's death, when she controlled the
resources of the duchy of Aquitaine. Even so, most were drawn
from her dower lands in Oléron. Most were personal, providing
support for family and friends – for her chaplain Roger, her granddaughter Alice of Blois and her protégée, the prioress Alice of
Brittany. After the deaths of the two Alices, their income would
revert to the abbey: clearly nuns from distinguished families at
Fontevraud could enjoy their own incomes.[21] Eleanor established
anniversary masses for herself and her family. She confirmed gifts
from members of her household, who were themselves donating
lands she had given them, like her handmaid Amiria Pantolf.[22]
The abbey necrology records that she gave a great gold gem-
encrusted processional cross, a gold chalice, several gold and

silver vases and silk vestments, and surrounded the abbey with a strong protective wall. She founded and had built a chapel dedicated to St Lawrence at Fontevraud for her own personal use. Perhaps it was alongside the residence, near the abbey gates. In 1199 she established Roger as its chaplain.[23]

Her interest in Fontevraud has been seen as a reflection of Henry II's devoted and generous patronage of the nunnery, in line with his Angevin and Anglo-Norman forbears. His aunt, Matilda of Anjou, was the second abbess of Fontevraud.[24] But Eleanor's family had their own tradition of support for Fontevraud, from her paternal grandmother, Philippa of Toulouse, and from her mother's family, the Châtellerault-Faye-Blaison-L'Île-Bouchard clan, which had placed at least four women there as nuns. Eleanor consented to a gift of Poitevin revenues to Fontevraud from Louis VII, as both toured Poitou and Saintonge before their departure on crusade.[25] The initiative was probably hers.

Most religious patronage had its political rationale, even that by the most egregiously pious of rulers. Some of Eleanor's gifts seem essentially strategic. Some were designed to rally support for John after Richard's death. The confirmation and gift to La Sauve-Majeure, for instance, was issued when she went to Bordeaux in the aftermath of Richard's death 'for the stability of the community and the good of the patrimony', and helped her to bring together the principal churchmen, nobles and powerful merchants of Bordeaux.[26] Eleanor followed Henry II and Richard in offering protection to Dalon in the Quercy. It was useful to cultivate a substantial Cistercian abbey, much favoured by the troublesome viscounts of Limoges, in a border zone.[27]

Why is Eleanor's record as religious patron so slim, given her resources as queen of England? It is surprising that Eleanor did not learn from her two mothers-in-law, or from the glowing reputation of previous duchesses of Aquitaine. Probably she preferred to give things, like the rock crystal vase, or the gold liturgical objects and fine silk vestments she gave to Fontevraud. But again, it is a thin record, especially in comparison to Empress Matilda, who gave an exquisite jewelled cross to the abbey of Le Valasse, jewels to Saint-Denis and the contents of her magnificent private chapel, replete with crosses, crowns, gospel books, liturgical vessels, reliquaries, silk vestments and altar cloths, to Le Bec.[28]

Like all elites, both lay and ecclesiastical, Eleanor had her own personal chapel, which travelled with her. The costs of moving it in its coffers, along with her incense, is listed in the pipe roll for 1159/60.[29] She was fond of incense, for one of her rare gifts was made in exchange for annual renders of it.[30] Her chapel would have contained a portable altar, chalices and vessels for the mass, altar cloths and vestments for her chaplains and books for her private devotion. Her gifts to Fontevraud probably came from her chapel.

It has been suggested that she owned a fine illustrated and gilded psalter (The Hague, Koninklijke Bibliotheek manuscript 76 F 13). Some of the saints in the calendar indicated that it was made in the Norman abbey of Fécamp, and it is usually dated to around 1180. It contains a striking image of a praying woman, presumably the first owner of the psalter. The blue and white pattern on the lining of her cloak has been taken for Angevin family heraldry, for it resembles the cloak lining of Henry II's father, Geoffrey of Anjou, on the famous enamel from his tomb. In fact, the pattern was the standard means of representing multi-skinned fur linings as shown in images of furriers in the stained-glass windows at Chartres and Bourges cathedrals. Besides, a close analysis of the saints in the calendar demonstrates that the psalter was produced not at Fécamp, but at the collegiate church of Ham-en-Vermandois in northeastern France. The names of the dead added to the calendar suggest that it was in the possession

Psalter, c. 1180. Often called the 'Fécamp' psalter, it was once thought to have been made at the Norman abbey of Fécamp but was in fact produced at the college of Ham-en-Vermandois. The kneeling female patron shown here has been identified as Eleanor of Aquitaine. Eleanor had no connection with Ham-en-Vermandois, but it is possible that the psalter was produced for Eleanor's unfortunate niece, Elizabeth of Vermandois, countess of Flanders.

of the family of the counts of Flanders in the thirteenth century. The original owner was not Eleanor, who was imprisoned in England when it was made, but just possibly her unfortunate niece, Elizabeth of Vermandois, countess of Flanders.[31]

The churchmen in Eleanor's household who dealt with her spiritual needs, the chaplains and almoners, were usually distinguished from the administrator clerks. There was some overlap. Roger the chaplain also acted as her notary, and her chaplain Peter doubled as her chancellor in 1140/41. Until 1189 she had a couple of clerics at a time. At the end of her life clergymen multiply in the witness lists to her acts, just like her knights, with as many as five serving concurrently. Two almoners are recorded: Richard in 1190 and Master William, who succeeded him in the 1190s. Apart from William the almoner, those who were qualified as 'Master' dealt with her administration rather than her spiritual life.[32]

We know most about Roger. In 1199 Eleanor provided for his living at her chapel of St Lawrence at Fontevraud, where he would say masses for her soul and the souls of her predecessors and her children. After his death the abbess would appoint a successor, to be supported by the income Eleanor had established for Roger. Roger is described as a brother of Fontevraud. Perhaps he had always been; perhaps this arrangement was made to allow him to retire into the community of Fontevraud. He had been one of Eleanor's clerics from the mid-1190s. In the frantic aftermath of Richard's death, Roger travelled with Eleanor to Bordeaux, Poitiers and Rouen. But he subscribed none of her acts after 1200, even those issued at Fontevraud. Perhaps he died.[33]

Eleanor's acts reveal some of the great churchmen who appeared in her entourage. Bishop John of Poitiers was an occasional attender during her rule at Poitiers between 1168 and 1173. Bishop John was no admirer of Ralph of Faye, 'our Luscus', and his relations with the queen were presumably respectful but cool. In the last few years of her life, there were three bishops on whom she depended: Helias, archbishop of Bordeaux, and even more Henry, bishop of Saintes, and her relation Maurice of Blaison, bishop of Poitiers. His appointment in 1198–9 suggests Eleanor had some influence upon the canons of Poitiers Cathedral. Perhaps Maurice benefitted from her patronage in the early stages of his career. He had been bishop of Nantes between 1185 and 1198. Little is known about Henry, bishop of Saintes from circa 1189 until 1213. Along with the bishop of Limoges, Sebrand Chabot, he accompanied Eleanor to Germany to secure Richard's release. Some of Eleanor's donations to Fontevraud were made on the advice of Bishops Henry and Maurice, and Maurice persuaded her to make restorations to Saint-Maixent.[34]

Isembert, master of the schools of Saintes, witnessed acts concerning La Rochelle for the queen. He visited Eleanor in England in 1192–4 – perhaps bringing moneys for Richard's ransom. He was a gifted engineer and built bridges at Saintes and La Rochelle, on the strength of which he was brought to London in 1202 by King John to help build London Bridge, presumably on Eleanor's recommendation.[35] Milo, abbot of Cistercian Le Pin, and Luke, abbot of Turpenay, stayed with Eleanor to support her as she dealt with Richard's death, for both had been close to Richard and present at his death. Milo was his almoner. One of her few gifts was made to the abbey of Turpenay in gratitude for Abbot Luke's solicitude for her son and for herself.[36] She consorted with the abbesses of Fontevraud – Matilda I, Audeberge (1164–c. 1180), Matilda II of Flanders (1187–94), Matilda III of Variville (1194–1204), the prioress and future abbess, Alice of Brittany – and with the prior William, usually at Fontevraud itself, though occasionally an abbess came to Eleanor. The abbots of Aquitaine attended Eleanor's court when they needed something from her, or when she was staying near or at their abbeys, but their presence was fleeting. None of them, not even from the ducal foundations of Montierneuf, Maillezais or Saint-Jean d'Angely, appears often in her entourage.

In her efforts to procure ecclesiastical preferment, Eleanor concentrated on her Châtellerault relatives rather than members of her household. Maurice of Blaison is an obvious case. One of Maurice's uncles, Ralph of Mirebeau, was dean of Poitiers Cathedral in the 1160s, presumably with Eleanor's help and to Bishop John's annoyance.[37] Her nephew Hugh of Châtellerault became dean of Saint-Hilaire at Poitiers, the venerable abbey in which the counts of Poitou were invested as count, and of which they were titular abbot.[38] Bartholomew of Vendôme, archbishop of Tours, was related to her indirectly through Ralph of Faye. At the start of Bartholomew's career, Eleanor arranged his appointment to a living in an English church belonging to Westminster Abbey. Bartholomew went on to become dean of Tours, and then archbishop. He may have been involved in the plan to send emotional letters to drive Pope Celestine to action over Richard's imprisonment, for some manuscripts have them sent in his name. He was close to both Ralph of Faye and Hugh of Sainte-Maure. He established a Faye cousin, John, in the Tours chapter; John became archbishop himself in 1208. Bartholomew officiated at Hugh of Sainte-Maure's funeral at Noyers in 1180. One wonders what role he played in the plotting of the early 1170s.[39] Eleanor wrote to Alexander III, and to Cardinal Hyacinth, the future Celestine III, on behalf of another ecclesiastical relative, Peter, the abbot of Saint-Maixent, whose monks wanted to depose him.[40]

Household clerks and chaplains who were not relations benefitted less from her patronage, apart from Roger, with his comfortable chaplaincy at Fontevraud, and a Master Solomon, her clerk, for whom she made some effort to obtain a post at Worcester Cathedral in the late 1150s.[41] If she could not, or perhaps would not, ensure glittering careers for her clerks, she was unlikely to attract the most impressive churchmen, either as administrators or as pastors. But perhaps that did not matter to a woman who was used to personal interaction with the greatest churchmen of the day.

When Eleanor died, she had outlived most of her children, as well as her parents, siblings, two husbands and two problematic uncles. Both Henry and Eleanor were devastated by the unexpected death of the Young King. Eleanor's grief for Richard and Joanna is clear; she was at both their deathbeds and thanked Abbot Luke of Turpenay for his support as she dealt with Richard's death. Presumably she mourned most of her family deeply; some, perhaps not at all.

Eleanor often asked for prayers for the souls of herself, her children, her husband, her parents and predecessors when she confirmed previous donations, or made one of her occasional outright gifts. Occasionally, she established the celebration of anniversaries. This was an expensive business, usually requiring an income stream. In the early 1160s the abbot of Reading wrote to Eleanor, in response to a request from her, offering her the benefits of confraternity, with prayers for her soul on the anniversary of her death, just as they would remember a member of the community. His letter suggests some affection between the queen and the community, perhaps because her precious first son, William, was buried at the abbey. The abbot described the commemorative liturgies within the church and chapter house, and the distribution of alms and food to the poor. There is no evidence of any funding to support it, and by the mid-thirteenth century Eleanor's anniversary was forgotten.[42]

Eleanor's requests for prayers and anniversary commemorations are in no way unusual. Commemoration of her ducal ancestors was important to her. She affirmed existing commemorative practices at ducal foundations, or ducal burial sites, like

Notre-Dame at Saintes, Saint-Maixent, Saint-Hilaire at Poitiers
or Montierneuf. Montierneuf was a Cluniac house on the out-
skirts of Poitiers, founded as a ducal mausoleum by Duke Guy-
Geoffrey by 1076. He was buried in the nave; Eleanor's grandfather
William IX was buried in the chapter house. A monk of the abbey
recorded the elaborate commemorations for a dead duke established by Guy-Geoffrey. They were remembered every day with
masses and psalms. On the anniversary of their death, their tombs
were draped in silks and lit by candles; every single precious
liturgical object or gold-bound holy book owned by the abbey
would be held or placed around their tomb. In 1126 William X
visited his father's tomb in the chapter house in the company
of the great men of the duchy. The monks showed Eleanor the

Act of Eleanor for the abbey of Montierneuf in Poitiers, given
on 4 May 1199, confirming the gifts of her father and ancestors,
'within a month of the death of my much-loved son, King Richard'.

Tomb of Eleanor's mother, Aenor of Châtellerault, duchess of Aquitaine, in the cloister of the abbey of Saint-Vincent at Nieul-sur-l'Autise. The original tomb covering is lost, but an elaborate canopy and sculptures of the Virgin and praying figures were added in the later 13th century.

charter which her father issued, recording his tears and filial affection as he 'felt his heart and entrails knotted with grief'. Her visit shortly after Richard's death, when she issued a charter of her own reciting the gifts of her ducal predecessors, must have been particularly moving.[43]

Eleanor's father was not buried at Montierneuf, for he died at Santiago de Compostela. There was no effort to repatriate his body: perhaps it was felt that he should remain at the goal of his pilgrimage. The bishop of Santiago, Diego Gelmírez, took care of his burial before the high altar.[44] Eleanor's mother was buried in the relatively modest Augustinian house of Saint-Vincent-de-Nieul, in the cloister, just outside the chapter house, so that the canons passed her tomb every time they processed between the church and chapter house. On one of her first visits to the duchy as queen of France, Eleanor persuaded Louis to make a generous donation to the abbey and take it under royal protection.[45]

Richard's was the soul for which Eleanor most often sought prayers, or established anniversaries, both before his death and after. Perhaps she thought his soul in need of help, for she made restitution for his depredations at Maillezais and Ste-Croix at Poitiers. Probably the drive was dynastic. Richard was the successor to her father, through herself, as duke of Aquitaine and count of Poitou. She did not forget her other children, but they were rarely named separately.

Eleanor asked for few prayers for Henry II. But then Henry did not ask for many for her beyond the early years of their marriage to around 1160, when she was so productive of sons, whose souls were also to be prayed for. Although Henry often requested prayers or anniversaries for his father and mother, the empress and his children, he forgot his wife long before her revolt. In a rare moment of what appears to have been joint grief, Eleanor and Henry established an anniversary for the murdered earl Patrick of Salisbury as well as themselves at Saint-Hilaire at Poitiers in 1168.[46]

Most of Eleanor's requests for prayers and anniversary celebrations for the souls of herself and her family were addressed to Fontevraud; most post-dated Richard's burial there. She set up two parallel strands of commemoration. In the great church of the abbey were held prayers and anniversaries for herself, for Henry, for all her Plantagenet children, for her daughter Alixe of Blois and granddaughter Alice, the young nun, and for her protégée, the prioress Alice of Brittany. At the same time, in her chapel of St Lawrence, her chaplain Roger and his successors celebrated the anniversaries of herself, her children, her antecedents and successors.[47] When in 1185 Henry forced Richard to relinquish Aquitaine to Eleanor so that Henry himself could repossess it, Eleanor gave £100 of annual ducal revenues, at Henry's request and assent, to the abbey, for the souls of all the family, for Henry himself, Richard, Geoffrey and John, her dead son Henry and her daughters – though the celebration of anniversaries was not specified.[48]

When they buried young William at the feet of Henry I at Reading Abbey, Henry and Eleanor probably intended the abbey as the family burial house. A prestigious Cluniac house, it had much in common with Montierneuf. But in 1170, when seriously ill in Normandy, Henry II announced his intention to be buried in the Limousin house of Grandmont, in the cloister beside the chapter house and the tomb of the saintly founder, Stephen of Muret – in the same position as Duchess Aenor at Nieul-sur-l'Autise. Henry had funded the new church at Grandmont and presented magnificent gifts, including a great gold dove. His entourage were shocked at his choice: Grandmont was not grand enough for a great prince.[49] Did Henry change his mind as he lay dying at Chinon and ask to be buried at nearby Fontevraud? Perhaps William Marshal, who arrived soon after the death, took the decision. It was an oppressively hot July, and Grandmont was much further to transport a decomposing corpse. Eleanor, semi-confined in England, had no say in the matter.

It was Richard and Joanna who transformed their father's burial place into a family mausoleum. On his deathbed Richard gave instructions for his burial. His viscera – the parts that would rot quickly – were to be buried at the Aquitanian abbey of Charroux; his heart alongside his brother, the Young King, at Rouen Cathedral; and his body at the feet of his father at Fontevraud. Eleanor, who was present, must have ordered the division of the body. She had the heart embalmed with mint, myrtle and rare eastern frankincense. She took his remains to Fontevraud, helped by Richard's almoner Milo, abbot of Le Pin, and the abbot of Turpenay.[50] Six months later, she took Joanna's body to Fontevraud for burial. Joanna died in Rouen and was buried initially in Rouen Cathedral alongside the Young King and Richard's heart. But Joanna had insisted on becoming a nun of Fontevraud on her deathbed, requesting burial in the nuns' cemetery. Eleanor ignored that aspect of her daughter's request and had her interred in the choir beside her brother and father, where in 1249 her son, Raymond VII of Toulouse, was buried at her feet.[51]

As Eleanor buried her two children, she must have reflected that she herself was unlikely to live for much longer. There was now no question but that she herself would be laid to rest at Fontevraud with her husband and her children. Perhaps she had it in mind for a long time. Henry's intended burial at Grandmont made no provision for his queen to be entombed alongside him. She commissioned two fine matched tomb effigies for the two

Tomb effigy of Joanna or Isabelle of Angoulême and Richard I, Fontevraud Abbey.

kings, showing them dressed in their royal regalia, as they had
lain on their biers for burial. It was rare to have life-sized effigies
of the dead on tombs, but Adela of Champagne had commissioned an effigy tomb for Louis VII at his Cistercian foundation
of Barbeaux after his death in 1180, and Eleanor's daughter Mary
commissioned an effigy tomb for her husband, Count Henry
of Champagne, at Troyes, after his death the following year.
Eleanor must have known about both tombs and commissioned
the tombs for her husband and her son at Fontevraud in emu-
lation. The sculptor had worked at Poitiers Cathedral. Perhaps
Eleanor also commissioned the smaller wooden tomb effigy for
Joanna. It is usually assumed to have been provided for Isabelle
of Angoulême. But Isabelle did not die until 1246, and the effigy
looks earlier than that, closer to 1200.

What of her own tomb, disappointingly rustic alongside those
of the two kings? Did she commission it herself? By the later
Middle Ages, it was normal for elites to order their own tombs,
overseeing the design before their deaths. That was rare in the
twelfth and thirteenth centuries. The tomb was usually left to
the executors of one's will, or to the discretion of one's spouse or
heirs.[52] But Eleanor had outlived most of her family, apart from
those who were far away, and she died at a time of political cata-
clysm. It must have been left to those who surrounded her at
Fontevraud to deal with her testament and provide for her tomb
– perhaps the prioress, Eleanor's very dear protégée, Alice of
Brittany, whom Henry II had once been accused of molesting.

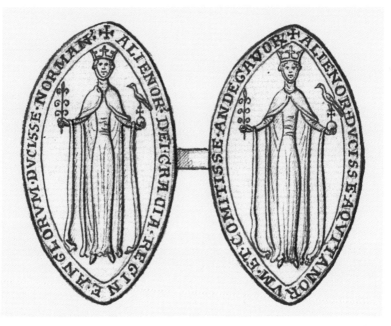

Drawings of Eleanor's double-sided seal of 1199, showing her in royal regalia on both sides, from *Chartularium monasterii Fontis-Ebraldi*.

NINE

Power

How much real power did Eleanor have? How did that vary through her long, politically and personally chequered career? How effectively, how successfully, did she wield the power that was hers? These are key questions when discussing any powerful figure – one can ask them of Henry II, Richard, John and Louis VII. There is the complicating factor that Eleanor was a woman wielding power.

Eleanor drew her authority – the authority that gave her legitimate political power – from two sources: that she was queen consort (not a queen regnant), firstly of France and then of England, and that she was in her own right countess of Poitou and duchess of Aquitaine. The dual basis of her authority was manifest on her seals. Her seal as queen of France has not survived, but it must have identified her as queen of France on one side and duchess of Aquitaine on the other, just as Louis VII's seal identified him as king on one side and duke on the other. Her first seal as queen of England was similarly double-sided, to show all her titles. Henry had a matching double-sided seal. Both Louis' and Henry's seals showed them in full royal regalia on the side that announced them as king, but as an aristocrat on horseback on the side announcing them as duke of Aquitaine. Similarly, Eleanor's first seal as queen of England showed her as a crowned queen on one side and an uncrowned duchess/countess on the other. However, by 1199 she had a new double-sided seal. Both sides show her in full English royal regalia, crowned, holding in one hand the orb surmounted by a dove, representing both peace and dominion, and in the other a flowering staff, Aaron's rod, based on the seals of previous queens of England. If people had forgotten that she had been the wife of the English king, Eleanor made sure to remind them.[1]

Being a queen rather than a duchess or countess mattered, as did being a king rather than a duke or count. Like a king, a queen was anointed with consecrated oil at her coronation. The ritual was derived from the anointing of priests. It made a queen, like the king, special, apart from the princes and barons of their lands. The queen was crowned and given a sceptre, smaller than the king's, but nonetheless a sign of her duty to 'partake in his kingship', as the coronation orders put it, and to ensure peace and justice for her people. Biblical queens were invoked at the coronation ceremony: Esther, who interceded with her husband for mercy and justice, but also Judith, who imposed punishment on the wicked. Coronation and anointing gave the queen the authority to act with reserve power should the king be ill or incapable, or absent. She could provide continuity as her sons succeeded. As a widow, she retained her special status as queen; her son might ask the queen dowager to 'partake in his kingship', for she had the authority to do so.[2]

Widowed queens made sure people remembered their status. Eleanor's mother-in-law, Empress Matilda, retained her imperial title – grander than that of queen – as widow of Emperor Henry v, though her second husband was the count of Anjou. Eleanor usually referred to her daughter Joanna as Queen of Sicily, not Countess of Toulouse.[3] John's widow, Isabelle of Angoulême, was furious when in 1241 the French king Louis ix treated her not as queen of England, but as an ordinary visitor, left standing in front of him.[4] So it was not surprising that Eleanor underscored her status as queen of England on both sides of her seal.

A queen's authority could be challenged by a disruptive or rebellious magnate or prelate – as could the authority of a king. In fact, it was not in the interests of the aristocracy to undermine the authority vested in the queen to act when her husband was absent, or during a minority, for they depended on their own wives to look after and defend their own lands if they were unable to do so. But women in positions of power often attracted adverse comment from political commentators. The Angevin court spawned a particularly engaged group of political commentators – the secular churchmen John of Salisbury, Ralph of Diceto, Walter Map, Gerald of Wales and Roger of Howden, and regular clergy such as Robert of Torigni, Richard of Devizes, William of Newburgh, Ralph of Coggeshall and Gervase of Canterbury. Many secular clergymen felt that their brilliance with the pen had not brought the worldly success they thought their due in a competitive court. Many distrusted all those who wielded worldly power. Most had sharp words for popes and bishops, as well as kings, queens and princes. Their views of powerful women were tainted by the inevitable misogyny of churchmen, themselves expected to adhere to sexual chastity, taught that the fall of man had been engineered by a woman with an apple. And whether commenting on powerful women or powerful men, ecclesiastical political commentators cannot be taken at face value. Abbot Suger is an unreliable witness, John of Salisbury and Walter Map purveyed entertaining gossip and Gerald of Wales's *Instruction for a Ruler* became a furious anti-Angevin diatribe.[5]

The reality for a woman in a position of power in the Middle Ages may have been less challenging than the bile of disappointed clerical writers suggests. Nevertheless, an institutionally patriarchal society expected those who led it, or had authority over it, to be men. As Archbishop Rotrou of Rouen told Eleanor, when he wrote to upbraid her for her revolt against Henry: 'man is the head of woman: woman is derived from man, woman is united to man, and she is subject to the power of man.'[6] The effectiveness of a woman's power and influence depended on the trust of their husbands or sons.

Eleanor was *suo jure*, through inheritance, duchess of Aquitaine and countess of Poitou, but she brought her title to her lands to her husbands, who ruled them in her right – as Eleanor and all her contemporaries, not just misogynistic churchmen, expected. Louis VII tried to retain the title of duke of Aquitaine after their divorce, holding Aquitaine in wardship for their daughters, who would eventually inherit the duchy.[7] When Eleanor produced a male heir with Henry II in 1153, that fiction was no longer tenable, and Louis stopped using the title. Louis took Eleanor with him on most of his visits to Aquitaine. He usually got her to corroborate or confirm gifts or concessions that he made to the Aquitanian Church or aristocracy. He had to be careful, because his hold on the duchy was not fully secure until Eleanor produced a son with Louis to inherit – which she did not. But there is no evidence that Louis gave Eleanor a say in the governance of her inheritance.

When Henry and Eleanor's first son was born in 1153, Henry's claim to be duke in right of his wife until his son was old enough to inherit was indisputable. From that point, Henry used the title Duke of Aquitaine along with his other titles.[8] Henry listened to Eleanor's advice on ruling Aquitaine, for he allowed Ralph of Faye to play a prominent role as seneschal of Poitou. Nevertheless, it was Henry who governed the duchy. He took Eleanor with him to Aquitaine less often than Louis did. She attested one act he issued for Aquitaine, for Fontevraud; sometimes they issued complementary acts of confirmation. But he issued many acts for Aquitaine with no reference to Eleanor whatsoever.[9]

In 1168 Henry established young Richard in Poitiers as future duke of Aquitaine, with Eleanor governing as regent duchess for her son. She sat in judgement in her court at Poitiers.[10] Many of her surviving acts date from this period. Most were issued with Richard's assent, or in their joint names.[11] Eleanor had Richard invested as count/duke of Poitou and Aquitaine in 1172. She, like everyone else, expected him to take over the rule of her inheritance when he reached his majority – a fluid concept, between the ages of fifteen and twenty-one – when she would retire to let him do so. Eleanor's mother-in-law, Empress Matilda, provided an example. When Henry was ready to rule England and Normandy, his mother, through whom he inherited them, stepped back.

During Richard's reign, Eleanor retained the title of Duchess of Aquitaine, using it on her seal and on any act that she issued. But Richard, when not on crusade or imprisoned, was an extremely active duke. He knew Aquitaine in a way that his father had not. He saw Aquitaine as an essential part of his dominions; for Henry II it was a distraction from his power base in Anjou, Normandy and England. Richard developed his own entourage among the Poitevin aristocracy, some, especially members of the Chauvigny and Chabot families, taken over from Eleanor's entourage.[12] But Richard needed a capable soldier to control the duchy. In 1196 he conferred the duchy of Aquitaine and the county of Poitou on his nephew, Eleanor's grandson, Otto of Saxony. Otto would have continued as ruler of Aquitaine, but for the enticing prospect of becoming emperor in 1198.

With Richard's unexpected death everything changed. John had none of Richard's knowledge of or connections with Aquitaine. Moreover, in western France, customary law favoured Arthur rather than John as heir. Between them, Eleanor and John concocted the arrangement which made John, not Arthur, Eleanor's heir to Poitou and Aquitaine. Eleanor did homage for Aquitaine to Philip Augustus, thus establishing her status as its duchess, before resigning Poitou and Aquitaine to John as her heir. John returned them to his mother, to hold as countess of

Poitou and duchess of Aquitaine for her lifetime, in her own right. The revenues of the duchy would accrue to her, for her to dispose of as she wished, though she could only alienate important ducal territories with his permission. Nevertheless, John continued to send orders from England. There was still an element of co-rule, perhaps on account of her age.[13]

The special nature of this arrangement makes it clear that, during Richard's reign, Eleanor's title to Aquitaine was essentially a status symbol. Richard and then Otto ruled the duchy. Richard and Otto received the revenues of the duchy, apart from those that constituted Eleanor's dower. Richard and Otto could dispose of the revenues and territories as they wished. Eleanor was only able to make gifts from her dower lands.

The changing reality of Eleanor's status is clearly visible in the acts that she issued for Aquitaine. She issued few during Richard's reign, hardly any when Otto was duke and a flood after Richard's death, when she made gifts to ecclesiastical institutions, to friends, to her household staff. Many reflected her desire to be generous to those she admired or cared about. But several were the political acts of a ruler – gifts of lands and revenues to the Aquitanian Church and aristocracy to persuade them to support John. Finally, in the last five years of her long life, she came into her inheritance.[14]

A QUEEN CONSORT WAS EXPECTED to play a role in the governance of her husband's kingdom – to 'partake in his kingship' – during his lifetime. In the first decade or so of her marriage to Henry, Eleanor acted as queen regent in England while Henry dealt with his continental lands. Briefly in 1165–6 she acted as his regent in Anjou, though with less success. In England, supported by Henry's administrators – as Henry himself would have been – she issued writs to order actions and compliance. She held court, confirming gifts made in her presence and sitting in judgement in Anjou, Normandy and England.[15] No one would have been surprised that the queen of England acted with such authority. All the Anglo-Norman kings had depended on their queens to act in their stead. Matilda I acted as regent in both Normandy and England when William the Conqueror was in the other polity; Matilda II, like Eleanor, as queen regent in England while Henry I dealt with Normandy. Matilda of Boulogne acted as queen regent when King Stephen was imprisoned. All proved wise and effective regents. Henry II himself depended not only on Eleanor in England, but on his mother, Empress Matilda, in the governance of Normandy.

The apogee of Eleanor's political power came in the five years between her husband's death and Richard's return from captivity. Richard depended on her to secure the succession in England, in effect as regent, while he dealt with the immediate fallout of Henry's death in France. According to Ralph of Diceto, Richard 'ordained that she accept power in the kingdom from her son . . . as if he had established under a general edict that all things should be disposed according to the command of the queen'.[16] She saw to justice for him, held court for him and made a royal progress round the kingdom for him, with her *curia reginalia* – 'a queenly court', as Roger of Howden put it.[17] Some have heard a note of misogyny in Roger's phrase – that a queenly court might be even more vicious or disorganized than a king's. But Roger generally appreciated the effectiveness of Eleanor's interventions, and Latin offered him 'kingly' or 'queenly' but not the gender neutral 'royal'.

Richard valued his mother's counsel and depended on her diplomatic skills to finalize the negotiation of Berengaria's marriage, to treat with Emperor Henry VI and deal with the pope in Rome. He did not name her as regent during the crusade, instead establishing a regency council, led by the justiciar, William Longchamp. But in the crisis of his imprisonment, the situation was rescued only by Eleanor's authority as anointed queen, by the force of her personality and the political assurance of someone with long experience of power – as is clear from all chroniclers, and from Richard's letters to Eleanor and members of the regency council. Richard wrote to her in March 1193: 'your prudence and discretion is the greatest cause of our land remaining in peaceful state until our arrival.'[18]

Louis VII never entrusted Eleanor with such an overt governing role, but then there was no need. He was not, like the Anglo-Norman kings, attempting to run more than one polity. When he went on crusade, and most of the times when he went to Aquitaine, he took Eleanor with him. There was neither the need nor the tradition for the queen to play so defined a role within the governance of the kingdom.

A queen, of France or England, had less defined roles. In earlier periods, she was in charge of the royal household. By the twelfth century, the household was a complex business, run by clerical and lay administrators. Now her role was as counsellor and advisor. As the coronation orders made manifest, she should model herself on the biblical Queen Esther and intercede with the king for mercy on his people. The queen's role as counsellor, advisor and intercessor with the king could bring her great power. If she was known to have the ear of the king, petitioners of all ranks, both lay and ecclesiastical, would approach the king through her. The problem for the historian is that this role leaves little or no trace, unless it is too flagrant or goes wrong. Then critical chroniclers will condemn the noxious influence of the queen – as they did when Eleanor fomented revolt.

As queen of France, Eleanor was at first too young to have much influence. Then her failure to provide an heir for Louis VII undermined her power at the French court. It made her isolated and in the end expendable. Increasingly, Louis' courtiers must have realized that they only needed to pay lip service to her

wishes, though St Bernard expected her to persuade Louis to make
peace with Theobald of Champagne. The mother of a future king
was in a very different position. Courtiers must make efforts to
retain her favour, for mothers of kings usually had the full confidence of their sons – as did Eleanor with Richard and John, or
Empress Matilda with Henry II.

As queen of England Eleanor was older, more experienced and
from the start the mother of a son and heir. Courtiers and other
petitioners sought her intercession with the king. Pope Anastasius
IV wrote to her as 'duchess of the Normans' in 1153 asking that
she 'diligently and effectively suggest' to her husband that he
restore favour to an abbot of Le Mont-Saint-Michel. A similar
letter was sent to Empress Matilda.[19] In 1157 John of Salisbury
depended on Eleanor and Becket – then chancellor – to persuade
Henry of John's innocence after unspecified accusations against
him at court.[20] The Becket camp briefly hoped that Eleanor and
Empress Matilda might persuade Count Philip of Flanders to reconcile Henry and Becket. Their hopes were soon concentrated
on the empress alone, but this fleeting reference reveals the range
and potential of Eleanor's diplomatic networks. Count Philip was
married to her niece, Elizabeth of Vermandois.[21] The monks of
Canterbury wrote to Eleanor in March 1191, January 1192 and
then in July 1198 asking for her intervention in their extended
clashes with their archbishops. Admittedly, they wrote to anyone
they thought could help them. In 1188 they appealed to Matilda
and Henry of Saxony, not Eleanor, to intercede with Henry II.
In 1198 they asked William Longchamp whether Richard could
be bribed.[22] Eleanor's position as ruler of Aquitaine alongside
young Richard from 1168 brought her direct power at a regional
level, but distanced her from her husband, his court and his most
important administrators. She lost the amorphous, indefinable,
uncertain power to persuade the king to do what she wanted.
But the confidence, competence and effectiveness with which

she prepared the way for Richard's accession and dealt with the imprisonment crisis suggests that, apart from the years of her own imprisonment, she had partaken fully in Henry's kingship, as the coronation order required the queen to do.

A queen was almost intrinsically a diplomat. She brought her own familial networks to her marriage and was expected to exploit them if they were useful, as were Eleanor's Iberian cousinships and networks to Henry, Richard and John. She was involved in most of the Angevin marriage strategies and arrangements. She had less opportunity to exploit her familial networks as queen of France, for Louis VII's ambitions did not extend to Iberia. She had no children or younger relations to arrange marriages for, apart from her sister, whose spectacularly unsuccessful marital partnership was arranged by the king.

The letter was one of the great tools of medieval diplomacy. The letters to Pope Celestine, problematic though they are, most likely reflect a genuine campaign of epistolary propaganda. Few letters survive. We have indications of several lost letters to and from Eleanor, like the one from the empress of Byzantium to Eleanor mentioned by Odo of Deuil, or the correspondence the monks of Canterbury asked her to undertake on their behalf to Richard and John in 1198. Eleanor's letters to Pope Alexander III and Cardinal Hyacinth interceding for her cousin, Abbot Peter of Saint-Maixent, both imply a more extended correspondence. Kings and queens, like most great churchmen, did not scratch their words on to parchment themselves. They instructed secretaries who specialized in the rhetorical structures and flourishes expected in well-confected letters. Eleanor had a large number of clerks, some of them masters, in her household. It is likely that she maintained a copious correspondence.

The extent and ways in which Eleanor exercised power in her long life are surprisingly inconsistent. She tasted active executive power: as regent for England, as ruler of Aquitaine with young

Richard, then as ruler of Aquitaine between 1199 and her death.
Her influence on Henry and at court was probably strong, though
would have diminished once she was established in Poitou in
1168. Her rebellion and long imprisonment deprived her of all
agency, at least initially. But she was still the mother of Henry's
children, and in the early 1180s Henry allowed her to take her
place within the family again. By the mid-1180s, if she did not
have freedom or access to her own resources, she did have influence, particularly through her closeness to Matilda of Saxony
and her family. As queen dowager, Eleanor's authority, energy
and political experience held the Angevin realm together at
Richard's accession, and during the crises of his imprisonment,
sudden death and John's disputed succession. She spent the years
from 1194 to 1199 largely in retirement, content to see Poitou
and Aquitaine ruled by Richard and Otto. But she was still politically engaged. The monks of Canterbury sought her influence
on her sons in 1198. Richard (presumably) involved her in the
plot to move Philip of Dreux from Rouen to Chinon, and she
probably operated her female familial networks to help Richard
entice Count Louis of Blois into an Angevin alliance.

Historians have often assumed that the woman who could
deliver the Angevin realm from existential threat as queen of
England must also have been a strong political force as queen
of France – not least because, as John of Salisbury said, Louis VII
loved Eleanor so passionately. The retirement of the old queen
Adela of Maurienne from court has been put down to Eleanor's
influence, as has the fall from favour of Abbot Suger, Louis' ill-
fated attempt to capture Toulouse and his support of Ralph of
Vermandois' marriage to Eleanor's sister. In short, every mis-
fortune in Louis' reign before the divorce has been ascribed to
the baleful influence of a powerful woman. But the retirement
of Adela of Maurienne – which did not last long – was probably
engineered by Suger rather than Eleanor. Suger himself had

many enemies at court, and Louis was turning to new younger advisors, such as Cadurc and Thierry Galeran, rather than those, like Suger, who had advised his father. Louis' attempt to claim Toulouse was certainly made as duke of Aquitaine in right of his wife. Eleanor may well have encouraged him, but there is no evidence she pushed him into it against his better judgement. No contemporary chronicler blamed Louis' invasion of Champagne on Eleanor. The churchmen blamed Ralph's rapacious sexual energy for the scandal. St Bernard did expect her to persuade Louis to come to peace with Count Theobald. But their conversation places Eleanor as a peripheral actor in the drama. If anything, it underlines her lack of potency. And it reminds us that a queen who had produced no heir after seven years of marriage was not in a strong position to influence her husband.

As queen of France, Eleanor was young, and then apparently infertile. The French court in which she operated was fractious and factional. Charter evidence, including Eleanor's own Aquitanian charters, suggest her opportunities to exercise power were limited. She had no opportunity to build her own power base. When she did oppose her husband on the crusade, she was simply forced to do what he wanted. It provided her with an unpleasant but useful training in the working of power in a royal court.[23]

Eleanor's record in handling power is also inconsistent. She did not use the soft power of religious patronage to build support among churchmen, in the way that so many canny elite women did, notably Matilda II of England, Empress Matilda, Mary of Champagne or Blanche of Castile. That support could be important. It helped Blanche of Castile withstand baronial revolt in the early days of her minority regency. Empress Matilda's long record of support for reformed monasticism allowed her to retain the respect of, and influence over, the churchmen around Becket, and to write to Becket as if he were a naughty boy: 'You will not be able to recover the king's grace, except by the greatest humility and conspicuous moderation.'[24] Eleanor did not have the religious credibility to do that.

Eleanor was a successful regent in England, perhaps because she worked with an impressive team of administrators. Her regency in Anjou had to be rescued by Henry because the aristocracy would not obey her. Her rule of Aquitaine alongside young Richard was at best a missed opportunity. She showed no interest in administrative rulership within Aquitaine, instead depending on the revenues that came from tightly administered Normandy and England. In her household and entourage she promoted her extended maternal family rather than able young clerks and the wider Aquitanian aristocracy. She did little to build regional ecclesiastical or aristocratic support for the new young duke.

It is often assumed that Aquitaine became a problem because the Angevin kings, Henry and then Richard, tried to impose on the aristocracy the sort of heavy-handed rule accepted in England and Normandy, and that this was unacceptable to an aristocracy which was used to a less confrontational, less interventionist and more consensual rule by its dukes. There were claims Earl Patrick was killed because the Poitevins resented King Henry curtailing their liberties.[25] Richard as king announced he did not want to violate the customs and laws of Poitou, by which the Poitevins settled their disputes by private war, rather than before the ruler's court – implying that that was what Henry had tried to do.[26] 'Exult Aquitaine, rejoice Poitou, because the king of the north no longer rules you,' wrote Richard the Poitevin of the revolt of 1173. Richard, detached from reality on his small island of Aix, hoped that the duchess of Aquitaine would return before long to her people.[27] It is true that the Aquitanian dukes sometimes struggled to impose themselves. At the beginning of the eleventh century, Duke William the Great resorted to a mutual treaty to control a quite minor lord, Hugh of Lusignan.[28] Many acts issued

by Dukes William ix and x portray the duke in the midst of the
great men of the duchy. The kings of France and England and
the dukes of Normandy usually set more distance between the
ruler and his men.

The most powerful and independent Aquitanian nobles,
the counts of Angoulême and La Marche, and the viscounts of
Limoges, dominated vital roads to the south; Dukes William ix
and x, Henry ii, Richard and John veered between marriage
alliances and military violence to control them and their vassals.
William ix or x married Duchess Aenor's sister to Count Vulgrin
of Angoulême; Henry ii married a daughter of Earl Reginald of
Cornwall to Aimer of Limoges, and a daughter of Ralph of Faye
to the lord of Ventadorn; John himself married the heiress to
Angoulême. Marriage alliances did not always hold and, as with
John's marriage to Isabelle of Angoulême, could create their own
fallout. The dukes and king/dukes had more territory and more
power within the county of Poitou, the Saintonge and Aunis.
Their dominance even here was uneven. William x wiped out
the Châtelaillon family, but others, like the Rancon, flourished
in the vacuum. Most of Louis vii's expeditions to Aquitaine aimed
to deal with contumacious or warring nobles. He let Geoffrey of
Rancon 'run' Aquitaine from 1149, to the despair of Suger and
Geoffrey of Loroux. In the end, Eleanor's hated nemesis, Thierry
Galeran, was sent to try to establish peace in Aquitaine.[29] Nobody
managed to deal with the Lusignan. This did matter, because
Lusignan itself is less than 16 kilometres (10 mi.) from Poitiers
and dominates one of the most important roads to the southwest.
There is a parallel with Montlhéry, which towered over the royal
road from Paris to Orleans in Capetian France. Philip i and Louis
the Fat finally defeated the Montlhéry clan: 'Make sure you don't
lose that castle,' said Philip to Louis the Fat, 'The trouble it has
caused has made me an old man.'[30] But the Lusignan family
remained ensconced in their castle, and flourished, winning

prestige and the crown of Jerusalem on crusade. They murdered Earl Patrick of Salisbury and forced Eleanor to give them the county of La Marche.

So Henry and Richard's attempt to control the Aquitanian nobility was not very different from, but sometimes more successful than, that of Louis VII or William IX and X. And despite Richard the Poitevin's fantasies, there is no evidence that Eleanor took a more consensual, diplomatic approach. She did nothing to mediate Richard's iron grip on Aquitaine in the 1190s, even when Richard seized lands from her Châtellerault cousins. When Henry II attacked the Thouars – also her cousins – in 1158, she urged him to destroy their citadel. When she ruled Aquitaine as regent for young Richard, she didn't court the nobility and attract them into her orbit. There were no favours to call in in 1199, when she tried to build support for John. Even her own cousins joined Arthur. And her attitude to the Angevin aristocracy was as imperious as that of her husband and her sons. She used Mercadier and his mercenaries to suppress those who rallied to Arthur in 1199, perhaps in revenge for their refusal to obey her in 1166.

Eleanor's political judgement was erratic. Of her close advisors, Mercadier was a thug and Ralph of Faye thuggish, irreverent, grasping and foolish. She knew that John was treacherous, vicious and untrustworthy, but she was determined that he inherit the whole sprawling Angevin realm. Was that to ensure that her revenues from England and Normandy could continue to reach her in Aquitaine?

Her participation in the uprising of 1173, on the advice of Ralph of Faye, was the biggest mistake of her long career. It is impossible to know how deeply implicated she was in planning the revolt. The prime movers were presumably the Young King and Louis VII, who stood to gain most. Louis built a formidable coalition, including the count of Flanders and the king of

Scotland. Did Eleanor assist her first husband in building the alliance against her second? Did she persuade Philip of Flanders, husband of her niece Elizabeth of Vermandois, to join it, as she and the empress persuaded him to work for peace between Becket and Henry? Or was she an accessory after the fact, responding to Young Henry's determination to challenge his father by taking his side when the plot was already well developed, and sending her younger sons to join him? Did she really believe that the Young King's youthful charm would prevail against the experience, the political and military acumen, of his father?

What did she hope to gain? Historians have speculated that she saw herself increasingly as duchess in her own right, that she saw things increasingly from an Aquitanian perspective, and that she came to resent Henry's control, as she administered Aquitaine from 1168. As for ambitions to rule as duchess in her own right, Eleanor knew that she would have to step back for Richard as he came of age, and that was imminent. Their close relationship meant she could have looked forward to many years as principal counsellor and advisor to the young duke. Her perspective was no more sympathetic to the bulk of the Aquitanian aristocracy than was Henry's, apart from her favour to members of her extended Châtellerault family. The Young King certainly did feel that his father and his father's administrators cramped his style and wrote to the pope to say so. Eleanor may have found Henry's administrators constricting, but she may equally have appreciated the experience of Richard of Ilchester or William of Lanvallay, not least in delivering her substantial English and Norman income.

Her reputation comes out of the revolt no better than she did herself. Either she conspired with her ex-husband to build a coalition to break the power of her present husband, or she rather carelessly encouraged her children to revolt against their father, with no obvious advantage to either herself or the younger children, and left it too late to escape herself. She could be prudent, but as Gervase of Canterbury observed, she was also *instabilis* – unreliable, perhaps more than anything else, careless.[31]

Epilogue: Finding Eleanor

Eleanor sometimes seems so close to us, so real. It seems easy to imagine her delight flirting with her uncle, her boredom with the sexual incompetence of her first husband, her excitement at finding herself with an energetic younger man, her bitter disappointment as his passion for her failed, the urge to use her influence with her sons to teach him a lesson . . . But all these are our projections onto her. And people, particularly men, were projecting their imagination, their fantasies, onto her from her revolt against Henry, and probably from her divorce from Louis. The legends and fantasies conceal her.

There is surprisingly little solid evidence beyond the legends and fantasies. Contemporary images of her, on her seals or on her tomb, are representations, not individualized portraits in any sense. We have pen portraits of her grandfather, her husbands and her sons, but not of Eleanor. When she married Louis, she was unremarkable and unremarked, described at best as very noble – which, given that she was heiress to Aquitaine, was stating the obvious. The Morigny chronicler hardly noticed her, but was enchanted by the slim good looks, grace and elegance of her husband. Gradually chroniclers describe her as 'beautiful', but only after the scandal of the divorce. Her reputation as a beauty grew with gossip. When Richard of Devizes described her as beautiful in the early 1190s, she was in her late sixties. Perhaps the unremarkable young girl improved with

age – as many do. Both her father and Henry the Young King
were described as tall and elegant. Perhaps she too was tall
and elegant, unlike Henry II and Richard, both of whom were
compact, with the Anglo-Norman family tendency towards
corpulence.

Only two contemporary chroniclers give brief character
sketches of her. Both were English monks – Richard of Devizes
and Gervase of Canterbury. Both knew her personally. Gervase
was shocked by her revolt against Henry, and even more by the
fact that she was dressed as a man when captured in 1173, but
appreciated her diplomatic handling of the battles between the
monks of Canterbury and their archbishops. Both admired her
decisive intervention during the crusade and imprisonment crisis.
Both seem unable to quite make her out. For Richard of Devizes,
she was 'an incomparable woman, beautiful and chaste, powerful
and modest, humble and eloquent, which is found so rarely in
women . . . and indefatigable in the face of all troubles, whose
effectiveness is the marvel of her age' – but he then tells us to
not mention the crusade.[1] For Gervase she was 'indeed a prudent woman, born of a noble dynasty', but '*instabilis*' – unsteady,
unreliable, unpredictable.[2]

Richard of Devizes is the chronicler who seems most sympathetic towards her. As a monk at Winchester, he probably knew
her quite well, for she often resided at the royal palace, including in her semi-confinement in the 1180s. But Eleanor never
built a close relationship with ecclesiastical institutions with a
tradition of history writing, so she had no literary champions,
in the way that writers from Le Bec, such as Robert of Torigni
and Stephen of Rouen, lauded Empress Matilda and Henry.
Fontevraud gave her shelter and the companionship of other
princesses. But it had no one who might provide a public encomium, or a poem to praise her life and works. Most surviving
letters sent to and by her were short and transactional. She

features in most letter collections only peripherally – apart from the collection of Peter of Blois.

Unlike so many of her elite contemporaries, both male and female, she left little concrete behind her. She didn't found a new abbey, or do very much in the way of building projects, either religious or secular, though she may have recommended Master Isembert the bridge-builder. Her gifts to ecclesiastical institutions were not conspicuously generous, and apart from the Eleanor Vase, they have all disappeared. She doubtless accepted the dedication of literary works to herself with grace, but as a literary patron she was receptive, not active. Her prodigious wealth seems to have been spent on the ephemera of courtly life – wines and spices, silks and furs, gilded saddles and gold chalices for herself, for those she loved and for those whose support or acquiescence must be bought, and horses for the many knights in her entourage. Of all these gifts and transactions, there is scarcely a trace.

Unlike so many of her contemporaries, indeed many of her family, both female and male, she made little use of patronage, either religious or cultural, as a lever of power. If anything, it seems that her preferred mode to exercise power was as coercive and military as Henry II and Richard. She enjoyed the company of knights, including William Marshal, Earl Patrick, Ralph of Faye, Andrew of Chauvigny and Mercadier. Her experience on Louis' ill-organized crusade ought to have been enough to put anyone off military adventures, but she joined Henry at Toulouse and Thouars and launched her own attacks on Angers and Le Mans. Arthur saw her as a military player to attack, not as an old lady in semi-monastic retirement. She was captured by Greek pirates, by the Lusignans, by Henry's forces. When many might have retired into monastic peace in their older age, she went on missions to Spain, Sicily, Rome and Germany, often travelling in winter. Her resilience and courage are unquestionable. She was also bold and decisive. She took the initiative in Antioch and told Richard to sell England to the emperor.

Her political record is mixed – sometimes prudent, but sometimes unsteady. She made terrible errors of judgement. She depended on the unreliable Ralph of Faye, but hated Thierry Galeran, who seems to have been a competent administrator and perhaps, given that he became a Templar, more morally serious than most courtiers. How could she think that her untried if charming oldest son and her ex-husband could get the better of Henry II – she who knew all three men well? What did she hope to gain when she encouraged her sons to revolt against their father? It is difficult to see a clear political rationale, which lays her open to suggestions that her revolt was motivated by spite against Henry.

On the other hand, she could be a formidable diplomat, particularly face to face. She was undaunted by popes, cardinals, archbishops, kings and emperors. She was eloquent, as Richard of Devizes noted. She must have known when to offer inducements and exactly what they might entail. She must have had an ease of manner, a naturalness in her dealings – perhaps that same engaging frankness with which she discussed intimate details of sex with Bernard of Clairvaux.

And there is no question that she saved the day when Richard was on crusade and during the crisis of his imprisonment. Like Winston Churchill during the Second World War, cometh the day, cometh the (wo)man. Like Churchill, she had precisely the skills, the qualities, the authority and the courage to handle the crisis; like Churchill, in other circumstances, her political skills and judgement had been uncertain.

Her personal life was as contradictory as her political record. She was herself the heiress to a great principality, but she needed a son to inherit it from her. A son did not materialize until she was nearly thirty, and in her first marriage, her infertility rendered her politically impotent. Her second marriage made her a matriarch. Motherhood became her. Through her sons, she had power, through her daughters, influence. Much of her diplomatic activity was devoted to familial marriage strategy, among them her winter journey to Castile to collect the granddaughter who would become, as she had been, queen of France.

What might she have said to the young Blanche of Castile, as they travelled back to France, some of the route, from Bordeaux north, the same as she herself had taken in 1137? Perhaps Eleanor advised taking more care of one's marriage than Eleanor had done, for Blanche would make much of, and draw personal and political strength from, her own good marriage. Perhaps Eleanor advised her granddaughter to take care that her sons did not squabble among themselves. Certainly Blanche ensured that her younger sons did not threaten Louis ix's rule, though there were undoubtedly tensions. Blanche seems to have learned from her grandmother's mistakes, for unlike Eleanor, she took care to build support from most sections of the Church, and from the second-rank aristocracy of the Capetian lands. Both enabled her to withstand the revolt of the great barons. Blanche was a great cultural and religious patron, where Eleanor was not. Blanche had her grandmother's boldness, resilience and courage, but she always took care; Eleanor often, it seems, did not.

Was Eleanor an exceptional woman – is that why she became a legend in her own times, and has attracted so much interest in both scholarly and popular culture ever since? Her political power was not exceptional. Her cultural and religious patronage was exceptional in the sense that she doesn't seem to have been as interested in it, or exploited it as a lever of power, compared to and in the way that most of her elite and powerful female contemporaries did. But she did live an exceptionally long life into which were crammed almost all the life experiences to which an aristocratic medieval woman might be subject. And Richard of Devizes thought her 'incomparable'.

CAN WE FIND ELEANOR OF AQUITAINE? She confused contemporaries with her contradictions. So much that she did was
ephemeral – the unrecorded gifts, the feasts, the diplomatic dis-
cussions. The pervasive legends hide her from us. The evidence
that does survive is fragmentary, difficult and deceptive. Just when
we think we have grasped her, she eludes us, just as her mythical
forbear, the she-devil duchess of Aquitaine, when cornered, flew
away through the church windows, taking some of her children
with her.

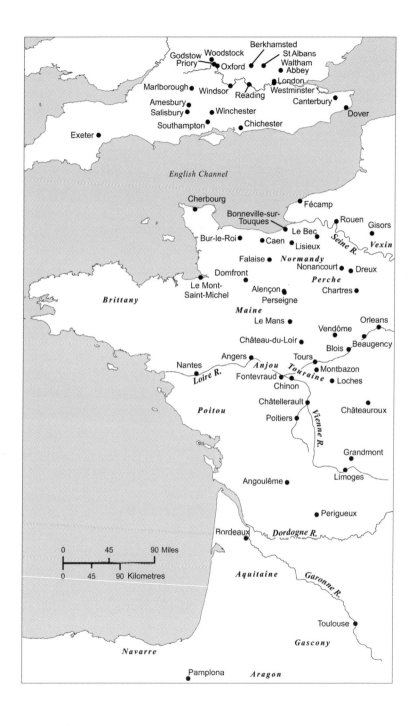

Berkhamsted
Woodstock
Godstow
Priory
Oxford
St Albans
Waltham
Abbey
London
Westminster
Marlborough
Windsor
Reading
Amesbury
Salisbury
Winchester
Canterbury
Southampton
Chichester
Dover
Exeter

English Channel

Cherbourg
Fécamp
Bonneville-sur-Touques
Rouen
Gisors
Le Bec
Seine R.
Vexin
Bur-le-Roi
Caen
Lisieux
Falaise
Normandy
Nonancourt
Dreux
Domfront
Perche
Le Mont-
Saint-Michel
Alençon
Chartres
Brittany
Perseigne
Maine
Le Mans
Orleans
Vendôme
Château-du-Loir
Blois
Beaugency
Angers
Tours
Touraine
Montbazon
Nantes
Loire R.
Anjou
Fontevraud
Loches
Chinon
Châtellerault
Châteauroux
Poitiers
Poitou
Vienne R.
Grandmont
Angoulême
Limoges
Perigueux
Bordeaux
Dordogne R.
Aquitaine
Garonne R.
Toulouse
Navarre
Gascony
Pamplona
Aragon

0   45   90 Miles

0   45   90 Kilometres

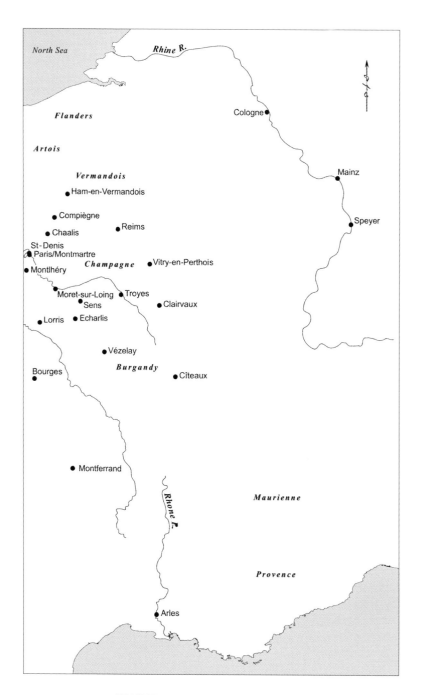

North Sea

Rhine R.

Flanders

Cologne ●

Artois

Mainz ●

Vermandois

● Ham-en-Vermandois

Speyer ●

● Compiègne

● Chaalis   ● Reims

St-Denis
Paris/Montmartre

Champagne   ● Vitry-en-Perthois

● Montlhéry

Moret-sur-Loing ● Troyes

● Sens   ● Clairvaux

● Lorris   ● Echarlis

● Vézelay

Bourges   Burgandy

●   ● Cîteaux

● Montferrand

Maurienne

Rhone R.

Provence

● Arles

FRANCE AND SOUTHERN ENGLAND

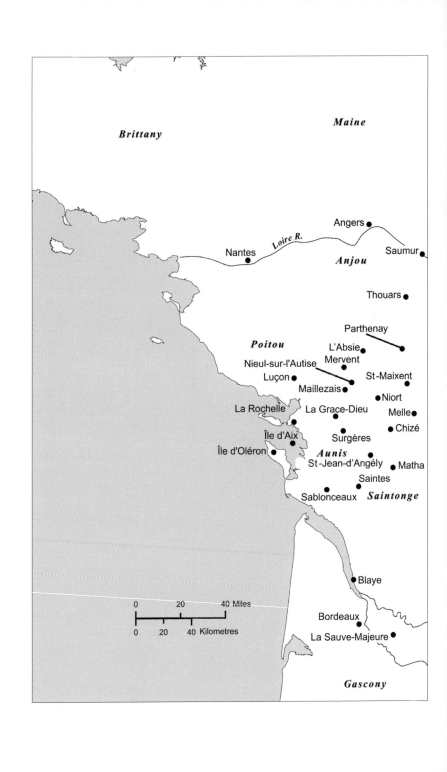

Brittany

Maine

Anjou

Angers

Nantes

Loire R.

Saumur

Thouars

Parthenay

Poitou

L'Absie

Mervent

Nieul-sur-l'Autise

Luçon

Maillezais

St-Maixent

Niort

La Rochelle

La Grace-Dieu

Melle

Chizé

Île d'Aix

Surgères

Île d'Oléron

Aunis

St-Jean-d'Angély

Matha

Saintes

Sablonceaux

Saintonge

Blaye

0   20   40 Miles

0   20   40 Kilometres

Bordeaux

La Sauve-Majeure

Gascony

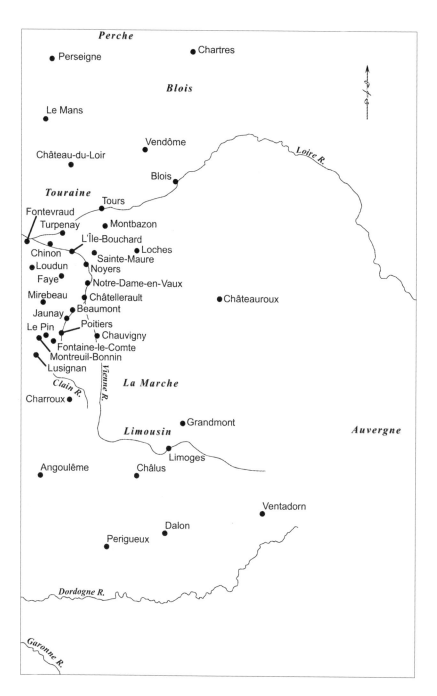

WESTERN FRANCE

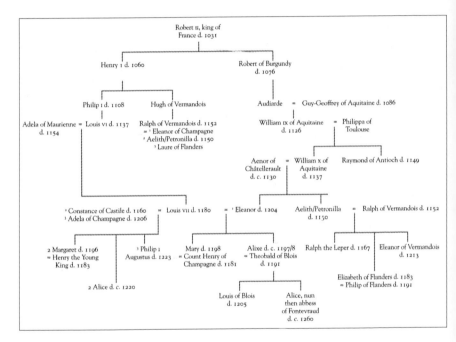

ELEANOR AND LOUIS VII

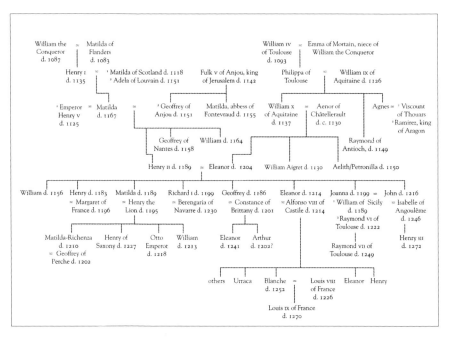

ELEANOR AND HENRY II

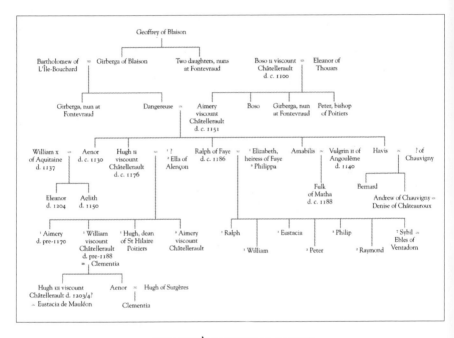

ELEANOR'S MATERNAL FAMILY

REFERENCES

Abbreviations

AHP   *Archives historiques du Poitou*

AHSA   *Archives historiques de la Saintonge et de l'Aunis*

GC   *Gallia Christiana*, 17 vols, ed. D. Sammarthani et al. (Paris, 1715–1865)

MGH   *Monumenta Germaniae Historica*

PL   *Patrologiae cursus completus . . . series Latina*, 221 vols, ed. J. P. Migne (Paris, 1844–1903)

PR   (cited by regnal year) *The Great Rolls of the Pipe for the Second, Third and Fourth Years of the Reign of King Henry II*, ed. Joseph Hunter, Record Commission (London, 1844); *The Great Rolls of the Pipe of the Reign of Henry II, 5th to 34th years*, 30 vols, Pipe Roll Society (London, 1884–1925); and *Great Roll of the Pipe*, new series, ed. Doris M. Stenton (London, 1925–)

RHF   *Recueil des historiens des Gaules et de la France*, 24 vols, ed. Martin Bouquet et al., new edn, published under the direction of Léopold Delisle (Paris, 1869–1904)

Rot. Chart.   T. D. Hardy, ed., *Rotuli chartarum, 1199–1216* (London, 1837)

Rot. Lit. Pat.   T. D. Hardy, ed., *Rotuli litterarum patentium in Turri Londinensi asservati* (London, 1835)

1 Queen of France

1 Jean Verdon, ed., *Chronique de Saint-Maixent* (Paris, 1979), pp. 194–5.

2 Alfred Richard, *Histoire des comtes de Poitou*, vol. II (Paris, 1903), pp. 2–53.

3 Geoffroi de Vigeois, *Chronica*, in *Novae bibliothecae manuscriptorum*, vol. II, ed. Père Labbé (Paris, 1657), p. 300.

4 Marjorie Chibnall, *The Empress Matilda: Queen Consort, Queen Mother and Lady of the English* (Oxford, 1991), pp. 50–63.

5 Suger, *Vie de Louis le Gros*, ed. Henri Waquet, 2nd edn (Paris, 1964), pp. 280–83; L. Mirot, ed., *La Chronique de Morigny*, 2nd edn (Paris, 1912), pp. 67–9; Richard, *Histoire des comtes*, pp. 55–61.

6 Mirot, ed., *Chronique de Morigny*, p. 70.

7 Suger, *Vie de Louis le Gros*, pp. 280–81; Mirot, ed., *Chronique de Morigny*, p. 67.

8 Achille Luchaire, *Études sur les actes de Louis VII* (Paris, 1885), p. 110, n. 35; L. M. de Richemond, ed., *Chartes de la Commanderie Magistrale du Temple de La Rochelle*, in AHSA, I (1874), pp. 25–6, n. i.

9 Walter Map, *De nugis curialium*, ed. C.N.L. Brooke and M. R. James, revd edn (Oxford, 1983), pp. 442–3; John of Salisbury, *The Historia Pontificalis of John of Salisbury*, ed. Marjorie Chibnall (Edinburgh, 1956), p. 61, '*fere puerili modo*'.

10 Lois L. Huneycutt, 'The Creation of a Crone: The Historical Reputation of Adelaide of Maurienne', in *Capetian Women*, ed. Kathleen Nolan (New York, 2003), pp. 27–43.

11 'Histoire du roi Louis VII', in *Vie de Louis VI le Gros, par Suger, suivie de l'Histoire du roi Louis VII*, ed. Auguste Molinier (Paris, 1887), p. 150.

12 Odo of Deuil, *De profectione Ludovici VII in Orientem: The Journey of Louis VII to the East*, ed. and trans. Virginia Berry, 2nd edn (New York, 1965), pp. 16–19.

13 John of Salisbury, *Historia Pontificalis*, p. 53; Luchaire, *Études sur les actes*, esp. nos 485, 504; Lindy Grant, *Abbot Suger of Saint Denis: Church and State in Early Twelfth-Century France* (London, 1998), pp. 142–55; Marcel Pacaut, *Louis VII et son royaume* (Paris, 1964), pp. 37–8.

14 Jean Dunbabin, *France in the Making, 843–1180* (Oxford, 1985), pp. 58–63, 173–9, 340–42.

15 T. Grasilier, ed., *Cartulaire de l'abbaye royale de Notre Dame de Saintes*, in *Cartulaires inédits de la Saintonge*, 2 vols (Niort, 1871), vol. II, p. 51, no. xlvii.

16 Luchaire, *Études sur les actes*, nos 270, 190, 64, 76, 78, 77, 176. See also Marie Hivergneaux, 'Queen Eleanor and Aquitaine, 1137–1189', in *Eleanor of Aquitaine, Lord and Lady*, ed. J. C. Parsons and Bonnie Wheeler (New York, 2003), pp. 56–63.

17 Luchaire, *Études sur les actes*, nos 35, 189, 180, 106.

18 Ibid., nos 77, 78.

19 This is clear in a letter to Suger as regent, RHF, vol. XV, p. 499.

20 'Histoire du roi Louis VII', pp. 151–4; for Louis' rule of Aquitaine, see Richard, *Histoire des comtes*, pp. 60–105.

21 Luchaire, *Études sur les actes*, nos 120, 268, 270, 180.

22 Grasilier, ed., *Cartulaire de l'abbaye royale*, p. 36, no. xxx.

23 Richard, *Histoire des comtes*, pp. 74–5.

24 'Histoire du roi Louis VII', pp. 156–7.

25 Grasilier, ed., *Cartulaire de l'abbaye royale*, p. 14, no. viii.

26 John of Salisbury, *Historia Pontificalis*, pp. 12–15.

27 Pacaut, *Louis VII*, pp. 39–46.

28 Geoffrey of Auxerre, 'Sancti Bernardi vita tertia', PL, vol. CLXXXV, col. 527.

29 See the list in 'Histoire du roi Louis VII', p. 159.

30 Luchaire, *Études sur les actes*, nos 188–92.

31 Mirot, ed., *Chronique de Morigny*, p. 86; Grant, *Abbot Suger*, pp. 156–7.

32 Odo of Deuil, *De profectione*, pp. 16–19.

33 Ibid., esp. pp. 56–7, 78–9.

34 Suger, *Œuvres*, vol. II, ed. Françoise Gasparri (Paris, 2001), pp. 32–9, esp. pp. 38–9; John of Salisbury, *Historia Pontificalis*, pp. 52–3; William of Tyre, *Chronique*, vol. II, ed. R.B.C. Huygens (Turnhout, 1986), pp. 754–5.

35 Louis' letters to Suger, RHF, vol. XV, pp. 513, 519; John of Salisbury, *Historia Pontificalis*, pp. 60–62.

36 Auguste Molinier and Auguste Lognon, *Obituaires de la Province de Sens*, vol. I (Paris, 1902–23), p. 494; 'Histoire du roi Louis VII', p. 161.

37 See, for example, Luchaire, *Études sur les actes*, no. 270.

38 André Salmon, ed., *Chronicon Turonense magnum*, in *Recueil des chroniques de Touraine* (Tours, 1854), p. 135.

39 Luchaire, *Études sur les actes*, no. 268.

40 Salmon, ed., *Chronicon Turonense*, p. 135; 'Histoire du roi Louis VII', p. 163; Robert of Torigni, *The Chronicle, AD 1100–1186*, in *The Chronography of Robert of Torigni*, vol. I, ed. Thomas N. Bisson (Oxford, 2020), pp. 160–61.

2 Queen of England

1 André Salmon, ed., *Chronicon Turonense magnum*, in *Recueil des chroniques de Touraine* (Tours, 1854), p. 135.

2 For her Anglo-Norman household, see Ralph V. Turner, *Eleanor of Aquitaine* (New Haven, CT, and London, 2009), pp. 153–4, 161–5. For her lack of English, Richard of Devizes, *The Chronicle of Richard of Devizes of the Time of King Richard the First*, ed. and trans. John T.

Appleby (London, 1963), p. 60; for Henry's languages, Walter Map, *De nugis curialium*, ed. C.N.L. Brooke and M. R. James, revd edn (Oxford, 1983), pp. 476–7.

3 Geoffroi de Vigeois, *Chronica*, in *Novae bibliothecae manuscriptorum*, vol. II, ed. Père Labbé (Paris, 1657), p. 308.

4 Nicholas Vincent, ed., *The Letters and Charters of Henry II*, 6 vols (Oxford, 2020), vol. II, nos 1048, 1182; vol. III, nos 1632–5; vol. IV, no. 2460; vol. V, no. 2911.

5 Turner, *Eleanor*, pp. 151–5; Marie Hivergneaux, 'Aliénor d'Aquitaine: le pouvoir d'une femme à la lumière de ses chartes (1152–1204)', in *La Cour Plantagenêt (1154–1204)*, ed. Martin Aurell (Poitiers, 2000), pp. 63–87.

6 Robert of Torigni, *The Chronicle, AD 1100–1186*, in *The Chronography of Robert of Torigni*, vol. I, ed. Thomas N. Bisson (Oxford, 2020), pp. 256–7.

7 See, for example, Vincent, ed., *The Letters and Charters of Henry II*, vol. I, nos 32a, 68; vol. II, nos 741, 845, 1042; vol. III, no. 1696; vol. IV, no. 2339; vol. V, no. 2638.

8 Richard Benjamin, 'A Forty-Year War: Toulouse and the Plantagenets, 1156–90', *Historical Research*, LXI (1988), pp. 270–85.

9 Richard the Poitevin, 'Ex chronico Richardi Pictaviensis', RHF, vol. XII, p. 417.

10 F. Villard, ed., *Recueil des documents relatifs à l'abbaye de Montierneuf de Poitiers*, AHP, vol. LIX (1973), pp. 135–6, no. 87; A. Richard, ed., *Chartes et documents pour servir à l'histoire de l'abbaye de Saint Maixent*, AHP, vol. XVI (1886), pp. 352–3, no. 335; Marie Hivergneaux, 'Autour d'Aliénor d'Aquitaine: entourage et pouvoir au prisme des chartes (1137–1189)', in *Plantagenêts et Capétiens: confrontations et héritages*, ed. Martin Aurell and N.-Y. Tonnerre (Turnhout, 2006), pp. 61–73.

11 Jacques Boussard, *Le Gouvernement de Henri II Plantagenêt* (Paris, 1956), pp. 353–9, 326.

12 Turner, *Eleanor*, pp. 153–4, 161–5; Nicholas Vincent, 'Henry II and the Poitevins', in *La Cour Plantagenêt*, ed. Aurell, pp. 103–35.

13 For Ralph of Faye, see, for example, PR 2 *Henry II*, pp. 11, 12; PR 16 *Henry II*, p. 164; for Saldebreuil, PR 16 *Henry II*, p. 14.

14 See, for example, PR 5 *Henry II*, pp. 41, 43; PR 6 *Henry II*, p. 47; PR 9 *Henry II*, pp. 54, 56.

15 See, for example, PR 3 *Henry II*, p. 105; PR 4 *Henry II*, pp. 171, 175; PR 6 *Henry II*, pp. 13, 49.

16 Robert of Torigni, *Chronicle*, vol. I, pp. 230–31, 224–5, 238–9, 264–5.

17 Stephen of Rouen, 'The "Draco Normannicus" of Étienne de
Rouen', in *Chronicles of the Reigns of Stephen, Henry II and Richard I*,
vol. II, ed. R. Howlett, Rolls Series (London, 1884–9), pp. 603, 663;
Martin Aurell, 'Henry II and Arthurian Legend', in *Henry II: New
Interpretations*, ed. Christopher Harper-Bill and Nicholas Vincent
(Woodbridge, 2007), pp. 362–94.

18 Nicholas Vincent, 'The Court of Henry II', in *Henry II: New
Interpretations*, ed. Harper-Bill and Vincent, pp. 278–334; Ian Short,
'Literary Culture at the Court of Henry II', ibid., pp. 335–61; Aurell,
'Henry II and Arthurian Legend'.

19 Robert of Torigni, *Chronicle*, vol. I, pp. 268–9; Roger of Howden,
Chronica Rogeri de Hovedene, 4 vols, ed. William Stubbs, Rolls Series
(London, 1868–71), vol. I, p. 273.

20 Louis Rédet, 'Documents pour l'histoire de l'église de St-Hilaire de
Poitiers', *Mémoires de la Société des Antiquaires de l'Ouest*, vol. XIV
(Poitiers, 1848 for 1847), pp. 180–81, no. 153.

21 A. J. Holden, ed., *The History of William Marshal*, vol. I (London,
2002), pp. 82–95, vv. 1864–83.

22 Howden, *Chronica*, vol. III, p. 167.

23 Geoffroi de Vigeois, *Chronica*, pp. 318–19.

24 Anne Duggan, ed., *The Correspondence of Thomas Becket,
Archbishop of Canterbury, 1162–1170*, 2 vols (Oxford, 2000),
vol. I, pp. 216–17. For the gift to Hugh of Châtellerault, see the
thirteenth-century inquest in *AHP*, vol. VIII (1879), pp. 63–72.
For Eleanor's household and entourage, see Nicholas Vincent,
'Patronage, Politics and Piety in the Charters of Eleanor of
Aquitaine', in *Plantagenêts et Capétiens*, ed. Aurell and Tonnerre,
esp. pp. 36–53; Hivergneaux, 'Autour d'Aliénor', pp. 61–73.

25 Paul Marchegay and Émile Mabille, eds, 'Chronicon Vindocinense
seu de Aquaria', in *Chroniques des églises d'Anjou* (Paris, 1869),
pp. 174–5.

26 C. Metais, ed., *Cartulaire Saintongeais de la Trinité de Vendôme*, AHSA,
XXII (1893), pp. 114–16, no. 70.

27 W. J. Miller and C.N.L. Brooke, eds, *The Letters of John of Salisbury*,
vol. II: *The Later Letters (1163–1180)* (Oxford, 1986), no. 212,
pp. 344–5.

28 Duggan, ed., *Correspondence of Thomas Becket*, vol. I, no. 34,
p. 129; it is clear from no. 31, p. 107, that Luscus is Ralph, who 'has
returned . . . with fullness of power . . . he has summoned the army
of Aquitaine' – as the seneschal would do.

29 Gerald of Wales, *Gemma ecclesiastica*, in *Giraldi Cambrensis opera*, 8 vols, ed. J. S. Brewer, J. Dimmock and G. F. Warner, Rolls Series (London, 1861–91), vol. II, p. 162.

30 John Jay Parry, ed. and trans., *The Art of Courtly Love by Andreas Capellanus* (New York, 1941), esp. pp. 57, 102–4 and 175: 'a court of ladies was assembled in Gascony' – which is not Poitiers.

31 Howden, *Chronica*, vol. II, pp. 14–15.

32 J. C. Robertson and J. B Sheppard, eds, *Materials for the History of Thomas Becket, Archbishop of Canterbury*, 7 vols, Rolls Series (London, 1875–85), vol. I, pp. 110–11; Robert of Torigni, *Chronicle*, vol. I, pp. 266–7; PR 13 Henry II, pp. 2–3, 5, 194; PR 14 Henry II, pp. 7, 15; Jitske Jasperse, *Medieval Women, Material Culture and Power: Matilda Plantagenet and Her Sisters* (Leeds, 2020), pp. 21–2; Stephen D. Church, 'The Date and Place of King John's Birth, Together with a Codicil on his Name', *Notes and Queries*, LXVII (2020), pp. 315–23 (pp. 319–20).

33 Act issued by Alfonso VIII, corroborated by Alfonso II in Julio Gonzalez, *El reino de Castilla en la epoca de Alfonso VIII*, 3 vols (Madrid, 1960), vol. I, photo opposite p. 192, full text opposite p. 193. See also Robert of Torigni, *Chronicle*, vol. I, pp. 284–5.

34 Robert of Torigni, *Chronicle*, vol. I, p. 291; Howden, *Chronica*, vol. II, p. 41.

35 Geoffroi de Vigeois, *Chronica*, p. 319.

36 Letter of Young King to Pope Alexander II, RHF, vol. XVI, pp. 643–8; Ralph of Diceto, 'Ymagines', in *Opera Historica: The Historical Works of Master Ralph of Diceto, Dean of London*, 2 vols, ed. W. Stubbs, Rolls Series (London, 1876), vol. I, p. 353.

37 Hivergneaux, 'Autour d'Aliénor', pp. 70–71.

38 Roger of Howden, *Gesta Regis Henrici Secundi Benedicti Abbatis*, 2 vols, ed. William Stubbs, Rolls Series (London, 1867), vol. I, p. 42.

39 Salmon, ed., *Chronicon Turonense*, p. 138; Howden, *Gesta Regis*, vol. I, p. 42; Diceto, 'Ymagines', vol. I, p. 350. For the revolt, see Matthew Strickland, *Henry the Young King, 1155–1183* (London and New Haven, CT, 2016), pp. 119–220; on Eleanor's role, pp. 134–8.

40 Gervase of Canterbury, 'Chronica Gervasii', in *Gervase of Canterbury: Historical Works*, 2 vols, ed. William Stubbs, Rolls Series (London, 1879–80), vol. I, p. 242.

41 Gerald of Wales, *Instruction for a Ruler: De principis instructione*, ed. Robert Bartlett (Oxford, 2018), pp. 696–7.

42 See, for example, PR *20 Henry II*, pp. 29, 34; PR *21 Henry II*, pp. 100, 106; PR *22 Henry II*, pp. 207, 211; PR *26 Henry II*, pp. 118, 119, 120–22; PR *28 Henry II*, pp. 109, 159. For the saddle, PR *25 Henry II*, p. 125. For Bellebell, PR *30 Henry II*, p. 134, though it has been argued that this entry refers to a 'bauble' for Henry; see Ian Short, 'Bellebelle: A Ghost Mistress for Henry', *Notes and Queries*, LXIV (2017), pp. 10–13.

43 'Magistri Thomae Agnelli Wellensis Archidiaconi sermo de morte et sepultura Henrici Regis Junioris', in *Radulphi de Coggeshall Chronicon Anglicanum*, ed. J. Stevenson, Rolls Series (London, 1875), pp. 265–73, esp. pp. 272–3; Robert of Torigni, *Chronicle*, vol. I, pp. 376–9; Strickland, *Henry the Young King*, pp. 305, 313–15.

44 Howden, *Chronica*, vol. II, pp. 278–9.

45 Howden, *Gesta Regis*, vol. I, p. 305.

46 Howden, *Chronica*, vol. II, p. 288.

47 Howden, *Gesta Regis*, vol. I, p. 337; Howden, *Chronica*, vol. II, p. 304; Diceto, 'Ymagines', vol. I, p. 40; P. Marchegay, 'Chartes de Fontevraud concernant L'Aunis et La Rochelle', *Bibliothèque de l'École de Chartes*, XIX (1858), pp. 330–31, no. i.

48 Howden, *Chronica*, vol. II, p. 309; Rigord, *Histoire de Philippe Auguste*, ed. E. Charpentier, G. Pon and Y. Chauvin (Paris, 2006), pp. 218–21, who says that Geoffrey died as a result of illness.

49 Howden, *Gesta Regis*, vol. I, pp. 313, 333–4; PR *30 Henry II*, pp. 58, 70, 134; PR *31 Henry II*, pp. 44, 206, 217; PR *33 Henry II*, pp. 39, 40, 158, 181, 194; PR *34 Henry II*, pp. 29, 148.

3 Queen Dowager

1 Roger of Howden, *Chronica Rogeri de Hovedene*, 4 vols, ed. William Stubbs, Rolls Series (London, 1868–71), vol. III, pp. 4–5; Ralph of Diceto, 'Ymagines', in *Opera Historica: The Historical Works of Master Ralph of Diceto, Dean of London*, 2 vols, ed. W. Stubbs, Rolls Series (London, 1876), vol. II, pp. 67–8. For this chapter see Jane Martindale, 'Eleanor of Aquitaine: The Last Years', in *King John: New Interpretations*, ed. S. D. Church (Woodbridge, 1999), pp. 137–64.

2 PR *1 Richard I*, pp. 223, 224.

3 Ibid., pp. 223–4; Howden, *Chronica*, vol. III, p. 7.

4 Diceto, 'Ymagines', vol. II, pp. 67–8.

5 Howden, *Chronica*, vol. III, pp. 28–32; Richard of Devizes, *The Chronicle of Richard of Devizes of the Time of King Richard the First*, ed. and trans. John T. Appleby (London, 1963), pp. 9, 13–14.

6 Howden, *Chronica*, vol. III, p. 99.

7 Ibid., pp. 95, 100; Diceto, 'Ymagines', vol. II, pp. 81, 83.

8 Howden, *Chronica*, vol. III, pp. 55, 61; Devizes, *The Chronicle*, pp. 17, 25.

9 Diceto, 'Ymagines', vol. II, p. 86.

10 Ibid., p. 83; Howden, *Chronica*, vol. III, p. 79.

11 Howden, *Chronica*, vol. III, pp. 134ff.; Diceto, 'Ymagines', vol. II, pp. 90–96.

12 Gerald of Wales, *Vita Galfridi*, in *Giraldi Cambrensis opera*, 8 vols, ed. J. S. Brewer, J. Dimmock and G. F. Warner, Rolls Series (London, 1861–91), vol. IV, pp. 420–21.

13 Ibid., pp. 410–12; Diceto, 'Ymagines', vol. II, p. 101.

14 A. J. Holden, ed., *The History of William Marshal*, vol. I (London, 2002), pp. 500–501, vv. 8972–9876.

15 John W. Baldwin, *The Government of Philip Augustus: Foundations of French Royal Power in the Middle Ages* (Berkeley, CA, 1986), pp. 80, 87–9; Devizes, *The Chronicle*, p. 58.

16 Devizes, *The Chronicle*, pp. 59–61.

17 Howden, *Chronica*, vol. III, pp. 204–5.

18 Devizes, *The Chronicle*, pp. 60–63; Howden, *Chronica*, vol. III, p. 207.

19 *Epistolae Cantuarensis, 1187–1199*, in *Chronicles and Memorials of Richard I*, 2 vols, ed. William Stubbs, Rolls Series (London, 1864–5), vol. II, nos cccxcix, cccci, cccciii, cccciv; Diceto, 'Ymagines', vol. II, p. 108.

20 PL, vol. CCVI, cols 1262–72, nos ii, iii, iv; Anne Duggan, 'On Finding the Voice of Eleanor of Aquitaine', in *Voix de femmes au Moyen Âge: actes du colloque du Centre d'Études Médiévales Anglaises de Paris-Sorbonne (26–27 mars 2010)*, ed. L. Carruthers, Association des Médiévistes Anglicistes de l'Énseignement Supérieur 32 (Paris, 2011), pp. 129–58; John D. Cott, *The Clerical Dilemma: Peter of Blois and Literate Culture in the Twelfth Century* (Washington, DC, 2009), esp. pp. 40–46, 283–4; B. A. Lees, 'The Letters of Queen Eleanor of Aquitaine to Pope Celestine III', *English Historical Review*, XXI (1906), pp. 78–93.

21 John of Salisbury, *The Historia Pontificalis of John of Salisbury*, ed. Marjorie Chibnall (Edinburgh, 1956), p. 62.

22 PL, vol. CCVII, cols 448–9, no. cliv.

23 PL, vol. CCVII, cols 187–90, no. lxiv, 428–32, no. cxliii.

24 Howden, *Chronica*, vol. III, pp. 210, 212.

25 Ibid., pp. 231–2; Diceto, 'Ymagines', vol. II, pp. 112–14.

26 Howden, *Chronica*, vol. iii, pp. 215, 275–6; Diceto, 'Ymagines', vol. ii, p. 113.
27 Howden, *Chronica*, vol. iii, pp. 202–3.
28 Ralph of Coggeshall, *Radulphi de Coggeshall Chronicon Anglicanum*, ed. J. Stevenson, Rolls Series (London, 1875), p. 62.
29 Howden, *Chronica*, vol. iii, p. 248.
30 Ibid., p. 252.
31 Jean-Marie Bienvenu, 'Aliénor d'Aquitaine et Fontevraud', *Cahiers de civilisation médiévale*, xxix (1986), p. 25.
32 Ibid., p. 25, n. 84.
33 Ibid., p. 25, nn. 85, 86.
34 PR 7 *Richard I*, p. 113; Howden, *Chronica*, vol. iii, p. 305.
35 PL, vol. ccvi, cols 1278–80, no. viii.
36 Howden, *Chronica*, vol. iv, pp. 40–41; William of Newburgh, *Historia rerum Anglicanum*, in *Chronicles of the Reigns of Stephen, Henry II and Richard I*, 4 vols, ed. Richard Howlett, Rolls Series (London, 1885–90), vol. ii, p. 493.
37 For Otto as duke, Alfred Richard, *Histoire des comtes de Poitou*, 2 vols (Paris, 1903), vol. ii, pp. 301–13.
38 Howden, *Chronica*, vol. iv, pp. 82–4; Roger of Wendover, *Flores historiarum*, 3 vols, ed. H. G. Hewlett, Rolls Series (London, 1886–9), vol. i, pp. 283–4.
39 Alexandre Teulet, H.-F. Delaborde and Élie Berger, eds, *Layettes du trésor des chartes*, 5 vols (Paris, 1863–1909), vol. i, p. 200, no. 489.
40 Howden, *Chronica*, vol. iv, pp. 86–7.
41 John Gillingham, *Richard I* (London and New Haven, CT, 1999), p. 298. Judith Everard, *Brittany and the Angevins: Province and Empire, 1158–1203* (Cambridge, 2000), pp. 149–75; J. C. Holt, 'Aliénor d'Aquitaine, Jean Sans-Terre et la succession de 1199', *Cahiers de civilisation médiévale*, xxix (1986), pp. 95–100.
42 Howden, *Chronica*, vol. iv, p. 88; Wendover, *Flores historiarum*, vol. i, p. 286.
43 Rigord, *Histoire de Philippe Auguste*, ed. E. Charpentier, G. Pon and Y. Chauvin (Paris, 2006), pp. 360–61; *Rot. Chart.*, pp. 30b, 31a, 31b. For John's orders for the government of Aquitaine, *Rot. Chart.*, pp. 30b, 31; *Rot. Lit. Pat.*, vol. i, pp. 12, 16, 17, 28b for the order of April 1203; Holt, 'Aliénor d'Aquitaine, Jean Sans-Terre', esp. p. 98.
44 See, for example, J. H. Round, ed., *Calendar of Documents Preserved in France, 918–1206* (London, 1899), pp. 450–51, no. 1248, for

Ste-Croix at Bordeaux; F. Villard, ed., *Recueil des documents relatifs à l'abbaye de Montierneuf de Poitiers*, AHP, vol. LIX (1973), pp. 182–6, no. 112.

45 *Rot. Chart.*, p. 4b; A. Giry, *Les Établissements de Rouen: études sur l'histoire des institutions municipales*, 2 vols (Paris 1883–5), vol. II, pp. 143–6, nos xxxii, xxxiii and I, p. 68, n. 1; Teulet et al., eds, *Layettes*, vol. I, pp. 208–9, no. 507; G. P. Cuttino, ed., *Gascon Register A*, 2 vols (London, 1975), vol. II, pp. 498–9, no. 162, pp. 497–8, no. 161.

46 Teulet et al., eds, *Layettes*, vol. I, p. 209, no. 508 and p. 211, no. 516; *Rot. Chart.*, p. 24b; C. Metais, ed., *Cartulaire Saintongeais de la Trinité de Vendôme*, Archives Historiques et L'Aunis, vol. XXII (1893), pp. 117–18, nos 72–3.

47 Colette Bowie, *The Daughters of Henry II and Eleanor of Aquitaine* (Turnhout, 2014), pp. 186–9.

48 A. W. Lewis, ed., *The Chronicle and Historical Notes of Bernard Itier* (Oxford, 2013), p. 60.

49 Wendover, *Flores historiarum*, vol. I, p. 293; Howden, *Chronica*, vol. IV, pp. 107, 114; Lindy Grant, *Blanche of Castile, Queen of France* (London, 2016), pp. 29–32.

50 *Rot. Chart.*, pp. 102b–103; Charles Higounet and A. Higounet-Nadal, eds, *Grand cartulaire de la Sauve-Majeure*, vol. II (Bordeaux, 1996), p. 732, no.1280; *Rot. Chart.*, p. 161; Teulet et al., eds, *Layettes*, vol. I, p. 247, no. 705.

51 Wendover, *Flores historiarum*, vol. I, pp. 313–14; Coggeshall, *Chronicon*, pp. 137–8; and *Rot. Lit. Pat.*, pp. 16, 22, 29, 30, 31.

4 Family and Dynasty

1 Alfred Richard, *Histoire des comtes de Poitou*, 2 vols (Paris, 1903), vol. I, pp. 383–497; Jane Martindale, '"Cavalaria et orgueill": Duke William IX of Aquitaine and the Historian', in *The Ideals and Practice of Medieval Knighthood*, vol. II, ed. C. Harper-Bill and R. Harvey (Woodbridge, 1988), pp. 87–116.

2 Richard, *Histoire des comtes*, vol. I, pp. 405–6, 437–8, 470, 473.

3 For William X, see Richard, *Histoire des comtes*, vol. II, pp. 1–53.

4 Geoffroi de Vigeois, *Chronica*, in *Novae bibliothecae manuscriptorum*, vol. II, ed. Père Labbé (Paris, 1657), p. 300.

5 Richard, *Histoire des comtes*, vol. I, p. 494.

6 Sidney Painter, 'The Houses of Lusignan and Châtellerault, 1150–1250', *Speculum*, XXX (1955), pp. 374–84.

7 Yannick Hillion, *Aliénor d'Aquitaine* (Paris, 2015), pp. 25–6. Though Geoffroi de Vigeois, *Chronica*, p. 304, claims that the name was invented for Eleanor – 'Alienor' as if 'alia Aenor' – another Aenor.

8 J. Boussard, ed., *Historia pontificum et comitum Engolismensium* (Paris, 1957), p. 42.

9 C. Chevalier, ed., *Cartulaire de l'abbaye de Noyers* (Tours, 1872), esp. p. 335, no. 310, p. 590, no. 562, p. 428, no. 394; Marie Hivergneaux, 'Autour d'Aliénor d'Aquitaine: entourage et pouvoir au prisme des chartes (1137–1189)', in *Plantagenêts et Capétiens: confrontations et héritages*, ed. Martin Aurell and N.-Y. Tonnerre (Turnhout, 2006), pp. 61–73; and Nicholas Vincent, 'Patronage, Politics and Piety in the Charters of Eleanor of Aquitaine', ibid., esp. pp. 36–53.

10 William of Tyre, *Chronique*, vol. ii, ed. R.B.C. Huygens (Turnhout, 1986), pp. 640–41; J. Phillips, 'A Note on the Origins of Raymond of Poitiers', *English Historical Review*, cvi (1991), pp. 66–7.

11 T. Evergates, *Henry the Liberal: Count of Champagne, 1127–1181* (Philadelphia, pa, 2016), pp. 68–70; T. Evergates, *Marie of France: Countess of Champagne, 1145–1198* (Philadelphia, pa, 2019), p. 8.

12 Elizabeth M. Hallam and Judith Everard, *Capetian France, 987–1328*, 2nd edn (London, 2001), pp. 99–100; John W. Baldwin, *The Government of Philip Augustus: Foundations of French Royal Power in the Middle Ages* (Berkeley, ca, 1986), pp. 15–6, 18.

13 John France, Neithard Bulst and Paul Reynolds, eds, *Rodulfus Glaber Opera* (Oxford, 1989), pp. 164–7.

14 Lois L. Huneycutt, 'The Creation of a Crone: The Historical Reputation of Adelaide of Maurienne', in *Capetian Women*, ed. Kathleen Nolan (New York, 2003), pp. 28, 34.

15 PR 11 *Henry ii*, p. 40; Geoffroi de Vigeois, *Chronica*, p. 324 for Marchisia of La Marche.

16 Margaret Howell, *Eleanor of Provence: Queenship in Thirteenth Century England* (Oxford, 1998), pp. 48–70.

17 Walter Map, *De nugis curialium*, ed. C.N.L. Brooke and M. R. James, revd edn (Oxford, 1983), pp. 454–5.

18 Achille Luchaire, *Études sur les actes de Louis vii* (Paris, 1885), no. 268.

19 Ibid., no. 270.

20 A. Richard, ed., *Chartes et documents pour servir à l'histoire de l'abbaye de Saint Maixent*, ahp, vol. xvi (1886), pp. 352–3, no. 335.

21 AHP, vol. viii (1879), pp. 63–72.

22 Painter, 'The Houses of Lusignan and Châtellerault', p. 84; Louis Rédet, 'Documents pour l'histoire de l'église de St-Hilaire

de Poitiers', in *Mémoires de la Société des Antiquaires de l'Ouest*,
vol. XIV (Poitiers, 1848 for 1847), esp. pp. 215–16; Jörg Peltzer,
'Les Évêques de l'empire Plantagenêt et les rois angevins: un tour
d'horizon', in *Plantagenêts et Capétiens*, ed. Aurell and Tonnerre,
pp. 469, 474.

23 Chevalier, ed., *Cartulaire de l'abbaye de Noyers*, p. 395, no. 364,
'cognomento Rumpe Stacha'; p. 470, no. 434, Elisabeth
Rumpestachia.

24 PR 6 *Richard I*, p. 9; PR 7 *Richard I*, p. 37.

25 Vincent, 'Patronage, Politics and Piety', esp. pp. 47–8; Hivergneaux,
'Autour d'Aliénor', esp. pp. 65–8; Marie Hivergneaux, 'Queen
Eleanor and Aquitaine, 1137–1189', in *Eleanor: Lord and Lady*,
ed. John Carmi Parsons and Bonnie Wheeler (New York, 2003),
p. 70; Painter, 'The Houses of Lusignan and Châtellerault', esp.
pp. 379–82; François Chamard, 'Chronologie historique des
vicomtes de Châtellerault', *Mémoires de la Société des Antiquaires
de l'Ouest*, XXXV (1870–71), pp. 79–122.

26 Frédérique Chauvenet, 'L'Entourage de Richard I Coeur de Lion
en Poitou et Aquitaine', in *La Cour Plantagenêt (1154–1204)*,
ed. Martin Aurell (Poitiers, 2000), pp. 141, 142; Ralph V. Turner,
'The Households of the Sons of Henry II', ibid., pp. 58–60.

27 Hivergneaux, 'Autour D'Aliénor', p. 73.

28 AHP, vol. VIII (1879), pp. 40–44.

29 Suger, *Vie de Louis le Gros*, ed. Henri Waquet, 2nd edn (Paris, 1964),
pp. 266–7.

30 Marcel Pacaut, *Louis VII et son royaume* (Paris, 1964), p. 31.

31 'Chronica de gestis consulum Andegavensis', in *Chroniques d'Anjou*,
2 vols, ed. Paul Marchegay and André Salmon (Cambridge, 2010),
vol. I, p. 71.

32 A. W. Lewis, *Royal Succession in Capetian France: Studies in Familial
Order and the State* (Cambridge, MA, 1981), pp. 58–64, esp. p. 61.

33 Marjorie Chibnall, *The Empress Matilda: Queen Consort, Queen
Mother and Lady of the English* (Oxford, 1991), pp. 167–8.

34 Lewis, *Royal Succession*, pp. 58–64.

35 Map, *De nugis curialium*, pp. 478–9.

36 Anne Duggan, ed., *The Correspondence of Thomas Becket, Archbishop
of Canterbury, 1162–1170*, 2 vols (Oxford, 2000), vol. I, p. 227.

37 Richard A. Jackson, ed., *Ordines coronationis Franciae: Texts and
Ordines for the Coronation of the Frankish and French Kings and
Queens in the Middle Ages*, 2 vols (Philadelphia, PA, 1995–2000),
vol. I, pp. 196–7, 214.

38 Gerald of Wales, *Instruction for a Ruler: De principis instructione*,
   ed. Robert Bartlett (Oxford, 2018), pp. 684–93.

39 Geoffrey of Auxerre, 'Sancti Bernardi vita tertia', PL, vol. CLXXXV,
   col. 527.

40 William of Newburgh, *Historia rerum Anglicanum*, in *Chronicles
   of the Reigns of Stephen, Henry II and Richard I*, 4 vols, ed.
   Richard Howlett, Rolls Series (London, 1885–90), vol. I,
   pp. 92–3.

41 John of Salisbury, *The Historia Pontificalis of John of Salisbury*,
   ed. Marjorie Chibnall (Edinburgh, 1956), p. 53.

42 Elisabeth Van Houts, 'Les Femmes dans la royaume Plantagenêt:
   gendre, politique et nature', in *Plantagenêts et Capétiens*, ed. Aurell
   and Tonnerre, pp. 99–102.

43 Robert of Torigni, *The Chronicle, AD 1100–1186*, in *The Chronography
   of Robert of Torigni*, 2 vols, ed. and trans. Thomas N. Bisson, Oxford
   Medieval Texts (Oxford, 2020), vol. I, pp. 180–81.

44 Colette Bowie, *The Daughters of Henry II and Eleanor of Aquitaine*
   (Turnhout, 2014), pp. 177–84, including naming patterns in the
   next generation.

45 Evergates, *Marie of France*, p. 2.

46 Lewis, *Royal Succession*, pp. 57–8, for Capetian naming patterns.

47 Bowie, *The Daughters*, esp. pp. 50–53, comprehensively refutes this
   charge.

48 Ibid., pp. 33–64.

49 Ibid., pp. 57–63.

50 'Historia comitum Andegavensium', in *Chroniques d'Anjou*, 2 vols,
   ed. Paul Marchegay and André Salmon (Cambridge, 2010), vol. I,
   pp. 342–3.

51 Matthew Strickland, *Henry the Young King, 1155–83* (London and
   New Haven, CT, 2016), pp. 34–40, 60–61.

52 Stephen Church, *King John* (London, 2015), pp. 4–6.

53 Gerald of Wales, *Instruction*, pp. 474–7, 481–5, 597–605.

54 John Gillingham, *Richard I* (London and New Haven, CT, 1999),
   pp. 67–75; Strickland, *Henry the Young King*, pp. 271–5, 282–301.

55 Jean-Marc Bienvenu, 'Aliénor d'Aquitaine et Fontevraud',
   Cahiers de civilisation médiévale, XXIX (1986), pp. 25–6.

56 PR 33 *Henry II*, pp. 40; PR 1 *Richard I*, pp. 223–4.

57 Strickland, *Henry the Young King*, pp. 27, 81, 194.

58 GC, vol. II, instrumenta (hereafter instr.), cols 389–90, no. x;
   Julio Gonzalez, *El reino de Castilla en la epoca de Alfonso VIII*,
   3 vols (Madrid, 1960), vol. III, pp. 208–10, no. 682.

59 PR 30 *Henry II*, pp. 58, 120, 134, 136, 137, 144, 150; PR 31 *Henry II*, pp. 206, 218; PR 32 *Henry II*, pp. 49, 168; PR 33 *Henry II*, pp. 40, 194, 203, 204, 212; PR 34 *Henry II*, pp. 14, 18, 71.

60 PR 34 *Henry II*, pp. 14, 18; Kathleen Thompson, *Power and Border Lordship in Medieval France: The County of the Perche, 1000–1226* (Woodbridge, 2002), pp. 109–110.

61 Bowie, *The Daughters*, pp. 186–9.

62 P. Marchegay, 'Chartes de Fontevraud concernant L'Aunis et La Rochelle', *Bibliothèque de l'École de Chartes*, XIX (1858), pp. 340–41.

63 Gillingham, *Richard I*, p. 313.

64 Evergates, *Marie of France*, esp. pp. 17, 56–7.

65 Gerald of Wales, *Vita Galfridi*, in *Giraldi Cambrensis opera*, 8 vols, ed. J. S. Brewer, J. Dimmock and G. F. Warner, Rolls Series (London, 1861–91), vol. IV, p. 416.

66 Paris, BNF ms Latin 5480, part I, p. 121; Alexandre Teulet, H.-F. Delaborde and Élie Berger, eds, *Layettes du trésor des chartes*, 5 vols (Paris, 1863–1909), vol. I, p. 200, no. 489.

67 Judith Everard, *Brittany and the Angevins: Province and Empire, 1158–1203* (Cambridge, 2000), pp. 155–74.

68 Richard of Devizes, *The Chronicle of Richard of Devizes of the Time of King Richard the First*, ed. and trans. John T. Appleby (London, 1963), p. 3.

69 Elisabeth van Houts, *Memory and Gender in Medieval Europe, 900–1200* (London, 1999), pp. 96–7 (identifying the woman as Eleanor, but dating the Gospel Book in the late 1180s, when Eleanor was back at the centre of the family); and Jitske Jasperse, *Medieval Women, Material Culture and Power: Matilda Plantagenet and Her Sisters* (Leeds, 2020), pp. 81–90, esp. 86–9, dating the book to the later 1170s, but dubious about the identification of the woman as Eleanor.

5 Marriage, Sex and Scandal

1 Richard of Devizes, *The Chronicle of Richard of Devizes of the Time of King Richard the First*, ed. and trans. John T. Appleby (London, 1963), pp. 25–6.

2 Geoffroi de Vigeois, *Chronica*, in *Novae bibliothecae manuscriptorum*, vol. II, ed. Père Labbé (Paris, 1657), p. 297; William of Malmesbury, *Gesta regum Anglorum*, 2 vols, ed. R.A.B. Mynors, R. M. Thompson and M. Winterbottom (Oxford, 1998–9), vol. II, pp. 782–5.

3 M. Chibnall, ed., *The Ecclesiastical History of Orderic Vitalis*, 6 vols (Oxford, 1969–80), vol. VI, pp. 258–61.

4 Malmesbury, *Gesta regum*, vol. II, pp. 784–5.

5 Gerald of Wales, *Instruction for a Ruler: De principis instructione*, ed. Robert Bartlett (Oxford, 2018), pp. 684–5. For legends around Eleanor, see Michael R. Evans, *Inventing Eleanor: The Medieval and Post-Medieval Image of Eleanor of Aquitaine* (London and New York, 2014), esp. pp. 19–43.

6 John of Salisbury, *The Historia Pontificalis of John of Salisbury*, ed. Marjorie Chibnall (Edinburgh, 1956), pp. 12–15.

7 Ralph of Diceto, 'Ymagines', in *Opera Historica: The Historical Works of Master Ralph of Diceto, Dean of London*, 2 vols, ed. W. Stubbs, Rolls Series (London, 1876), vol. I, p. 402; Roger of Howden, *Chronica Rogeri de Hovedene*, 4 vols, ed. William Stubbs, Rolls Series (London, 1868–71), vol. II, pp. 82–3.

8 Bruno Scott James, ed. and trans., *The Letters of St Bernard of Clairvaux*, 2nd edn (Stroud, 1998), nos 294–302, pp. 361–73, esp. pp. 364–8.

9 Geoffrey of Auxerre, 'Sancti Bernardi vita tertia', PL, vol. CLXXXV, col. 527.

10 Suger, *Œuvres*, vol. II, ed. Françoise Gasparri (Paris, 2001), pp. 38–9.

11 Gerhoh of Reichersberg, 'De investigatione Antichristi', MGH, *Libellus de lite*, vol. III (Hanover, 1897), p. 376.

12 John of Salisbury, *Historia Pontificalis*, pp. 52–3.

13 Scott James, ed. and trans., *The Letters of St Bernard*, no. 300, p. 371.

14 John of Salisbury, *Historia Pontificalis*, pp. 61–2.

15 William of Tyre, *Chronique*, vol. II, ed. R.B.C. Huygens (Turnhout, 1986), pp. 754–5.

16 Linda Paterson, *Singing the Crusades* (Cambridge, 2018), pp. 33–4, for Marcabru, 'Cortesamen vouill comenssar'; Luciano Rossi, ed., *Cercamon, Œuvres poétiques* (Paris, 2009), pp. 164–9; George Wolf and Roy Rosenstein, *The Poetry of Cercamon and Jaufre Rudel* (New York and London, 1983), p. 5.

17 Anne Duggan, ed., *The Correspondence of Thomas Becket, Archbishop of Canterbury, 1162–1170*, 2 vols (Oxford, 2000), vol. I, pp. 216–17.

18 Gerald of Wales, *Instruction*, pp. 684–5.

19 Matthew Paris, *Chronica majora*, 7 vols, ed. H. R. Luard, Rolls Series (London, 1872–83), vol. II, p. 186.

20 Gerald of Wales, *Instruction*, pp. 688–9; Philippe Mousket, *Chronique rimée*, 2 vols, ed. Frédérique de Reiffenberg (Brussels, 1836–8), vol. II, pp. 248–9, vv. 18685–18817.

21 Samuel N. Rosenberg, trans., *Tales of a Minstrel of Reims in the Thirteenth Century*, introduction by William Chester Jordan,

annotated by Randall Todd Pippinger (Washington, DC, 2022),
pp. 5–7.

22 Richard the Poitevin, 'Ex chronico Richardi Pictaviensis', RHF,
vol. XII, p. 417.

23 Walter Map, *De nugis curialium*, ed. C.N.L. Brooke and M. R. James,
revd edn (Oxford, 1983), pp. 474–7; Gerald of Wales, *Instruction*,
pp. 686–9.

24 Robert of Torigni, *The Chronicle, AD 1100–1186*, in *The
Chronography of Robert of Torigni*, 2 vols, ed. and trans. Thomas
N. Bisson (Oxford, 2020), vol. I, p. 298.

25 Roger of Howden, *Gesta Regis Henrici Secundi Benedicti Abbatis*,
2 vols, ed. William Stubbs, Rolls Series (London, 1867), vol. I, p. 42.

26 Diceto, 'Ymagines', vol. I, pp. 355–66. See Michael Staunton, *The
Historians of Angevin England* (Oxford, 2017), pp. 78–9, 187–90.

27 John Jay Parry, ed. and trans., *The Art of Courtly Love by Andreas
Capellanus* (New York, 1941), esp. pp. 168–70, 172, 106–7.

28 Richard the Poitevin, 'Ex chronico', pp. 419–20.

29 Guernes de Pont Saint-Maxence, *La Vie de Saint Thomas*, 2 vols,
ed. and trans. Jacques T. E. Thomas (Louvain/Paris, 2002), vol. I,
pp. 346–7.

30 Diceto, 'Ymagines', vol. II, p. 67.

31 Roger of Howden, *Chronica Rogeri de Hovedene*, 4 vols, ed. William
Stubbs, Rolls Series (London, 1868–71), vol. III, pp. 167–8.

32 Evans, *Inventing Eleanor*, pp. 35–7.

33 Howden, *Gesta*, vol. II, p. 78.

34 W. J. Miller and C.N.L. Brooke, eds, *The Letters of John of Salisbury*,
vol. II: *The Later Letters (1163–1180)* (Oxford, 1986), no. 279,
pp. 602–3; Judith Everard, *Brittany and the Angevins: Province and
Empire, 1158–1203* (Cambridge, 2000), p. 46.

35 John Gillingham, *Richard I* (London and New Haven, CT, 1999),
pp. 82, 142, reviews the evidence.

36 PR 33 *Henry II*, pp. 15, 40; PR 34 *Henry II*, pp. 14, 21; PR 1 *Richard I*,
pp. 217, 223, 224.

37 Evans, *Inventing Eleanor*, pp. 19–43; Ralph V. Turner, *Eleanor of
Aquitaine* (New Haven, CT, and London, 2009), pp. 299–313;
Daniel Power, 'The Stripping of a Queen: Eleanor in Thirteenth-
Century Norman Tradition', in *The World of Eleanor of Aquitaine:
Literature and Society in Southern France between the Eleventh
and Thirteenth Centuries*, ed. Marcus Bull and Catherine Léglu
(Woodbridge, 2005), pp. 115–35, esp. pp. 124–31; Lindy Grant,
Blanche of Castile (London, 2016), pp. 323–4, 103–4, 111.

38 Rosenberg, trans., *Tales of a Minstrel of Reims*, pp. 83–4.

39 Mousket, *Chronique*, vol. II, p. 618, vv. 29, 160–75; Rosenberg, trans., *Tales of a Minstrel of Reims*, p. 151.

40 Gerald of Wales, *Instruction*, pp. 688–9.

6 The Eagle with the Spread Wings

1 Richard the Poitevin, 'Ex chronico Richardi Pictaviensis', RHF, vol. XII, pp. 419–20; and see Élie Berger, *Notice sur divers manuscrits de la Bibliothèque Vaticane. Richard le Poitevin, moine de Cluny, historien et poète*, Bibliothèque des Écoles françaises d'Athènes et de Rome, vol. XI (Paris, 1879), esp. pp. 47–51.

2 George T. Beech, 'The Eleanor Vase, William IX of Aquitaine and Muslim Spain', *Gesta*, XXXII (1993), pp. 3–10.

3 Richard Benjamin, 'A Forty-Year War: Toulouse and the Plantagenets, 1156–90', *Historical Research*, LXI (1988), pp. 270–85, for the Angevins and Aragon.

4 PR 34 *Henry II*, pp. 14, 18.

5 Suger, *Vie de Louis le Gros*, ed. Henri Waquet, 2nd edn (Paris, 1964), pp. 224–5; Nicolo Pasero, ed., *Guglielmo IX d'Aquitania. Poesie* (Modena, 1973), no. XI, p. 278.

6 T. Grasilier, ed., *Cartulaire de l'abbaye royale de Notre Dame de Saintes*, in *Cartulaires inédits de la Saintonge*, 2 vols (Niort, 1871), vol. II, p. ii; Alfred Richard, *Histoire des comtes de Poitou*, vol. I (Paris, 1903), pp. 462–3.

7 Jean-Hervé Foulon, 'Un représentant de la spiritualité canoniale au XIIe siècle: Geoffroi de Loroux', in *Les Chanoines réguliers*, ed. M. Parisse (Saint-Étienne, 2009), pp. 71–115; Jean-Hervé Foulon, *Eglise et réforme au Moyen Âge. Papauté, milieux réformateurs et ecclésiologie dans les Pays de la Loire au tournant des XIe au XIIe siècles* (Brussels, 2008); Jean-Yves Tilliette, 'La Vie culturelle dans l'ouest de la France au temps de Baudri de Bourgueil', in *Robert d'Arbrissel et la vie religieuse dans l'ouest de la France*, ed. Jacques Dalarun (Turnhout, 2004), pp. 71–86.

8 For troubadours and the issue of Eleanor's relations with them, see Ruth Harvey, 'Eleanor of Aquitaine and the Troubadours', in *The World of Eleanor of Aquitaine: Literature and Society in Southern France between the Eleventh and Thirteenth Centuries*, ed. Marcus Bull and Catherine Léglu (Woodbridge, 2005), pp. 101–14; Ruth Harvey, 'Courtly Culture in Medieval Occitania', in *The Troubadours: An Introduction*, ed. Simon Gault and Sarah Kay

(Cambridge, 1999), pp. 8–27; George Wolf and Roy Rosenstein, *The Poetry of Cercamon and Jaufre Rudel* (New York and London, 1983); Simon Gaunt, Ruth Harvey and Linda Paterson, eds, *Marcabru: A Critical Edition* (Cambridge, 2000); Linda Paterson, *Singing the Crusades* (Cambridge, 2018), esp. pp. 25–38; Cynthia Robinson, 'Courtly Courts as Sites of Cultural Interaction: The Case of Two Caskets', in *Culture politique des Plantagenêts (1154–1224)*, ed. Martin Aurell (Poitiers, 2003), esp. pp. 104–10, on exchanges with Iberian Islamic poetry. For Duke William's poem featuring the big red cat, Pasero, ed., *Guglielmo IX d'Aquitania*, pp. 125–32.

9 Geoffroi de Vigeois, *Chronica*, in *Novae bibliothecae manuscriptorum*, vol. II, ed. Père Labbé (Paris, 1657), p. 291.

10 G. Gouiran, 'Bertran de Born: un maître pour les princes Plantagenêts?', in *Culture politique des Plantagenêts*, ed. Aurell, pp. 129–41, esp. p. 132.

11 Mary O'Neill, *Courtly Love Songs of Medieval France: Transmission and Style in Trouvère Repertoire* (Oxford, 2006), esp. pp. 1–12.

12 Nicholas Vincent, 'The Court of Henry II', in *Henry II: New Interpretations*, ed. Christopher Harper-Bill and Nicholas Vincent (Woodbridge, 2007), esp. pp. 319–34; Ian Short, 'Literary Culture at the Court of Henry II', ibid., pp. 335–61; Charity Urbaniski, *Writing History for the King: Henry II and the Politics of Vernacular Historiography* (Ithaca, NY, 2013), esp. pp. 149–97; Judith Weiss, *Wace's Roman de Brut: A History of the English. Text and Translation* (Exeter, 2002), esp. pp. xii–xiii; Glynn Burgess and Douglas Kelly, eds and trans, *The Roman de Troie by Benoît de Sainte-Maure* (Woodbridge, 2018), pp. 4–7 and p. 207, vv. 13457–70.

13 Martin Aurell, 'Henry II and Arthurian Legend', in *Henry II: New Interpretations*, ed. Harper-Bill and Vincent, pp. 362–94; Jean Flori, *Aliénor d'Aquitaine* (Paris, 2004), pp. 415–42.

14 *GC*, vol. II, instr., col. 470, no. XVI: 'in curia . . . sub umbraculo'.

15 Helgaud de Fleury, *Vie de Robert le Pieux. Epitoma vitae Regis Rotberti Pii*, ed. R.-H. Bautier and G. Labory (Paris 1965), pp. 100–101, 112–13.

16 PR 2 *Henry II*, p. 5; PR 4 *Henry II*, p. 175; PR 5 *Henry II*, p. 25.

17 Beech, 'The Eleanor Vase'.

7 Riches

1 Walter Map, *De nugis curialium*, ed. C.N.L. Brooke and M. R. James, revd edn (Oxford, 1983), pp. 450–51.
2 John W. Baldwin, *The Government of Philip Augustus: Foundations of French Royal Power in the Middle Ages* (Berkeley, CA, 1986), pp. 37–73, 137–75, 220–58.
3 For Eleanor's income and resources, Ralph V. Turner, *Eleanor of Aquitaine* (New Haven, CT, and London, 2009), pp. 165–7, 260–61.
4 Ralph of Diceto, 'Ymagines', in *Opera Historica: The Historical Works of Master Ralph of Diceto, Dean of London*, 2 vols, ed. W. Stubbs, Rolls Series (London, 1876), vol. I, pp. 293–4.
5 L. M. de Richemond, 'Chartes de la commanderie magistrale du Temple de La Rochelle', AHSA, I (1874), pp. 25–6, no. 1.
6 T. Grasilier, ed., *Cartulaire de l'abbaye royale de Notre Dame de Saintes*, in *Cartulaires inédits de la Saintonge*, 2 vols (Niort, 1871), vol. II, p. 14, no. viii, privilege of Pope Eugenius III, 1146.
7 Achille Luchaire, *Études sur les actes de Louis VII* (Paris, 1885), nos 18, 177, 138.
8 'Histoire du roi Louis VII', in *Vie de Louis VI le Gros, par Suger, suivie de l'Histoire du roi Louis VII*, ed. Auguste Molinier (Paris, 1887), p. 150.
9 Nicholas Vincent, ed., *The Letters and Charters of Henry II*, 6 vols (Oxford, 2020), vol. I, pp. 44–8, no. 45; vol. V, pp. 174–81, nos 2765–6; Turner, *Eleanor*, pp. 236–7.
10 Roger of Howden, *Chronica Rogeri de Hovedene*, 4 vols, ed. William Stubbs, Rolls Series (London, 1868–71), vol. III, p. 27; Richard of Devizes, *The Chronicle of Richard of Devizes of the Time of King Richard the First*, ed. and trans. John T. Appleby (London, 1963), p. 14.
11 J. W. Baldwin, ed., *Les Registres de Philippe Auguste* (Paris, 1992), pp. 54–5 for Eleanor's Norman dower; p. 469 for Richard's dower for Berengaria, 1191; pp. 471–2 for Berengaria's English lands, which includes some of Eleanor's English dower, for example, Berkhamsted, and must postdate her death (it is not on the earliest Register A, but is in the later Registers C, f. 77v and E f. 169); pp. 485–6 for John's dower for Isabelle of Angoulême, August 1200. For Isabelle obtaining Eleanor's English dower after her death, *Rot. Chart.*, p. 128a and b. See also Nicholas Vincent, 'Isabelle of Angoulême: John's Jezebel', in *King John, New Interpretations*, ed. Stephen Church (Woodbridge, 1999), pp. 185–92, on the queens' dower arrangements.

12 For living expenses see, for example, PR 2 Henry II, p. 40; PR 4 Henry II, pp. 112, 157; PR 5 Henry II, pp. 41, 58; PR 6 Henry II, pp. 16, 49; PR 10 Henry II, p. 25.

13 Turner, Eleanor, p. 166.

14 J. H. Round, ed., Calendar of Documents Preserved in France, 918–1206 (London, 1899), nos 1090 and 1107; Rot. Chart., pp. 10b, 7b–8, 25.

15 T. Stapleton, ed., Magni rotuli scaccarii Normanniae sub regibus Angliae, 2 vols (London, 1840), vol. I, 1195 roll, p. 234; vol. II, 1198 roll, pp. 352, 369.

16 London, British Library ms. Additional charter 54007.

17 Alexandre Teulet, H.-F. Delaborde and Élie Berger, eds, Layettes du trésor des chartes, 5 vols (Paris, 1863–1909), vol. I, p. 209, no. 508 (Andrew of Chauvigny); Rot. Chart., pp. 25–25b (William Maingot); Rot. Chart., p. 24b (Ralph of Mauléon).

18 AHP, vol. VIII (1879), 'Hec est inquesta vicecomitis de Castri Eraudi de venatione in Moleria', p. 64.

19 Nicholas Vincent, 'Patronage, Politics and Piety in the Charters of Eleanor of Aquitaine', in Plantagenêts et Capétiens: confrontations et héritages, ed. Martin Aurell and N.-Y. Tonnerre (Turnhout, 2006), pp. 21–5; Turner, Eleanor, esp. pp. 129–30.

20 Matthew Paris, Chronica majora, 7 vols, ed. H. R. Luard, Rolls Series (London, 1872–83), vol. VI, Addimenta, p. 385. The Latin is compacted and has been read to suggest that Richard himself had studied alongside Eleanor in his youth – but he would surely not have described her as a 'mate': 'quem de dono cuiusdam reginae Alienorae obtinuerat, quia conscolares in sua iuventute extiterat et sodales. Fuerat autem gemma antea ipsius reginae A.'

21 Adam and Roger, Rot. Chart., pp. 25 and 71b; William, Rot. Lit. Pat., pp. 28b, 31.

22 Vincent, ed., The Letters and Charters of Henry II, vol. III, pp. 326–7, no. 1679.

23 A. J. Holden, ed., The History of William Marshal, vol. I (London, 2002), v. 9508, pp. 482–3.

24 Ibid., vv. 1864–83, pp. 94–7.

25 Vincent, 'Patronage, Politics and Piety', pp. 50–51; Turner, Eleanor, p. 285.

26 Lindy Grant, Blanche of Castile (London, 2016), pp. 118–19.

27 Vincent, ed., The Letters and Charters of Henry II, vol. IV, no. 2569, p. 665.

28 Stapleton, ed., *Magni rotuli scaccarii Normanniae*, vol. II, 1198 roll, pp. 352–4, 495–6.

29 *RHF*, vol. XV, esp. pp. 486, 500, 514; Jacques Boussard, *Le Gouvernement d'Henri II Plantagenêt* (Paris, 1956), pp. 312, 319–29.

30 See, for example, *PR 5 Henry II*, p. 1; *PR 14 Henry II*, p. 2.

31 Grasilier, ed., *Cartulaire de l'abbaye royale*, p. 36, no. xxx.

32 Vincent, ed., *The Letters and Charters of Henry II*, vol. IV, pp. 315–18, no. 2221.

33 For Eleanor's early acts, see F. Villard, ed., *Recueil des documents relatifs à l'abbaye de Montierneuf de Poitiers*, AHP, vol. LIX (1973), pp. 135–6, no. 87; A. Richard, ed., *Chartes et documents pour servir à l'histoire de l'abbaye de Saint Maixent*, AHP, vol. XVI (1886), pp. 352–3, no. 335.

34 For Eleanor's household, see Turner, *Eleanor*, pp. 161–7, 276–7; Vincent, 'Patronage, Politics and Piety'; Marie Hivergneaux, 'Autour d'Aliénor d'Aquitaine: entourage et pouvoir au prisme des chartes (1137–1189)', in *Plantagenêts et Capétiens*, ed. Aurell and Tonnerre, pp. 61–73.

8 Prayer

1 Jean-Hervé Foulon, 'Une conscience profane à l'aube du XIIe siècle, Guillaume IX d'Aquitaine, 1086–1126', in *Guerriers et moines: conversion et sainteté aristocratiques dans l'Occident médiévale (XIe–XIIe siècles)*, ed. Michel Lauwers (Antibes, 2000), pp. 503–35.

2 Alfred Richard, *Histoire des comtes de Poitou*, 2 vols (Paris, 1903), vol. II, pp. 20–49.

3 L. Mirot, ed., *La Chronique de Morigny*, 2nd edn (Paris, 1912), p. 74.

4 *GC*, vol. II, instr., cols 370–71, no. liii; Jean-Hervé Foulon, 'Un représentant de la spiritualité canoniale au XIIe siècle: Geoffroi de Loroux', in *Les Chanoines réguliers*, ed. Michel Parisse (Saint-Étienne, 2009), pp. 71–115.

5 *GC*, vol. II, instr., col. 387, no. viii.

6 'Documents concernant le prieuré de Saint-Denis-en-Vaux', AHP, vol. VII (1878), pp. 346–7, no. i; Suger, *Vie de Louis le Gros*, ed. Henri Waquet, 2nd edn (Paris, 1964), pp. 48–9; Lindy Grant, *Abbot Suger of Saint Denis: Church and State in Early Twelfth-Century France* (London, 1998), pp. 81–2.

7 Marcel Pacaut, *Louis VII et son royaume* (Paris, 1964), pp. 39–90.

8 John of Salisbury, *The Historia Pontificalis of John of Salisbury*, ed. Marjorie Chibnall (Edinburgh, 1956), p. 62.

9 Anne Duggan, 'On Finding the Voice of Eleanor of Aquitaine',
   in *Voix de femmes au Moyen Âge: actes du colloque du Centre
   d'Études Médiévales Anglaises de Paris-Sorbonne (26–27 mars
   2010)*, ed. L. Carruthers, Association des Médiévistes
   Anglicistes de l'Énseignement Supérieur 32 (Paris, 2011),
   pp. 129–58.

10 P. Marchegay, 'Chartes de Fontevraud concernant L'Aunis et
   La Rochelle', *Bibliothèque de l'École de Chartes*, XIX (1858),
   p. 323; Richard, *Histoire des comtes*, vol. II, pp. 9–10, 47–9.

11 Jean-Marc Bienvenu, Robert Favreau and Georges Pon, eds,
   *Grand cartulaire de Fontevraud (pancarta et cartularium abbatissae
   et ordinis Fontis Ebraudi)*, 2 vols (Poitiers, 2000–2005). See, for
   example, vol. I, nos 51, 52, 30, 170, 62, 298, 316, 326, 455, 520,
   and vol. II, nos 710, 772, 868. Henri Beauchet-Filleau and Charles
   Clergé, *Dictionnaire historique et généalogique des familles de Poitou*,
   5 vols (Poitiers, 1891–1909), vol. I, p. 320.

12 C. Chevalier, ed., *Cartulaire de l'abbaye de Noyers* (Tours, 1872).
   See, for example, nos 20, 148, 335, 394, 525, 555, 562, 590 and
   no. 613, burial of Hugh of Sainte-Maure, no. 494, burial of Viscount
   Aimery, probably around 1151.

13 PL, vol. CLVII, cols 204–5, 202; and Richard, *Histoire des comtes*,
   vol. I, pp. 438, 470, 473.

14 Richard, *Histoire des comtes*, vol. II, pp. 12, 45; see also F. Villard,
   ed., *Recueil des documents relatifs à l'abbaye de Montierneuf de
   Poitiers*, AHP, vol. LIX (1973), no. 78, pp. 121–4.

15 Lois L. Huneycutt, 'The Creation of a Crone: The Historical
   Reputation of Adelaide of Maurienne', in *Capetian Women*,
   ed. Kathleen Nolan (New York, 2003), p. 34; Marjorie Chibnall,
   The Empress Matilda (Oxford, 1991), pp. 177–94; Lois L. Huneycutt,
   'Alianora Regina Anglorum: Eleanor of Aquitaine and Her Anglo-
   Norman Predecessors as Queens of England', in *Eleanor of Aquitaine:
   Lord and Lady*, ed. Bonnie Wheeler and John Carmi Parsons (New
   York, 2003), esp. pp. 129–30.

16 Jean-Marc Bienvenu, 'Aliénor d'Aquitaine et Fontevraud', *Cahiers
   de civilisation médiévale*, XXIX (1986), p. 26, n. 98.

17 See, for example, Villard, ed., *Recueil des documents relatifs à l'abbaye
   de Montierneuf*, pp. 135–6, no. 87, pp. 182–6, no. 112.

18 P. de Monsabert, 'Documents inédits pour servir à l'histoire de
   l'abbaye de Sainte-Croix de Poitiers', *Revue Mabillon*, IX (1913),
   pp. 74–5, no. 11; J. Besly, *Histoire des comtes de Poictou et ducs de
   Guyenne* (Paris, 1647), pp. 497–8.

19 L. M. de Richemond, 'Chartes de la commanderie magistrale du
    Temple de La Rochelle', AHSA, I (1874), pp. 25–6, no. 1, pp. 30–31,
    no. 6; Achille Luchaire, *Études sur les actes de Louis VII* (Paris, 1885),
    p. 110, no. 35 and p. 150, no. 176; C. Metais, ed., *Cartulaire
    Saintongeais de la Trinité de Vendôme*, AHSA, XXII (1893), pp. 98–100,
    no. lix; Nicholas Vincent, ed., *The Letters and Charters of Henry II*,
    6 vols (Oxford, 2020), vol. III, p. 327, no. 1679 for Luçon and vol. IV,
    no. 2569, p. 665 for Surgères; for La Sauve see Thomas Rymer, ed.,
    Foedera, Conventiones, Literae (London, 1741), vol. V, pp. 79–80; for
    Turpenay, see Alexandre Teulet, H.-F. Delaborde and Élie Berger,
    eds, *Layettes du trésor des chartes*, 5 vols (Paris, 1863–1909), vol. I,
    p. 200, no. 489. See also Nicholas Vincent, 'Patronage, Politics and
    Piety in the Charters of Eleanor of Aquitaine', in *Plantagenêts et
    Capétiens: confrontations et héritages*, ed. Martin Aurell and N.-Y.
    Tonnerre (Turnhout, 2006), pp. 21–5; Ralph V. Turner, *Eleanor of
    Aquitaine* (New Haven, CT, and London, 2009), esp. pp. 59–60,
    129–30.

20 Bienvenu, 'Aliénor d'Aquitaine et Fontevraud'.

21 Marchegay, 'Chartes de Fontevraud', pp. 337–41, nos 1, 2, 3 and 4.

22 J. H. Round, ed., *Calendar of Documents Preserved in France,
    918–1206* (London, 1899), no. 1090.

23 Marchegay, 'Chartes de Fontevraud', no. 3; for the necrology, see
    Bienvenu, 'Aliénor d'Aquitaine et Fontevraud', p. 26, n. 98.

24 Jean-Marc Bienvenu, 'Henri II Plantagenet et Fontevraud', *Cahiers
    de civilisation médiévale*, CXLV/CXLVI (1994), pp. 25–32; Bienvenu,
    'Aliénor d'Aquitaine et Fontevraud'.

25 Luchaire, *Études sur les actes*, no. 189.

26 Rymer, ed., *Foedera*, vol. V, pp. 79–80.

27 A. W. Lewis, 'Six Charters of Henry II and His Family for the Abbey
    of Dalon', *English Historical Review*, CX (1995), pp. 652–65.

28 'Draco Normannicus, addimenta', in *Chronicles of the Reigns of
    Stephen, Henry II and Richard I*, vol. II, ed. R. Howlett, Rolls Series
    (London, 1885), pp. 758–60. See also Nicolas Hatot, '*Augusta*
    Matilda and the Valasse Reliquary Cross: *Translatio Crucis* from the
    Holy Roman Empire to the Plantagenet Realm', *British
    Archaeological Association Journal*, CLXXII (2019), pp. 95–130.

29 PR 6 Henry II, p. 49.

30 *Rot. Chart.*, pp. 7b–8, 10b.

31 Walter Cahn, *Romanesque Manuscripts: The Twelfth Century*, 2 vols
    (London, 1996), vol. II, pp. 160–61, no. 134; Jesús Rodríguez Viejo,
    'Royal Manuscript Patronage in Late Ducal Normandy: A Context

for the Female Patron Portrait of the *Fécamp Psalter* (c. 1180)',
Cerae: An Australasian Journal of Medieval and Early Modern Studies,
III (2016), pp. 1–33, esp. pp. 15–16, identifies the patron as Eleanor,
but see also Stéphane Lecouteux, 'Les Calendriers et les litanies des
saints dans les manuscrits liturgiques de l'abbaye Bénédictine de la
Trinité de Fécamp (XIe–XVIe siècles)', *Revue Bénédictine*, CXXX (2020),
pp. 123–64, esp. pp. 153–4, for the definitive association of the
psalter with Ham-en-Vermandois.

32 Vincent, 'Patronage, Politics and Piety', pp. 41–2.

33 Turner, *Eleanor*, p. 288; London, British Library, ms. Additional
charter 54007; Marchegay, 'Chartes de Fontevraud', pp. 339–40, no. 3;
for Roger in Bordeaux and Normandy, see Rymer, ed., *Foedera*, vol. V,
pp. 79–80, and Teulet et al., eds, *Layettes*, vol. I, p. 209, no. 508.

34 See, for example, Marchegay, 'Chartes de Fontevraud', pp. 339–40,
no. 3 and pp. 340–41; A. Richard, ed., *Chartes et documents pour
servir à l'histoire de l'abbaye de Saint Maixent*, AHP, vol. XVIII (1886),
pp. 16–18, nos 402–3. See also Jörg Peltzer, 'Les Évêques de l'empire
Plantagenêt et les rois angevins: un tour d'horizon', in *Plantagenêts et
Capétiens*, ed. Aurell and Tonnerre, pp. 461–84.

35 Round, ed., *Calendar*, no. 1096; R. Ransford, ed., *The Early Charters
of the Augustinian Canons of Waltham Abbey, Essex, 1062–1230*
(Woodbridge, 1989), p. 194, no. 287; *Rot. Lit. Pat.*, p. 9b; Robert
Favreau, 'Les Débuts de la ville de La Rochelle', *Cahiers de
civilisation médiévale*, CXVII (1987), pp. 3–32 (pp. 18–19).

36 Teulet et al., eds, *Layettes*, vol. I, p. 200, no. 489.

37 GC, vol. II, col. 1215.

38 Sidney Painter, 'The Houses of Lusignan and Châtellerault,
1150–1250', *Speculum*, XXX (1955), p. 84; Louis Rédet, 'Documents
pour l'histoire de l'église de St-Hilaire de Poitiers', in *Mémoires de la
Société des Antiquaires de l'Ouest*, vol. XIV (Poitiers, 1848 for 1847),
esp. pp. 215–16.

39 Turner, *Eleanor*, pp. 163–4; Emma Mason, ed., *Westminster Abbey
Charters, 1066–c.1214* (London, 1988), pp. 298–9, no. 463;
Chevalier, ed., *Cartulaire de l'abbaye de Noyers*, no. 613; Peltzer,
'Les Évêques de l'empire Plantagenêt', esp. pp. 461, 467–75.

40 Luc D'Achery, *Prospectus novae editionis Spicilegium, et veterum
Analectorum*, 3 vols (Paris, 1721–3), vol. III, cols 528–9.

41 W. J. Millor and H. E. Butler, eds, *The Letters of John of Salisbury:
The Early Letters* (London, 1955), pp. 151–2; PR 2–4 Henry II, p. 13.

42 C. R. Cheney, 'A Monastic Letter of Fraternity to Eleanor of
Aquitaine', *English Historical Review*, LI (1936), pp. 488–93.

43 Cécile Treffort, 'La Mémoire d'un duc dans un écrin de pierre: le tombeau de Guy-Geoffroi à Saint-Jean Montierneuf de Poitiers', *Cahiers de civilisation médiévale*, CLXXXVII (2004), pp. 249–59; Villard, ed., *Recueil des documents relatifs à l'abbaye de Montierneuf*, pp. 115–20, no. 76, pp. 135–6, no. 87 and pp. 182–6, no. 112.

44 Jean Verdon, ed., *Chronique de Saint-Maixent* (Paris, 1979), pp. 194–5.

45 Luchaire, *Études sur les actes*, no. 77, p. 124, full text in GC, vol. II, instr., cols 385–6.

46 Rédet, 'Documents pour l'histoire de l'église de St-Hilaire', pp. 180–81, no. 153.

47 London, British Library ms. Additional charter 54007; Marchegay, 'Chartes de Fontevraud', pp. 337–8, no. 1, pp. 338–9, no. 2, pp. 340–41.

48 Marchegay, 'Chartes de Fontevraud', pp. 330–31, no. 1.

49 Roger of Howden, *Gesta Regis Henrici Secundi Benedicti Abbatis*, 2 vols, ed. William Stubbs, Rolls Series (London, 1867), vol. I, p. 7.

50 Roger of Howden, *Chronica Rogeri de Hovedene*, 4 vols, ed. William Stubbs, Rolls Series (London, 1868–71), vol. IV, p. 84; P. Charlier et al., 'The Embalmed Heart of Richard the Lionheart (1199 AD): A Biological and Anthropological Analysis', *Scientific Reports*, III (2013), article no. 1296.

51 Colette Bowie, *The Daughters of Henry II and Eleanor of Aquitaine* (Turnhout, 2014), pp. 186–7; for Raymond's will see Teulet et al., eds, *Layettes*, vol. III, no. 3802.

52 B. Filliol-Braquet, 'La Sculpture du xiiie siècle dans les églises d'Anjou', in *Saint Louis et L'Anjou*, ed. Etienne Vacquet (Angers, 2014), pp. 248–53; Kathleen Nolan, *Queens in Stone and Silver: The Creation of a Visual Imagery of Queenship in Capetian France* (New York, 2009), pp. 99–113, though this assumes Eleanor ordered her own tomb.

9 Power

1 Kathleen Nolan, *Queens in Stone and Silver: The Creation of a Visual Imagery of Queenship in Capetian France* (New York, 2009), pp. 70–86; François Eygun, *Sigillographie de Poitou jusqu'en 1515* (Poitiers, 1938), pp. 159–60; Elizabeth A. R. Brown, 'Eleanor of Aquitaine Reconsidered: The Woman and Her Seasons', in *Eleanor of Aquitaine: Lord and Lady*, ed. Bonnie Wheeler and John Carmi Parsons (New York, 2003), esp. pp. 20–27.

2 Richard A. Jackson, ed., *Ordines coronationis Franciae: Texts and Ordines for the Coronation of the Frankish and French Kings and Queens in the Middle Ages*, 2 vols (Philadelphia, PA, 1995–2000), vol. I, pp. 196–7, 214–16. The coronation orders in France and England were similar, in both cases derived from Carolingian coronation liturgies.

3 See, for example, J. H. Round, ed., *Calendar of Documents Preserved in France, 918–1206* (London, 1899), no. 1090, n. 4.

4 Léopold Delisle, 'Mémoire sur une lettre inédite adressée à la Reine Blanche par un habitant de La Rochelle', *Bibliothèque de l'École de Chartes*, fourth series, II (1856), pp. 513–55 (pp. 525–6).

5 For the Angevin writers, see Michael Staunton, *The Historians of Angevin England* (Oxford, 2017); for Suger, see Lindy Grant, *Abbot Suger of Saint Denis: Church and State in Early Twelfth-Century France* (London, 1998), esp. pp. 32–42.

6 PL, vol. CCVII, cols 448–9, no. cliv.

7 Robert of Torigni, *The Chronicle, AD 1100–1186*, in *The Chronography of Robert of Torigni*, 2 vols, ed. and trans. Thomas N. Bisson (Oxford, 2020), vol. I, pp. 162–3.

8 Nicholas Vincent, ed., *The Letters and Charters of Henry II*, 6 vols (Oxford, 2020), vol. VI, see, for example, p. 141, no. 3857, p. 182, no. 3924, pp. 192–3, no. 3939.

9 Ibid., vol. II, no. 1048, attesting; vol. I, no. 285, assenting; vol. II, nos 1063, 1202; vol. III, no. 1679; vol. IV, nos 2081 and 2306; vol. VI, nos 3979 and 3982, complementary acts; vol. I, nos 32a, 68; vol. II, nos 741, 845, 1042; vol. III, no. 1696; vol. IV, no. 2339; vol. V, no. 2638, with no reference to Eleanor.

10 See, for example, P. Marchegay, *Cartulaires du Bas-Poitou* (Les Roches-Baritaud, 1877), p. 109, no. 24; C. Metais, ed., *Cartulaire Saintongeais de la Trinité de Vendôme*, AHSA, XXII (1893), pp. 114–16, no. 70.

11 Vincent, ed., *The Letters and Charters of Henry II*, vol. I, no. 562; A. W. Lewis, 'Six Charters of Henry II and His Family for the Abbey of Dalon', *English Historical Review*, CX (1995), pp. 652–65 (pp. 659–61), no. 2; P. Marchegay, 'Chartes de Fontevraud concernant L'Aunis et La Rochelle', *Bibliothèque de l'École de Chartes*, XIX (1858), pp. 135–6; J.-L. Lacurie, *Histoire de l'abbaye de Maillezais depuis sa fondation jusqu'à nos jours* (Fontenay-le-Comte, 1852), pp. 271–2, no. 50; E. Clouzot, ed., *Cartulaire de l'abbaye de Notre-Dame de la Merci-Dieu, autrement dite de Bécheron*, AHP, vol. XXXIV (1905), pp. 78–9, no. 87.

12 F. Chauvenet, 'L'Entourage de Richard Coeur de Lion', in *La Cour Plantagenêt (1154–1204)*, ed. Martin Aurell (Poitiers, 2000), pp. 137–49.

13 For John's orders for the government of Aquitaine, *Rot. Chart.*, pp. 30b, 31; *Rot. Lit. Pat.*, vol. I, pp. 12, 16, 17 and 28b for the order of April 1203.

14 Marie Hivergneaux, 'Aliénor d'Aquitaine: le pouvoir d'une femme à la lumière de ses chartes (1152–1204)', in *La Cour Plantagenêt*, ed. Aurell, pp. 63–87.

15 See, for example, Anne Duggan, 'On Finding the Voice of Eleanor of Aquitaine', in *Voix de femmes au Moyen Âge: actes du colloque du Centre d'Études Médiévales Anglaises de Paris-Sorbonne (26–27 mars 2010)*, ed. L. Carruthers (Paris, 2011), pp. 140–41; B. R. Kemp, ed., *Reading Abbey Cartularies*, 2 vols (London, 1986, 1987), vol. I, pp. 357–8, no. 466 and p. 358, no. 467; Clovis Brunel, ed., *Recueil des actes des comtes de Ponthieu (1026–1279)* (Paris, 1930), pp. 117–19, no. 80, for a case involving the monks of Perseigne settled 'in the court of the lady queen of England'; for a gift made at her court in Normandy, GC, vol. XI, instr., col. 82, no. 16.

16 Ralph of Diceto, 'Ymagines', in *Opera Historica: The Historical Works of Master Ralph of Diceto, Dean of London*, 2 vols, ed. W. Stubbs, Rolls Series (London, 1876), vol. II, p. 67.

17 Roger of Howden, *Chronica Rogeri de Hovedene*, 4 vols, ed. William Stubbs, Rolls Series (London, 1868–71), vol. III, pp. 4–5.

18 *Epistolae Cantuarensis, 1187–1199*, in *Chronicles and Memorials of Richard I*, 2 vols, ed. William Stubbs, Rolls Series (London, 1864–5), vol. II, no. cccxcix.

19 S. Loewenfeld, *Epistolae pontificum Romanae ineditae* (Graz, 1959), nos 215, 216.

20 W. J. Millor and H. E. Butler, eds, *The Letters of John of Salisbury: The Early Letters*, (London, 1955), p. 51.

21 W. J. Miller and C.N.L. Brooke, eds, *The Letters of John of Salisbury*, vol. II: *The Later Letters (1163–1180)* (Oxford, 1986), no. 152, pp. 52–3; for Matilda's role, see Marjorie Chibnall, *The Empress Matilda: Queen Consort, Queen Mother and Lady of the English* (Oxford, 1991), pp. 168–72.

22 *Epistolae Cantuarensis*, to Eleanor, no. ccclii, p. 332, no. cccxciii, p. 358, no. ccchlxxii, pp. 437–8; to Matilda and Henry of Saxony, no. clxxx, pp. 158–9; to Longchamp, no. cccchlxxiii, pp. 438–9.

23 Michael Evans, 'The Missing Queen? Eleanor of Aquitaine in the Early Reign of Louis VII', in *Louis VII and His World*, ed. M. L. Bardot and L. W. Marvin (Leiden, 2018), pp. 105–13.

24 Anne Duggan, ed., *The Correspondence of Thomas Becket, Archbishop of Canterbury, 1162–1170*, 2 vols (Oxford, 2000), vol. I, no. 49, pp. 210–13.

25 Gervase of Canterbury, 'Chronica Gervasii', in *Gervase of Canterbury: Historical Works*, 2 vols, ed. William Stubbs, Rolls Series (London, 1879–80), vol. I, p. 205.

26 Howden, *Chronica*, vol. III, p. 255.

27 Richard the Poitevin, 'Ex chronico Richardi Pictaviensis', RHF, vol. XII, cols 419–20.

28 Jane Martindale, 'Conventum inter Guillelmum Aquitanorum comitem et Hugonem Chiliarchum', *English Historical Review*, LXXXIV (1969), pp. 528–53.

29 RHF, vol. XV, col. 524, no. cix.

30 Suger, *Vie de Louis le Gros*, ed. Henri Waquet, 2nd edn (Paris, 1964), pp. 38–9.

31 Gervase of Canterbury, 'Chronica', vol. I, p. 242, 'Erat enim prudens femina valde, nobilibus orta natalibus, sed instabilis'.

Epilogue: Finding Eleanor

1 Richard of Devizes, *The Chronicle of Richard of Devizes of the Time of King Richard the First*, ed. and trans. John T. Appleby (London, 1963), pp. 25–6.

2 Gervase of Canterbury, 'Chronica Gervasii', in *Gervase of Canterbury: Historical Works*, 2 vols, ed. William Stubbs, Rolls Series (London, 1879–80), vol. I, p. 242.

SELECT BIBLIOGRAPHY

This short bibliography contains the key publications that informed this book and provides further reading. It includes some very useful collections on Eleanor herself, and the Plantagenets.

Primary Sources

Gerald of Wales, *Instruction for a Ruler: De principis instructione*, ed. Robert Bartlett (Oxford, 2018)

Gervase of Canterbury, 'Chronica Gervasii', in *Gervase of Canterbury: Historical Works*, 2 vols, ed. William Stubbs, Rolls Series (London, 1879–80)

John of Salisbury, *The Historia Pontificalis of John of Salisbury*, ed. Marjorie Chibnall (Edinburgh, 1956)

Ralph of Diceto, *Opera Historica: The Historical Works of Master Ralph of Diceto, Dean of London*, 2 vols, ed. W. Stubbs, Rolls Series (London, 1876)

Richard of Devizes, *The Chronicle of Richard of Devizes of the Time of King Richard the First*, ed. and trans. John T. Appleby (London, 1963)

Robert of Torigni, *The Chronicle, AD 1100–1186*, in *The Chronography of Robert of Torigni*, 2 vols, ed. and trans. Thomas N. Bisson, Oxford Medieval Texts (Oxford, 2020)

Roger of Howden, *Gesta Regis Henrici Secundi Benedicti Abbatis*, 2 vols, ed. William Stubbs, Rolls Series (London, 1867)

—, *Chronica Rogeri de Hovedene*, 4 vols, ed. William Stubbs, Rolls Series (London, 1868–71)

Vincent, Nicholas, ed., *The Letters and Charters of Henry II*, 6 vols (Oxford, 2020)

Secondary Sources

Aurell, Martin, 'Henry II and Arthurian Legend', in *Henry II: New Interpretations*, ed. Christopher Harper-Bill and Nicholas Vincent (Woodbridge, 2007), pp. 362–94

—, ed., *La Cour Plantagenêt (1154–1204)* (Poitiers, 2000)

—, ed., *Culture politique des Plantagenêts (1154–1224)* (Poitiers, 2003)

—, and N.-Y. Tonnerre, eds, *Plantagenêts et Capétiens: confrontations et héritages* (Turnhout, 2006)

Baldwin, John W., *The Government of Philip Augustus: Foundations of French Royal Power in the Middle Ages* (Berkeley, CA, 1986)

Bienvenu, Jean-Marc, 'Aliénor d'Aquitaine et Fontevraud', *Cahiers de civilisation médiévale*, XXIX (1986), pp. 15–27

Bowie, Colette, *The Daughters of Henry II and Eleanor of Aquitaine* (Turnhout, 2014)

Brown, Elizabeth A. R., 'Eleanor of Aquitaine Reconsidered: The Woman and Her Seasons', in *Eleanor of Aquitaine: Lord and Lady*, ed. Bonnie Wheeler and John Carmi Parsons (New York, 2003), pp. 20–27

Bull, Marcus, and Catherine Léglu, eds, *The World of Eleanor of Aquitaine: Literature and Society in Southern France between the Eleventh and Thirteenth Centuries* (Woodbridge, 2005)

Chibnall, Marjorie, *The Empress Matilda: Queen Consort, Queen Mother and Lady of the English* (Oxford, 1991)

Church, Stephen, ed., *King John, New Interpretations* (Woodbridge, 1999)

Duggan, Anne, 'On Finding the Voice of Eleanor of Aquitaine', in *Voix de femmes au Moyen Âge: actes du colloque du Centre d'Études Médiévales Anglaises de Paris-Sorbonne (26–27 mars 2010)*, ed. L. Carruthers (Paris, 2011), pp. 129–58

Evans, Michael R., *Inventing Eleanor: The Medieval and Post-Medieval Image of Eleanor of Aquitaine* (London and New York, 2014)

Everard, Judith, *Brittany and the Angevins: Province and Empire, 1158–1203* (Cambridge, 2000)

Evergates, Theodore, *Marie of France, Countess of Champagne, 1145–1198* (Philadelphia, PA, 2019)

Gillingham, John, *Richard I* (London and New Haven, CT, 1999)

Grant, Lindy, *Abbot Suger of Saint Denis: Church and State in Early Twelfth-Century France* (London, 1998)

—, *Blanche of Castile* (London, 2016)

Harper-Bill, Christopher, and Nicholas Vincent, eds, *Henry II: New Interpretations* (Woodbridge, 2007)

Harvey, Ruth, 'The Two Wives of the "First Troubadour", Duke William IX of Aquitaine', *Journal of Medieval History*, XIX (1993), pp. 307–25

—, 'Eleanor of Aquitaine and the Troubadours', in *The World of Eleanor of Aquitaine: Literature and Society in Southern France between the Eleventh and Thirteenth Centuries*, ed. Marcus Bull and Catherine Léglu (Woodbridge, 2005), pp. 187–212

Hivergneaux, Marie, 'Aliénor d'Aquitaine: le pouvoir d'une femme
    à la lumière de ses chartes (1152–1204)', in *La Cour Plantagenêt
    (1154–1204)*, ed. Martin Aurell (Poitiers, 2000), pp. 63–87
——, 'Queen Eleanor and Aquitaine, 1137–1189', in *Eleanor of Aquitaine:
    Lord and Lady*, ed. Bonnie Wheeler and John Carmi Parsons (New
    York, 2003), pp. 55–76
——, 'Autour d'Aliénor d'Aquitaine: entourage et pouvoir au prisme des
    chartes (1137–1189)', in *Plantagenêts et Capétiens: confrontations et
    héritages*, ed. Martin Aurell and N.-Y. Tonnerre (Turnhout, 2006),
    pp. 61–73
Huneycutt, Lois L., '*Alianora Regina Anglorum*: Eleanor of Aquitaine and
    her Anglo-Norman Predecessors as Queens of England', in *Eleanor
    of Aquitaine: Lord and Lady*, ed. Bonnie Wheeler and John Carmi
    Parsons (New York, 2003), pp. 115–32
Martindale, Jane, '"Cavalaria et orgueill": Duke William IX of Aquitaine
    and the Historian', in *The Ideals and Practice of Medieval Knighthood*,
    vol. II, ed. C. Harper-Bill and R. Harvey (Woodbridge, 1988),
    pp. 87–116
——, 'Eleanor of Aquitaine', in *Richard Coeur de Lion in History and Myth*,
    ed. Janet Nelson (London, 1992), pp. 17–50
——, 'Eleanor of Aquitaine: The Last Years', in *King John: New
    Interpretations*, ed. S. D. Church (Woodbridge, 1999), pp. 137–64
Nolan, Kathleen, *Queens in Stone and Silver: The Creation of a Visual
    Imagery of Queenship in Capetian France* (New York, 2009)
Richard, Alfred, *Histoire des comtes de Poitou*, 2 vols (Paris, 1903)
Staunton, Michael, *The Historians of Angevin England* (Oxford, 2017)
Strickland, Matthew, *Henry the Young King, 1155–83* (London and
    New Haven, CT, 2016)
Turner, Ralph V., *Eleanor of Aquitaine* (London and New Haven, CT,
    2009)
Vincent, Nicholas, 'Henry II and the Poitevins', in *La Cour Plantagenêt
    (1154–1204)*, ed. Martin Aurell (Poitiers, 2000), pp. 103–35
——, 'Patronage, Politics and Piety in the Charters of Eleanor of
    Aquitaine', in *Plantagenêts et Capétiens: confrontations et héritages*,
    ed. Martin Aurell and N.-Y. Tonnerre (Turnhout, 2006), pp. 17–60
Wheeler, Bonnie, and John Carmi Parsons, eds, *Eleanor of Aquitaine:
    Lord and Lady* (New York, 2003)

ACKNOWLEDGEMENTS

I would like to thank Professor Nicholas Vincent for letting me have a copy of his collection of Eleanor's acts, which will be published in the fairly near future. It would have been impossible to do the research for this book without it. But I know that it is still a work in progress, so I have not given references to it, since extra acts may still be found and the numbering may change. Dr Rowan Watson very kindly gave me some books from the library of Dr Jane Martindale, who had for many years been working on a biography of Eleanor. Jane's health declined as I started working on this book and, sadly, she died as I was completing it. Her articles have been foundational for an understanding of Eleanor and of Aquitaine. Professor Ruth Harvey was extremely helpful as I struggled with the vexed troubadour issue. And I have had many illuminating chats with colleagues at seminars and conferences, particularly the Anglo-Norman Studies conference. Dr Florian Meunier, curator at the Louvre, gave me a special viewing of the Eleanor Vase. Dr Katie Phillips produced the family trees and Gordon Thompson the maps. When I needed to photograph sites in the Loire and Aquitaine, Clare Pillman was happy to do the driving and turn a research trip into a holiday. The Île d'Aix, where poor Richard the Poitevin went slightly mad, is now completely charming, but it is easy to see why Mirebeau, over which so many squabbled and where Eleanor was nearly captured by her grandson Arthur, does not feature on any tourist trails.

PHOTO ACKNOWLEDGEMENTS

The author and publishers wish to express their thanks to the sources listed below for illustrative material and/or permission to reproduce it. Some locations of artworks are also given below, in the interest of brevity:

Archives départementales de la Vienne, Poitiers (Pièce Restaurée 40): p. 146; Bibliotheque de l'Arsenal, Paris (MS 1186 réserve, f. 122v): p. 57; Bibliothèque nationale de France, Paris: pp. 18 (MS NAL 779, f. 177v), 54 (MS Latin 9230, f. 8), 61 (MS Français 12473, f. 128r), 82 (MS Français 794, f. 27r), 110 (MS Français 794, f. 184r), 111 (MS Français 123, f. 229r), 152 (MS Latin 5480 (1), f. 265); British Library, London: pp. 70 (Royal MS 14 B VI, membrane 6), 121 (Cotton MS Nero D I, f. 146v, photo Bridgeman Images); Michael R. Evans/Shutterstock.com: p. 150; photos Lindy Grant: pp. 6, 8, 14 (Musée du Donjon de Niort), 30, 34, 52 (Herzog Anton Ulrich-Museum, Braunschweig), 98, 117, 133, 147; Herzog August Bibliothek, Wolfenbüttel (Cod. Guelf. 105 Noviss. 2°, f. 171v), photo © HAB Wolfenbüttel (CC BY-SA 4.0): p. 79; Koninklijke Bibliotheek, The Hague (MS 76 F 13, f. 28v), photo courtesy Koninklijke Bibliotheek, The Hague: p. 141; photo courtesy Dr Elizabeth Matthew: p. 39; photo © Ministère de la Culture, Médiathèque du patrimoine et de la photographie, Dist. RMN-Grand Palais/ Franck Genestoux: p. 80; photo © RMN-Grand Palais (Musée du Louvre, Paris)/Daniel Arnaudet/Dist. Photo SCALA, Florence: p. 113; courtesy Gordon Thompson, GISP: pp. 176–7, 178–9; Wikimedia Commons: p. 31 (photo Florian Pépellin, CC BY-SA 4.0).

INDEX

Page numbers in *italics* refer to illustrations

Louis VI, the Fat, king of France
12–13, *18*, 102, 115, 166
Louis VII, king of France, 8–9,
12–22, *18*, 25, 29, 30, 40,
45, 63, 65, 67–9, 71–2, 78,
84–91, 93, 94, 96, 104–5,
113, 114–15, 118–19, 122,
134, 139, 160–61, 163–4,
167–8, 170–73
as duke of Aquitaine 15–16,
22, 72, 118, 156, 167
family of *18*, 67–8, 78
and rebellion of 1173–4 37–8
Luçon 123, 138
Luke, abbot of Turpenay 143,
145, 149
Lusignan, lords of 26, 30–31, 66,
124, 165–7
see also Hugh of Lusignan

Maillezais, abbey of 15, 138, 144,
148
Maingot family 62
William 32, 35–6, 53
Mainz, archbishop of (Conrad
of Wittelsbach) 48, 49, 135
Manasser Bisset 24
Marcabru 88–9, 104–5, 108
Marchisia 64, 79
Margaret of France *18*, 37, 39, 74
Martin Algais 53
Mary of France, countess of
Champagne *18*, 19, 34, 63, 71,
76–7, 82, 93, 96, 106–7, 109,
110, 111, 130, 137, 151, 164
Matilda, empress 11, 24–5, 30,
63, 68, 71–2, 78, 79, 80, 96,
135–6, 140, 154, 157, 159,
161, 164, 171
Matilda II, queen of England 96,
136–7, 159, 164

Matilda of Anjou, abbess of
Fontevraud 63, 139, 143
Matilda of England, duchess of
Saxony 27, 35, 40, 42, 51–2,
70, 71–2, 75–7, 79, 80, 106,
137, 161, 163
Matilda-Richenza of Saxony,
countess of Perche 40, 51–2,
75–7, 102, 137
Matthew of Angers, master 24,
127, 129
Matthew of Montmorency 13
Mauléon family 26
Ralph of 53
Maurice of Blaison, bishop of
Poitiers 66, 143–4
Maurice of Craon 36
Maurienne, county of 36
Alice of 75, 101
see also Adela of Maurienne,
queen of France
Mercadier 53, 56, 130, 167, 172
Merlin, prophesies of 29, 42, 91,
93, 99, 109
Mervent 11, 118, 120, 125
Milo, abbot of Le Pin 143, 149
Minstrel of Reims, the 90,
95–6
Mirebeau 36, 56, 67, 124
Montbazon 120
Montferrand 36, 101

Nieul-sur-l'Autise, abbey of St
Vincent 11, 16, 22, 65, 132,
147–8, *147*
Niort 11, 31, 75, 83, 120
castle *31*
Nonancourt 42
Normandy 24, 39, 44, 52–4, 56,
58, 60, 67–8, 74, 116–17,
119–20, 127, 129